CANCAN!

CANCAN!

David Price

cygnus arts

London **Cygnus Arts**
Madison & Teaneck **Fairleigh Dickinson University Press**

Published in the United Kingdom by
Cygnus Arts, a division of Golden Cockerel Press
16 Barter Street
London
WC1A 2AH

Published in the United States of America by
Fairleigh Dickinson University Press
Associated University Presses
440 Forsgate Drive
Cranbury
NJ 08512

First published 1998

ISBN 1 900541 50 5
ISBN 0 8386 3820 1

BRITISH LIBRARY CATALOGUING-IN-PUBLICATION DATA
A catalogue record for this book is available from the British Library

LIBRARY OF CONGRESS CATALOGUING-IN-PUBLICATION DATA
Price, David.
    Cancan! / David Price.
       p.   cm.
    Includes bibliographical references (p.) and index.
    ISBN 0-8386-3820-1 (alk. paper)
    1. Cancans—History. 2. Dance—History. 3. Cancans—France—History. 4. Cancans—Social Aspects. 5. Cancans—Social Aspects—France. 6. Paris (France)—Social life and customs—19th century.
    I. Title.
    GV1781.P75   1998
    792.7'8—dc21

                                     98-21956
                                     CIP

PRINTED IN THE UNITED KINGDOM BY MARTINS THE PRINTERS

CONTENTS

ILLUSTRATIONS

COLOUR ILLUSTRATIONS (between pp. 118 and 119)

PREFACE

THIS BOOK IS SOMETHING OF A LABOUR OF LOVE, CARRIED OUT WITH THE intention of investigating the history of the cancan and what has made it special for so many ordinary people, artists, writers, film directors and composers—and me. I first saw the cancan in 1966 at a young age and was captivated by what I knew was a little bit 'naughty', but was also so full of life, colour and humour, unlike (I have come to believe) any other dance or stage activity.

Research for the book took a long time—years—and the picture research was difficult, time-consuming and expensive. I did not manage to acquire all the illustrations I had wanted; for example there are no stills from *Can-Can* because 20th Century Fox wanted to charge far too much for them and because I was told that I would have to get special permission from Frank Sinatra for their use. I would also like to have done some more general research in the United States, but my resources (money) would not stretch that far. So the book is not perfect, but perfection is impossible.

Cancan! will, I hope, satisfy the curiosity of anyone who has ever wondered how the dance came into being and expose the surprising number of myths that exist about its origins and development. It should satisfy the need for such a book which has been reported to me by people in the dance world and also interest those who enjoy operetta, musicals, ballet, music hall and other forms of popular entertainment. But mainly I hope that it will please those, who like myself, find the cancan, when performed well (which does not necessarily mean by professional companies) such a thrilling, exciting experience.

There are many people I need to thank for their help and support in the completion of the book. First of all, my family, and particularly my wife, Rosanna, whose idea it was in the first place, and her mother and father who have always had faith in the future of the project. Rosanna's sister, Anya, has been invaluable as my French representative, chasing up picture sources in Paris and elsewhere, and helping me with translations of some rather obscure texts. Ivor Guest, the chairman of the Royal Academy of Dancing, has been a great help and enthusiastic supporter of the enterprise, and I am also grateful to him for lending me some of the illustrations. I would like to thank Graeme Cruickshank and Jane Pritchard for providing me with some important archive material and Denise Collett-Simpson and Mandy Payne, the librarians at the Royal Academy of Dancing, for their help during my research. Needless to say, the interviewees referred to in the last chapter are deserving of special thanks.

CANCAN!

FIG. 1. La Goulue, the most famous cancan dancer ever, thanks largely to the works of the artist Toulouse-Lautrec. Her brief period of stardom at the Elysée-Montmartre and at the Moulin Rouge made her rich, but she was to die thirty years later in poverty. *Roger-Viollet.*

INTRODUCTION / THE 'NAUGHTY NINETIES'
Society, The Arts . . . and Ladies' Underwear

"The cancan ignores, disdains and eliminates all that recalls rules, regulations and method . . .
it is above all a dance of liberty." Rigolboche, *Memoires*

IMAGINE THE SCENE: A PARISIAN DANCE HALL AT THE TURN OF THE CENTURY. THE audience is composed of the rich, and the not so rich. Aristocrats, even royalty, mix with working people, artisans, laundresses, factory workers, shop girls—all of whom have come to enjoy a notorious spectacle. There is an atmosphere of anticipation. People who have been entertained during the evening by a series of singers, dancers, acrobats and jugglers are now poised to be excited, aroused and some, no doubt, just prepared to be shocked.

Suddenly, a fanfare sounds from the orchestra and from all around the hall young women appear, running onto the dance floor squealing and holding up and shaking their skirts, revealing a mass of frothy, lacy white petticoats, frilly bloomers and black stockings. Some of them perform cartwheels as they rush across the floor. The orchestra begins to play the galop from Offenbach's *Orpheus in the Underworld*, and the girls begin a wild dance in the middle of the hall, kicking their legs high into the air.

Occasionally, some of the dancers turn, bend over, and toss their skirts over their backs, shamelessly displaying their derrières. Some men in the audience throw their hats in the air in their excitement, others stare in open-mouthed astonishment. Women in the audience are more restrained, some amused by the male reaction, others infected by the exuberance of the dance—and perhaps a few jealous of the freedom that the dancers enjoy with their cheeky protest at the conventions of contemporary society.

The climax of the show approaches with the dancers performing individual feats of enthusiastic acrobatics, while fellow members of the troupe stand in a semicircle, appearing almost demure in comparison, but undermining any illusion of this by continuing to hold up their skirts and treating the spectators to a feast of snowy-white lingerie. The solo performers become even more daring by expertly kicking off the top hats of some English visitors, and one surprises a too serious-looking gentleman by collapsing in his lap, and then quickly removing herself to the intense amusement of his female companion.

As the final bars of the music sound, the girls form up again and rush down the dance floor, give a final series of high kicks, and then all leap into the air and descend in unison, performing the splits and triumphantly flourishing their petticoats.

Suddenly, with shrieks of excitement, they exit as they had come in, with a flash of frills, ribbons and black stockings, and with the last one throwing her skirts over her head again to give the audience a final look at the lacy drawers covering her bottom.

This is a flavour of what many believe the atmosphere of dance halls in Paris would have been at the turn of the century, when the scandalous cancan was in vogue. But was it really like this, or is this just a popular myth, spread by Hollywood films? In fact, the Parisian cancan was not a choreographed, chorus-line style of dance until some years later. The cancan went through a number of phases in its development, and the dance as performed by a group of young women, carefully choreographed to leave the impression of a degree of spontaneity, only really appeared in the 1920s. In its earlier evocations, the dance was mainly a vehicle for individual stars, each of whom had her own trademark. There are numerous other myths associated with this one dance, for example: that Offenbach invented it; that it was created at the Moulin Rouge; that the dancers were all prostitutes; that it was frequently danced without knickers; or that it was officially banned by the authorities in France, Great Britain or the United States. None of these is absolutely true, but, as with most myths, there is some truth in all of them, even if only a grain.

The cancan certainly had its controversial aspects, and it was viewed as shocking by many, because it dared to challenge social and moral conventions of the time. Nevertheless, it was being performed in most of the major cities of Europe and North America in the 1890s and early 1900s. It had become something of a device with which to undermine Victorian values, and was part of a growing movement for change. The Victorian period, from the 1830s until 1900, had already passed through a number of distinct phases, and the evolution of the cancan in many ways reflected these. Political events in Paris tended to influence fashions and society not only in France but in most countries of Europe and America in the nineteenth century, and the variations of monarchy, empire and republic all had an effect on the history of the cancan.

The most significant political change in this respect was the defeat of the French army by the Prussians in 1870 at the Battle of Sedan and the consequent fall of the Second Empire. The Prussian army laid siege to Paris until early in 1871, and German unification was in effect declared in the Hall of Mirrors at Versailles, where the king of Prussia was proclaimed emperor of Germany on 18 January. If all this were not enough humiliation, the French were forced to pay a huge indemnity for the war and had to cede the territories of Alsace and Lorraine. In the ensuing chaos and despondency generated by these events, workers and revolutionaries declared the Paris Commune in opposition to the new National Assembly. The Commune was supported by various socialist groups and was motivated by a number of disparate factors, in particular class hatred of the bourgeoisie, distrust of politicians in general, patriotic fervour and hatred of Germans. The Commune's symbolic nature need not be of concern here; suffice it to say that its leaders may have had laudable aims to begin with but that they ended by ruling with terror, and that it was finally crushed by government troops who took savage reprisals. More than seven thousand people were deported following the Commune's defeat, leaving an even more dissatisfied working class. The upper classes, in turn, now felt an increased fear of left-wing revolution.[1] In short, the Third Republic hardly had auspicious beginnings.

The cancan of the 1880s and 1890s was almost indistinguishable from that of the Second Empire, except for the change in dress fashions and an increasing degree of skirt manipulation. But the social milieu in which it was performed had considerably changed. This was reflected in the name for the dance: the word "cancan" itself had bourgeois associations and now was irrevocably tainted with the former, discredited régime, and so the more proletarian name *chahut* was readopted.[2] In the immediate postwar years the dance survived in the sort of working-class dance halls in which it had originated, so the use of the word *chahut* to describe it was appropriate.[3] That it persisted when the cancan became an entertainment for all classes was at least partly because no one wished to be reminded of the empire's frivolous excesses or of the sort of women who had danced the cancan in those days. The dance of the *fin de siècle* was also known as the *quadrille naturaliste*, a term first coined in the 1840s and now used to describe the professional performances at the Moulin Rouge and elsewhere.[4]

The end of empire signalled the demise of a carefree atmosphere supporting some the most glittering of dancing gardens that had fostered the cancan's development.[5] The golden era of the Carnival balls, at which hundreds of revellers had taken part in the dance, was also now effectively over.[6] These changes were brought about by the collapse of the existing social order, which ultimately resulted in the cancan abandoning its roots as an amateur, participatory dance in favour of full-blown, professional entertainment.

When performed today, the cancan at its best provides a fascinating display of Victorian underwear, which in the final decade of the nineteenth century was the most extravagant ever seen (or usually not seen of course). At this time, the high kicks which are so characteristic of the dance were still regarded as unseemly in an era struggling to break free from Victorian moral standards. In fact it had been the kicks and other exaggerated gestures with legs and arms, rather than the exhibition of underwear, that had shocked and disturbed the sensibilities of polite society when the dance first appeared around 1830. The cancan was originally performed by both men and women, and the manipulation of skirts and petticoats to produce a subtly erotic effect only became a feature much later in its evolution. The embryonic cancan also involved a great deal of bodily contact between male and female participants, which was certainly not acceptable to the middle and upper classes.[7] The high kicks were initially performed only by the men, but when the women joined in they inevitably revealed their undergarments, and often much more, because drawers or knickers only became commonly worn in the 1850s. This was another factor which gave the cancan notoriety in its early years.

The flimsy, revealing clothing of the Empire style in France had been ousted as moral standards were raised, and by the time the July revolution in 1830 ushered in the 'bourgeois monarchy' of Louis Philippe, both women and men were wearing more modest dress. Young people unsurprisingly reacted against constraints on pleasure in whatever way they could, and the cancan was part of their protest. The young women who first joined their male partners in the new dance were not able to indulge in the athletic feats of the men because of their long skirts and underskirts, unless of course they lifted them up to enable their legs to have free movement. This was quite out of the question for 'respectable' women, and so the dancers of the cancan during the first decades of its development tended to be working girls and prostitutes.

Displays of sex and sexuality were strongly disapproved of in the Victorian era, at least in public, and women were covered with more layers of clothing than at any time before or since. There was a significant easing up of the strict morality normally associated with this era both during the Second Empire and towards the end of the century, and in these periods the cancan flourished. This more liberal attitude was reflected in styles of women's dress; at the end of the century this meant increasingly erotic underwear, while in the 1850s and 1860s it was characterised by the popularity of the more revealing crinoline. Prior to the arrival of the crinoline, fashion had dictated that women should fill out their skirts with more and more petticoats, and eventually it had seemed simpler (and much less heavy!) to provide the width with a garment stiffened with hoops. It was soon found that the crinoline offered many opportunities for a sight of women's legs, because the skirt tended to swing like a bell from the waist. Hence during strong winds, while negotiating staircases, or even when simply sitting down carelessly, knees and even thighs frequently became visible. The crinoline also allowed more freedom of movement for amateur cancan dancers, who could lift the edges of their skirts and kick up their legs, unencumbered by too many petticoats.

The crinoline's tendency to expose the lower limbs would surely have led swiftly to its rejection in conditions of strict moral standards, and that it persisted for several years is indicative of a more relaxed atmosphere. In France, Empress Eugénie and the ladies of her court helped to popularise the new garment, and, according to Aileen Ribeiro, managed to imbue the swaying movement of their skirts with a "delicate sexual quality".[8] Most middle-class women adopted the crinoline, and they even expected their maidservants to wear it.[9] Its dominance of fashion covered much of the period of the Second Empire, which was known for its gaiety and licence. As legs were now often more visible, boots generally replaced pumps for everyday wear, and more consideration was given to them by the fashion-conscious. They became increasingly attractive and ornate, and it is somewhat ironic, but apparently inevitable, that the use of boots to hide women's ankles only resulted in making them more fascinating for men.[10] The cancan is often presented today with the women wearing ankle boots that are often referred to in a more general context in the twentieth-century fashion vocabulary as 'cancan' boots.

In addition to encouraging the wearing of boots, the crinoline was also responsible for making drawers a standard item of underwear for the first time.[11] They had originally appeared in the Empire period, but the return to longer, fuller skirts with layers of underskirts had made them unnecessary for warmth. They had been popular with prostitutes, who found wearing them was more sexually attractive than wearing nothing, partly because they were originally 'open'—i.e. they consisted merely of two tubes of material, joined at the waist—and possibly partly because the feel of them on the legs was

FIG. 2. The Empress Eugénie, consort to Napoléon III, wearing a dress with the notorious crinoline which she helped to popularise as a fashion in the Second Empire. The crinoline's revealing nature was evidence of more sexually liberated times. *Private Collection.*

CRINOLINE AGAIN!

Charles. "Confound the Hoops, just when I want to make my neat Speech about being '*nearer and dearer*' too!"

FIG. 3. The crinoline was the subject of much humour on both sides of the English Channel, but it was nevertheless viewed as a sexy garment. Men had to keep their distance because of the width of the skirts, but this only increased women's allure. PUNCH, *9 October 1858, by permission of the British Library.*

stimulating if you were used to nothing at all. In addition, drawers were also evidence that female legs existed, a fact that it had been previously considered improper to acknowledge. The initial reluctance of respectable women, afraid of being classed as whores, was overcome when it was realised that some degree of modesty was necessary under their crinolined skirts.[12]

The crinoline could have been seen as a formidable garment, enclosing each woman in a rigid cage, keeping men a bay, but the fact that women were thus so inaccessible only served to increase their allure, as did the changes in leg fashions described above. If this were not enough, women's necklines, especially on evening dresses, were often cut low in the *décolleté* style. Women's fashions thus seemed designed to enhance their appeal for men, and women knew well how to exploit the situation.

Hypocritical attitudes to sexuality prevailed throughout most of the Victorian era, and while a woman's body was mostly hidden from view, the absolutely essential item of underwear at the time was the corset, which simply served to accentuate her shape. This garment, which was the subject of much controversy, due to a certain obsession with tight lacing, was sexually attractive for men, and it seems likely that women, despite their obviously restricted movement, were proud of the figures that could be achieved with their 'stays'. The concept of the tyranny of Victorian fashion, so often alluded to as almost a sinister method of keeping women subjugated to men's desires, may have been largely exaggerated. An absurd collection of medical theories were invented attesting to the advantages of tight lacing for both health and morality, and, once corsets had been identified as symbolic of male domination, a similar number of scare stories were spread to discourage women from wearing them. *Very* tight lacing was of course dangerous to health, but, according to Aileen Ribeiro, it is unlikely that corsets when worn properly caused any harm. For some women, tight lacing may have been a method of providing sexual thrills in itself, but most would have merely viewed the corset as a means to good outline.[13]

It is true that corseted ladies were sometimes unable to breathe deeply, which, in general, did not matter, as middle- and upper-class women were expected to be idle and dependent. Women who did not wear corsets were considered to be immoral—loose in more ways than one. Perhaps surprisingly, it is clear from contemporary photographs that most cancan dancers of the naughty nineties wore corsets. The sight of women wearing fashionable clothes and cavorting about in an energetic and apparently depraved manner

MILLIONS OF LADIES
All over the English-speaking World
WEAR C B CORSETS.

Ladies desiring to place their friends under an obligation recommend them to wear

C B *CORSETS,*

and it is by recommendation of this sort that the demand for these beautiful Corsets—gigantic beyond all precedent—has been created. The need for paying high prices for Corsets has passed away, for the most perfect shaped Corsets the world produces can be now obtained at prices so moderate as to be within the reach of every lady, even those of the most modest means. Excellent qualities can be bought from Drapers and Outfitters everywhere at

2/11, 3/11, 4/11, 6/11, 8/11, 10/6, 15/6, & 21/-
WHOLESALE ONLY:
Messrs. BAYER & CO., London Wall, E.C.
RETAIL EVERYWHERE.

FIG. 4. Towards the end of the century, corsets became more erotic garments and mass-production meant that relatively ornate examples, decorated with ribbons and lace, were within the reach of more ordinary women. THE LADY'S REALM, *vol. 6 (1898), by permission of the British Library, P.P.6004.OG.*

PETTICOAT FOR EVENING WEAR IN PINK AND MAUVE BROCADE, FLOUNCED WITH ACCORDION-PLEATED MAUVE MOUSSELINE-DE-SOIE, EDGED WITH PINK SATIN BÉBÉ RIBBON, AND TRIMMED WITH A WIDER PINK RIBBON IN "TRUE LOVERS'" KNOTS.

LINGERIE.
(*Sketched at Swears & Wells', Regent Street.*)

FIGS. 5. AND 6. Turn-of-the-century petticoats were the most extravagant and beautiful ever produced. These drawings accompanied an article by Mrs E. Pritchard, who, in *The Cult of Chiffon*, advised that certain types of underwear could save a failing marriage. THE LADY'S REALM, *vol. 5 (1898), by permission of the British Library,* P.P.6004.OG.

must have been disconcerting for the average citizen. The dancers themselves appear to have been unrestricted by their stays, although Lottie Collins, who danced her own version of the cancan while singing 'Ta-ra-ra-boom-de-ay', was often to be found fainting in the wings after her show—but this probably had more to do with the number of encores that her ecstatic audiences persuaded her to give them.[14]

The cancan made a virtue out of the major feature of late-nineteenth-century underwear: luxurious petticoats and knickers. Finer materials had been introduced for undergarments, including silk, and they were now decorated with hand embroidery, lace and ribbons threaded through the material. Corsets, which had been purely functional items, were often similarly adorned, and became truly erotic. A revolt against corset wearing promoted by the rational dress movement in the twilight of the Victorian era had little effect, and luxury and extravagance became the order of the day. All items of underwear were affected, and the use of satins and lace, and the *froufrou* rustle of layers of silk continued into the early Edwardian period.[15]

Lacy camisoles and drawers with pastel-coloured ribbons, and layers and layers of petticoats were a must for the fashionable *fin-de-siècle* woman. Prior to the 1870s and 1880s, lace had been used in petticoats only where it showed, i.e. at the edge of the skirt. In the Second Empire, most attention was given to the ornamentation of the bodice and skirt of a dress, especially as the size of the skirt meant that there was much scope for this. In the post-empire decades, skirts became plainer, but clearly the fashion designers were not to be deprived of an outlet for their extravagant tendencies for long. From about 1872, flounces of embroidery or lace, reaching above the knees, were used on the outer petticoat, and four or five plain white ones were worn underneath that. Evening petticoats became even more elaborate, with trimmings of lace and lace-edged flounces up as far as the waist, with still more delicate flounces over them. For the seamstresses who worked on these magnificent creations, it must have seemed a tragedy that they were not for public display. Drawers also became more elaborate, and complemented the petticoats with lace, embroidery and ribbons. Women were aware of the fascination that their beautiful undergarments held for the opposite sex, and, by lifting the edges of their skirts a little—which was necessary to some extent to avoid tripping over—contrived to show off a few of the frills to their admirers. Some wore petticoats of moreen, which gave an intriguing rustle as they walked.[16]

Silk stockings were supported by garters until the late 1870s, when the appearance of suspender belts gave women a choice. Garters remained in use for many years, and photographs of cancan dancers in the 1890s almost without exception show them with garters, not suspenders. This may be because suspenders only became attached to the corset at the turn of the century, but whatever the reason it seems that the vision of cancan dancers in short frilly knickers and suspenders belongs to the twentieth century, not the nineteenth. Nevertheless, according to James Laver, it was 'French' dancers appearing at the Alhambra Theatre in London's Leicester Square in 1876 that first promoted suspenders in Britain, great excitement being engendered by the sight of "naked thighs with suspenders stretched across them to keep up the stockings".[17] The most popular colour for the stockings themselves increasingly was black, often with ornate patterns woven into the silk. The contrast between the black stockings and the white petticoats became a major attraction, not only in the cancan. The revelation of the dainty ankle, covered with patterned black silk stocking and surrounded by a profusion of white lace, as a woman raised her skirts a few inches to cross the street, was an extremely erotic image in the late nineteenth century.

At the beginning of the twentieth century, despite a growing movement in favour of women becoming more active, in particular through the increasingly popular pastime of cycling, fashions continued to emphasise the feminine. As the Cunningtons said:

Edwardian underclothes developed a degree of eroticism never previously attempted . . . women had learned much, since the 1870s, of the art of suggestion . . . they invented a silhouette of fictitious curves, massive above, with rivulets of lacy embroidery trickling over the surface down to a whirlpool of froth at the foot.[18]

James Laver describes a particularly ornate example of an Edwardian petticoat, made of yellow brocade and black lace, and wonders "what could be the possible use of such elaborate undergarments for a respectable woman".[19] Perhaps the answer is provided by Mrs Pritchard in *The Cult of Chiffon* when she recommends certain types of underwear to save a failing marriage. She says that women should spend as much as a fifth of their incomes on it.[20] In fact, women now had much more choice of dress, and they tended to wear more practical clothes for sports and work, while continuing to dress in the most luxurious and feminine costumes for social occasions.

Many men in the nineteenth century never even saw the wonders of their wives' underwear. Comte Muffat in Emile Zola's novel *Nana* is unsettled by being introduced to Nana in her theatre dressing room because in nineteen years of marriage he "had never seen the Comtesse Muffat putting on her garters".[21] Zola was writing about the Second Empire period, but from the point of view of later in the century. Very little had changed, and in middle- and upper-class households a woman was still helped with her dressing and undressing by a housemaid in a separate room adjoining the bedroom, and her husband only usually saw her either fully dressed or in her nightgown. Married couples often had separate rooms. This amount of separation in the

FIG. 7. Domestic bliss: a pretty parlourmaid could be useful to a Victorian woman who wished to keep her husband occupied. Middle-class men expected their wives to produce a large family, but not to enjoy sex. PUNCH, *21 April 1894, by permission of the British Library, P.P.5270.*

READY, AYE READY!

The New Parlour-Maid. "MISTRESS TOLD ME TO TELL YOU SHE WAS NOT AT HOME, SIR."

He. "OH—ER—REALLY! THEN TELL HER I DIDN'T CALL!"

bourgeois marriage seems to have been as common in France as in supposedly less liberal Britain.[22]

It is tempting to believe that the extent of Victorian prudery has been exaggerated in popular myth. Surely a woman who was inclined to wearing sexually attractive clothes would most likely have been a sexual being in other ways? However, it was part of the Victorian belief system that a girl was innocent of all forms of sensuality.[23] For example, bathing was a rare event, and even when it took place it was not socially acceptable to bathe naked, so teenage girls and women would continue to wear their chemises in the bath. Some girls were trained to close their eyes when changing their underwear, in case they should catch sight of their own nudity.[24] Sex tended to be a taboo subject in most families, but on the other hand, a married woman was expected to have, and indeed usually had, a number of children, and so there was a certain inconsistency. If sexual relations were avoided, this was probably mostly because of the unsatisfactory methods of contraception: the prospect of giving birth could seem distinctly unattractive to a woman who had experienced the pain it involved, or the mental anguish that often happened because of infant mortality. These problems sometimes led to a woman putting a stop to sex altogether,[25] leaving her husband to seek his sexual satisfaction elsewhere, possibly with the same chambermaid who helped with his wife's dressing. Some wives went so far as to employ pretty maids in order to keep their husbands occupied, and, in tune with the hypocrisy of the age, maids who became pregnant after being seduced by their masters were often sacked and ended up being forced into prostitution.[26]

Prostitution in France was strictly controlled through a system of licensed brothels and individual licences issued to some women, the *filles isolées*, to work from home. Girls who worked in the brothels, known as *maisons closes*, were strictly controlled, unable even to leave the building six days out of seven. They were also not allowed to parade in the streets or appear at doors or windows. Prostitutes who tried to work independently were ruthlessly hounded by the police, and forcibly licensed in some form.[27] Licensing ensured that prostitutes were able to be given regular medical examinations, a humiliating operation recorded in a painting by Toulouse-Lautrec. Syphilis was a major problem in the nineteenth century and needed to be kept in check, but the prostitutes' clients were not subjected to such humiliation. If the attitude of Guy de Maupassant is anything to go by, they needed to be. When he contracted syphilis he wrote to a friend: "I've got the pox. At last! . . . That means I'm no longer afraid of catching it, so I screw the whores of the street and those who prowl the highways. After doing it I tell them, 'I've got the pox'. They're scared. As for me, I just laugh."[28]

Many French prostitutes moved to London, where they could ply their trade with less official harassment. Nevertheless, *Paris by Night*, a guide to Paris for the man about town published in London in 1871, said that there were an estimated thirty-five thousand prostitutes in the French capital at the time, and only about five thousand of these were licensed. To this number has to be added working girls who were spare-time prostitutes.[29] Laundresses were particularly

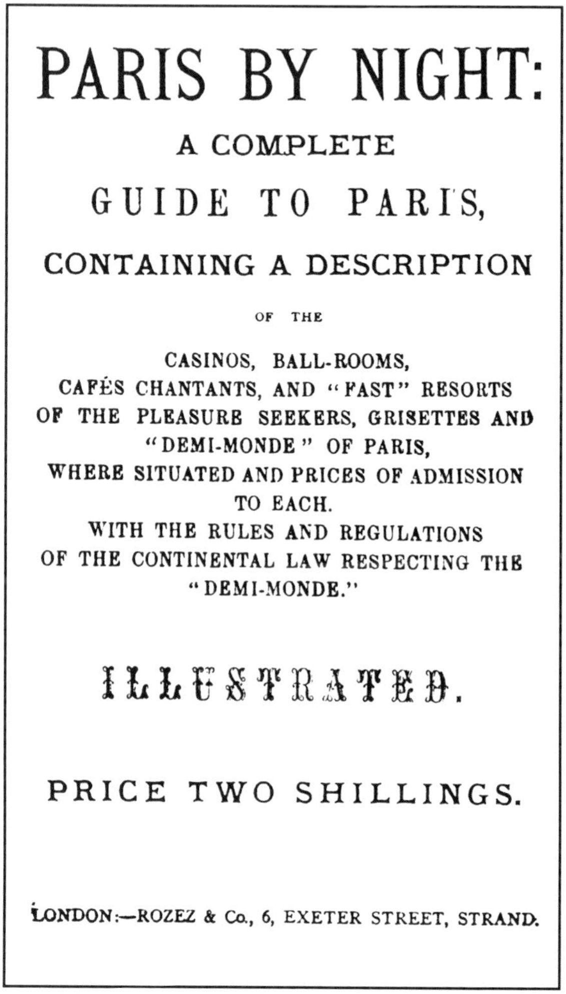

FIG. 8. The inside cover of *Paris by Night*, one of a number of similar guides to the pleasures of the French capital produced from the Second Empire to the Belle Epoque. The unequivocal message seemed to be that Paris was designed purely for enjoyment's sake. *By permission of the British Library, 12331.B.5.*

PARIS BY NIGHT:

A COMPLETE

GUIDE TO PARIS,

CONTAINING A DESCRIPTION

OF THE

CASINOS, BALL-ROOMS,
CAFÉS CHANTANTS, AND "FAST" RESORTS
OF THE PLEASURE SEEKERS, GRISETTES AND
"DEMI-MONDE" OF PARIS,
WHERE SITUATED AND PRICES OF ADMISSION
TO EACH.
WITH THE RULES AND REGULATIONS
OF THE CONTINENTAL LAW RESPECTING THE
"DEMI-MONDE."

ILLUSTRATED.

PRICE TWO SHILLINGS.

LONDON:—ROZEZ & Co., 6, EXETER STREET, STRAND.

inclined towards this activity, as they had endless opportunities for sexual liaisons while delivering clothes to rich clients.[30] Towards the end of the century, the police took a much more relaxed view of prostitution, and the number of *maisons closes* began to decline as it became easier for prostitutes to operate in public.[31] Popular places to find customers were the *café-concerts*, music halls and dance halls. The *promenoir* of the Folies Bergère was notorious as a market for prostitution, as was the promenade of the Alhambra in London.[32]

The high number of prostitutes was reflection of the fact that in France their profession attracted far less moral opprobrium than it did in other countries of Europe. *Paris by Night* remarked that the "Parisian nymphs of the pavé are never styled 'unfortunates' as with us. Such a term would not be acknowledged by our gay neighbours."[33] Many teenage boys gained their first experience of sex in a brothel and during school holidays they often displaced the regular clients. Some brothels had impressive, ornate interiors and offered a range of services to suit their clients' complex requirements. As if to emphasize

FIG. 9. The rue des Moulins brothel, as portrayed by Toulouse-Lautrec. Prostitution in France was strictly controlled through a system of licensed brothels and individual licences, but the law was becoming more relaxed towards the end of the century. *Toulouse-Lautrec,* Au salon de la rue des Moulins, *Musée Toulouse-Lautrec, Albi.*

the acceptance of prostitution, a directory of ladies of the night, the *Guide Rose*, acquired semi-official status.[34]

Double standards existed throughout Europe and America in the Victorian era. Some men who were pillars of society, ostensibly happily married with several children, made no attempt to please either themselves or their wives sexually within the marriage, and instead visited prostitutes. A confused notion of romantic love, found in the writings of novelists, poets and moralists, which had set the married woman on a pedestal as an ideal of purity and godliness, had at the same time enhanced the status of the prostitute as a provider of pleasure which was impossible with a wife.[35] Some 'respectable' women may secretly have enjoyed sex and had good sexual relationships with their husbands, or other men, but it was unwise to admit this, because any indication of sexual enjoyment on the part of a woman, even with her husband, could be seen as offensive and shocking—behaviour which only befitted a whore. So a man could condemn his wife for displaying any sexual prowess, but be prepared to pay a prostitute to fulfil the same role.

Whereas members of the middle and upper classes were in general anxious to preserve their image of respectability, the very cream of society seemed less concerned about appearances within their circle. Sexual freedom was much greater for women as well as for men among the aristocracy, and this has been attributed to their greater general boredom. The women had very little with which to occupy themselves apart from social visits, walking and driving. Servants were in the charge of a steward or housekeeper, and children were looked after in an organised way by nannies, governesses and tutors. Sex became acceptable as a release from the tedium, and in England Lady Arundel was able openly to consort with the painter Basil Hodges, Lord Torrington with Lady Molesworth, Lord Abingdon with Lady Jersey, Lord Hartington with the Duchess of Manchester and Lord Walpole with Lady Lincoln.[36] Similar behaviour was recorded in France, and even lesbian relationships were acknowledged. In the Second Empire, Countess Trubetzkoi and the Marquise

FIG. 10. A courtesan being dressed by her maid, as illustrated by *Le Courrier français*. The elaborate nature of women's dress meant that such intimate contact between servant and mistress was very necessary and it sometimes led to affairs between them. LE COURRIER FRANÇAIS, *9 June 1889, by permission of the British Library*, M.F.85.

— Eugénie, je vais au grand prix, tu sais ce que c'est?...
— Oui, madame, c'est le plus qu'un homme puisse donner

Adda were not afraid to carry out their love affair in public, exchanging caresses without inhibitions. Ladies also frequently fell in love with their maids, the latter being the only people with whom they had any form of regular intimate contact. Such a liaison could be exploited by a maid, aware that society could be scandalised if the affair became public—probably less on account of its homosexual nature than because it was a relationship between people of different classes. In one well-publicised case, a member of the aristocracy accused a young and pretty chambermaid of stealing his wife's jewellery. In court it was eventually revealed that the lady concerned had given the jewellery to her servant in exchange for sexual favours. During the trial several other marquises and duchesses were exposed as having had lesbian affairs.[37]

While lower-class women often appeared more intelligent than their husbands and usually ruled the home, the upper classes tended to expect women to be not only idle but also stupid. Education for girls was extremely limited, and men consequently found their wives poor conversationalists. Girls were not permitted to read novels or attend theatre performances except on very rare occasions, and grew up with a very narrow view of the world. Although contact with the opposite sex after marriage brought a chance of improving the mind, the gap in educational opportunities tended to be perpetuated through customs such as the traditional separation of the sexes after the meal at dinner parties.[38] It is not surprising that the high-class courtesans or *cocottes* who were so much a feature of mid- to late Victorian society, and were as witty in their conversation as they were expert at pleasing men sexually, should have been so admired by men and women. Having said that, high-society ladies rarely came into direct contact with the *demi-mondaines*, except in gambling halls and at watering places such as Spa, Baden-Baden and Monte Carlo. Here they were often embarrassed to find that their wardrobe was inferior to that of the *cocottes*, and that they were now faced with direct competition for their husbands' attentions.[39]

There were several different categories of *demi-mondaine* in Paris, and the terms *grisette, lorette, crevette, cocodette, cocotte, grande cocotte* and *grande horizontale* were all used at different times to mean women who received their income primarily from men whose mistresses they had become on a more or less formal basis. The most sought after were the *grandes cocottes* of the Second Empire and the *grandes horizontales* of the turn of the century. These women were the most expensive, and thus conferred on their lovers a certain status. The *grisettes* were originally working-class girls employed as dressmakers or milliners. During the time of the Directory they acquired a reputation for having loose morals, and in the 1830s were much sought after by the students from the Latin Quarter who taught them to dance the cancan at the public dancing gardens. The term *grisette* gradually came to mean any girl of easy virtue originating from the working class, and was sometimes regarded as synonymous with prostitute. The aforementioned guide to Paris describes *grisettes* as simply *cocottes* in their apprenticeship "who had found out that a silk dress was easier to get than a cotton one, and a rollicking free life with the students more tempting than the laborious one of the work-room".[40] When Franz Lehár came to write *The Merry Widow* in 1905 he called the cancan-dancing tarts who appear in Act Three *grisettes*, although by this time it had become an outdated term. Between the *grisettes* and the *grandes cocottes* were the *cocodettes*, among whom were some of the most famous cancan dancers of the Second Empire, such as Rigolboche and Finette la Bordelaise. These women may have lacked the sophistication of the *cocottes* but nevertheless were able to earn enough money from their many lovers to dress very well.

For an aspiring courtesan of the Second Empire, the cancan may have been considered a form of advertising, and she may only have needed to dance a few times before being 'adopted' by a rich patron of the dance hall. A certain Blanche d'Antigny danced the cancan at the age of fourteen at the Closerie des Lilas (later the Bal Bullier), where she was observed by a rich Wallachian, who seduced her and took her away with him to Bucharest. She soon left him and was reputed to have made several other conquests before returning to Paris two years later. This time she chose the fashionable Bal Mabille for her dancing exploits. A drama critic who saw her there recommended her to the Théâtre de la Porte St-Martin, and she was engaged to play the living statue of Helen in *Faust*. She took a number of roles in light-operatic productions and was relatively successful, but it appears she eventually became bored with the theatre and pursued a career as a high-class courtesan.[41]

FIG. 11. Blanche d'Antigny's life history was even more fascinating than that of Nana, Emile Zola's fictional 'heroine', said by some to have been based on Blanche. This photograph shows her dressed for one of her theatrical roles. *Mary Evans Picture Library.*

Blanche d'Antigny was one possible model for Zola's Nana, who is to be found dancing at the Reine Blanche, the Elysée-Montmartre and other *bals* of Paris in his novel *L'Assommoir*. She later (in *Nana*) moves through a brief career as an actress to become a wealthy courtesan. Zola's novels accurately portray the down side of life under the Second Empire in Paris, but there were unquestionably positive aspects as well which he often tends to ignore. Morals may have been lax, but at least there was less hypocrisy than at other times in the nineteenth century. *Le Figaro* once taunted the dancing master Markowski for sending out invitations admitting the bearer plus *une amie*. Why, asked the paper, did he not simply say *sa biche* (his mistress)? [42]

The courtesans were a symbol of the opulence of the Second Empire, but as Zola's novels show, there was still plenty of poverty in the cities and in rural communities. When France was defeated in the war against Prussia, many attributed their country's weaknesses directly to the courtesans, and even before the fall of the empire, they were not tolerated by certain sections of society. When the celebrated Cora Pearl, an English-born courtesan who was perhaps the most notorious in Second Empire Paris, appeared as Cupid in a production of Offenbach's *Orpheus in the Underworld*, she was initially given a warm reception by her fans. But during the twelfth performance she was booed off stage by socialist students who viewed her as epitomising the decadent luxury of the era. [43]

It would be a mistake to assume that every dancer was a potential prostitute. True, in the Second Empire the famous cancan dancers were *cocodettes*, but in the 1880s and 1890s some girls danced as a way of supplementing the meagre wages they received as seamstresses or laundresses, and possibly as a way of avoiding being tempted into amateur prostitution. The future for working-class girls was somewhat grim: marriage was socially necessary, and often meant domestic prison, with beatings from their husbands being a regular occurrence. By the 1890s, there were signs of some of the barriers between the classes being broken down, as department stores were selling fashionable clothes at affordable prices, and education was becoming more widely available. Some of the benefits of this limited revolution filtered down to the working class, and the frustrations of relative poverty were alleviated. [44] Nevertheless, working-class women still suffered, and they knew that there was a chance that performing the cancan at one of the dance halls would lead to stardom, as it did for Louise Weber (La Goulue).

The famous *grandes horizontales* of the *fin de siècle*, Liane de Pougy and La Belle Otéro, inhabited a different world from La Goulue and Jane Avril, and other professional cancan dancers. It is possible that La Goulue involved herself in prostitution before becoming established as a dancer, and Jane Avril was the daughter of Elise Richepin, a Second Empire courtesan, but despite these links, neither had any desire to pursue the career of a true *demi-mondaine*. In fact, Jane Avril strongly and successfully resisted attempts by her mother to force her into prostitution. [45] La Belle Otéro was an accomplished Spanish dancer who performed at the Folies Bergère, but most of her contemporaries had few such talents and they were satisfied with doing little else in public than merely looking beautiful at society balls or driving in the Bois de Boulogne.

Generally French, or French-educated, the sophisticated ladies of the night were almost accepted in respectable society, and certainly many women admired them and copied their styles of dress. Fashion in general was dictated by Paris, and dictated to Paris by the high-class courtesans, who could afford all sorts of expensive, impractical frivolities in their clothes. One of Liane de Pougy's ballgowns would have cost one thousand francs or more—well over the annual wage paid to her maid.[46] Unsurprisingly, these women also led the way in underwear styles. Back in the 1860s, the courtesans who had so popularised the crinoline were quick to adopt the replacement style, with its tight-fitting bodice accentuating the figure, although, paradoxically, some continued to wear the crinoline long after it had gone out of fashion at the court of the Empress Eugénie.[47] Its ostentatious nature added to their allure, especially when their dresses were decorated with the latest designs and accessories, but no doubt the undergarment's revealing tendency was also prominent in the minds of the wearers.

The *grandes horizontales* held a fascination for Victorians in France, Britain and, to some extent, America as well. Men were certainly dominant in middle- and upper-class society, but these women clearly knew how to exploit male patronage to their great advantage. Formerly, it had been dangerous to consort with a prostitute, and syphilis was still widespread at the end of the nineteenth century, but the high-class tart was a different proposition entirely. She took great care with hygiene, and her clients could apparently indulge in the pleasures of the flesh with impunity—the 'wages of sin' no longer having to be paid. 'Respectable' women and marriage as an institution were thus often felt to be under threat, especially as the courtesans seemed more intelligent than the average wife.[48]

The male sex may therefore appear to have had the best of both worlds, and women's resentment at this situation soon began to be felt. The traditional idleness expected of the 'gentle sex' was replaced by a striving for activity in sport, and particularly cycling. Middle-class women especially had a new feeling of independence, and many also took up office work for the first time at the turn of the century. Wives became less afraid of making their sexual demands clear and stated that there was a limit to the amount of children they would be prepared to bear. By the end of the century it had become almost unfashionable to have more than two children. At the same time, women generally became more overtly sexual beings and shocked their husbands by flirting with other men. Adultery by wives also became more common, despite a legal system in France that treated such activity as a crime while it allowed their husbands to have as many mistresses as they liked.[49] Divorce also became more acceptable in the 1890s, and the divorced woman was increasingly the object of hostility from male critics who resented her freedom, particularly as her formerly married state implied that she was sexually experienced. The classic 'gay divorcee' also knew how to enhance her sexual charms through her dress.[50]

The composer Lehár claimed to have had first-hand experience of the new liberated behaviour of women while on a trip to England in the early 1900s. During the steamer crossing from France, he became acquainted with a young woman who had recognised him as the composer of *The Merry Widow*. Before reaching Dover, the mutual attraction between the two of them became strong enough for them to agree to continue their liaison in London. Lehár recounted that they both consumed large amounts of champagne in a private room attached to Romano's, a fashionable restaurant. The following evening, George Edwardes, the impresario, took Lehár to a society party where the composer was astonished to find that his host's wife was his lover from the Channel crossing. He admired her duplicity—when introducing herself on the ferry she had claimed to be a Grosvenor Street mannequin—and later tried unsuccessfully to persuade librettists to use his experience as the basis for the plot for an operetta. Unfortunately it seems that they found his story to be too incredible. [51]

In a sense, the cancan symbolises the revolution in women's attitudes.

FIG. 12. Franz Lehár, the Hungarian composer of *The Merry Widow*, was attracted to Paris like many foreigners, but he was surprised to find some English women were as liberated as their French counterparts in the *belle époque*. *Theatre Museum, V&A Picture Library.*

The dancers display their legs and their underwear brazenly, completely unconcerned about conventional morality, and, what is more, they seem to be enjoying this expression of their sexuality. The high kicks, similarly, signify a disdain for the role that women have been allocated in society. Men were just as jealous in the nineteenth century as in any era, but somehow in the atmosphere of Victorian society, when morality had become almost institutionalised, they felt that they had more of a right to demand fidelity from their wives and mistresses. The sight of women flaunting their charms in such a way may have been stimulating to most men, but not a few found the notions of such freedoms on the part of the opposite sex disturbing.

It may be thought that *cancaneuses* were drawn exclusively from the working class, being more brash and less hampered by social conventions. Most *were* from the lower classes, but a number had an above average education. Grille d'Egout had been a schoolteacher, and Jane Avril was an intelligent woman who acted as secretary to Arsène Houssaye, the theatre director and writer.[52] This was sometimes reflected in the style and individuality of the their dancing: Jane Avril was viewed as refined and subtle, whereas La Goulue was considered vulgar and outrageous (and very much admired for these qualities).

Towards the end of the century there was something of a return of the sense of freedom in France which had been experienced to a limited extent in the 1850s and 1860s—the time of the crinoline, and the first heyday of the cancan. But this time there was none of the experience of confidence in the status of the nation—more a feeling of trepidation about the approaching twentieth century. Confidence in absolutes had largely disappeared: scientific reasoning had failed to provide the answer to life's woes, and so many people turned to all sorts of other forms of release from their humdrum lives. Throughout the Victorian period, the middle classes frequently felt bored, and while in the 1860s men resorted to simple pleasures, like the company of prostitutes, and visited the theatres and *bals publics*, leaving their wives at home, in the 1890s other forms of stimulation were becoming increasingly popular, or at least talked about. Drugs and mysticism were often discussed in journals of the day, giving the impression that they were fashionable pursuits. Sexual perversions were also frequently indulged in by some, more because they were felt to be desirable or fashionable rather than because of any particular natural inclination.[53]

Middle-class men may well have felt somewhat confused by the new era, the *fin-de-siècle* decadence that seemed to be all around them, but probably worse that any of this was that women were beginning to assert themselves more and becoming more active in work and recreation. Most important were the subtle changes in women's attitudes to sex and having children, and the fact that husbands found their dominance in marriage increasingly under threat, particularly in the bedroom.

In the light of all these changes, the cancan itself may seem in retrospect to have been a relatively harmless and healthy pursuit. But for all but the most blasé Parisians it was as much a sign of decadence as were the activities described above. Its popularity in the Second Empire was rooted in its origins as an improvised participatory activity, and it symbolised the unrestrained mood of the age. In the 1890s and early 1900s it was much more of an entertainment, glorifying frilly underwear, but at the same time it represented a turning point in the position of women in society. The likes of La Goulue and Jane Avril were not dependent on male patronage like the courtesans who made their names as *cancaneuses* in the 1850s. Instead, the new stars of the cancan were professionals, who took great pride in their art.[54] Their dancing was an unashamed demonstration of female sexuality, and is a significant indication of women's relative emancipation. For many people, such notions were profoundly shocking. French provincials and foreigners visiting Paris who chanced on a performance by La Goulue may have returned home believing that their world had been turned upside down. For many amongst the middle classes in Paris, the behaviour of the cancan dancers at the Moulin Rouge and elsewhere was a worrying symptom of a disintegration of society, which the anarchists were trying to bring about. Bomb-throwing incidents had become so common in the 1880s and 1890s that there were regular columns in the newspapers entitled 'Dynamite' giving details of the latest events. The terrorist activities finally came to an end with the assassination of President Sadi Carnot in 1894.[55]

Despite these violent episodes, Paris remained a cosmopolitan centre and was now being marketed as the pleasure capital of Europe. Central to this campaign was a series of international exhibitions which attracted thousands of visitors from abroad and for whom the entertainment industry did its best to cater. There was a vast expansion in the number of cabaret venues, providing a range of acts of varying quality with often somewhat risqué content. Without doubt the most famous of these as far as foreigners were concerned were the cancan dancers of Montmartre, but the cancan was just one of many exciting entertainments in the Parisian theatres and music halls of the 1890s. Scientific advances, such as X-rays, were used to provide thrills of a sort, and there were also the first examples of 'moving pictures' shown as part of the music-hall bill. In keeping with the increased interest in the mystical or the bizarre, illusionists and magicians were very popular. The introduction of limelight in many theatres had provided the opportunity for clever effects, often enhanced by using tinsel and sequins on costumes.[56] Electric lighting when it appeared was less satisfactory than limelight in projecting a magical quality. In great demand then as now were the cabaret singers, whose sometimes coarse songs showed a similar disdain for convention as did the cancan. Most famous of these were the well-known subjects of Toulouse-Lautrec, Aristide Bruant and Yvette Guilbert.

Even in this age of decadence, when it might have been thought that anything would have been tolerated on the Parisian stage, there were certain sights that were found to be unacceptable. When Colette gave her lover the Marquise de Belbeuf, who was dressed as a man, a long passionate kiss on the stage of the Moulin Rouge, whistles, boos and shouts from the audience were followed by a rain of coins, cushions and opera glasses. It seemed that Montmartre could tolerate lesbian behaviour in public, but not as entertainment.[57]

The dancers of Montmartre were also at the forefront of a revolution in the arts, when realism was fast being overtaken by expressionist forms. Doubt and uncertainty, which in the period after defeat in the Franco-Prussian War had meant gloom and despondency in Paris, now encouraged experimentation and a feeling that it was necessary to live for today, as no one knew what the new century would bring. Members of the artistic establishment in Paris imposed severe restrictions on creativity, and were remarkably conservative in other ways too. The cancan was inspiration for many of Paris's avant-garde artistic community, sometimes directly, as in the case of Toulouse-Lautrec, but mostly indirectly, by firing enthusiasm for creativity with its daring and its exuberance. Magazines such as *Le Courrier français* and *Le Mirliton* frequently contained illustrations of dancers at the *bals* of Paris, and sometimes used such images to make almost political statements. Whether painters and writers were merely reporting 'everyday life' at the end of the century, or were consciously trying to shock, or at least provoke, there is little point in considering, as it was most likely something of both. More importantly, many people *were* shocked,

Salut à la Province et à l'Etranger!

FIG. 13. As this cover of *Le Courrier français* shows, the cancan was felt to be a more recognisable symbol of Paris for provincials and foreigners than the newly built Eiffel Tower. The dance was often employed satirically in this magazine. LE COURRIER FRANÇAIS, *12 May 1889, by permission of the British Library*, M.F.85.

and this only served to encourage the artists to push the boundaries even further. It was entirely consistent with the dance's image for a republican magazine in England to be called the *London Cancan*. Describing itself as "A True Exponent of Nineteenth Century Thought and Reflex of Nineteenth Century Character", it appeared towards the end of 1881 and only seems to have lasted for one issue.[58]

Political movements in other countries were motivated by a feeling of the need for change, while others grew up as a reaction to the perceived decadence that was creeping in. Russia in particular was torn between the need to modernise and a resentment of foreign interference. Performances of the cancan in St Petersburg were the most visible sign of Western 'immorality' creeping into Russia in the 1870s and were condemned by populist revolutionaries.[59] This rejection of Western 'decadent' values was later fostered by communist leaders, notably Stalin, during the 1930s, and Khrushchev, who again used the cancan as a symbol of the moral failure of the West after his visit to Hollywood in the late 1950s.

The cancan has provided a stimulus to artistic endeavour well into the twentieth century. Many operettas and musicals and a number of major films have featured the dance, and writers and artists have continued to be fascinated by the era represented by the captivating *danseuses* of the Moulin Rouge and other places of entertainment found in 1890s Paris. Tourists of course still expect to find the artistic milieu in the city today, which is why the Place du Tertre is always full of painters, and why so many cabarets still present their versions of the cancan.

This book is intended to be a celebration of the cancan and what it has meant for dancers, musicians, artists, writers, film directors and others over the past one hundred and fifty years. It aims to evoke the spirit of the 'naughty nineties' and provide a taste of the excitement, beauty and sheer joy of the dance. It may also explain how the cancan has managed to survive and remain popular so many years after its first appearance, why it is still sought after by visitors to Paris, from elsewhere in France and abroad, and why it remains for many people such a potent erotic image in our supposedly liberated times.

CHAPTER 1 / HOW IT ALL BEGAN
From the 1830s to the Second Empire

THE ORIGIN OF THE CANCAN IS A LITTLE OBSCURE AND IT CAN BE SAID TO HAVE evolved rather than anyone having invented it. The professional, choreographed form that began to take shape in the 1890s in Paris was a far cry from the dance that emerged in public *bals* in the 1830s. In fact, comparisons between the naughty-nineties version, so redolent of the foreigners' image of 'Gay Paree', and the strictly amateur dance of the outer boulevards sixty years earlier might lead one to assume that they should be classified separately. Severe confusion often results from historians and commentators referring to them both as 'the cancan', without further explanation, leading many people to believe that something like the familiar stage dance existed in the 1830s. In fact, the history of the cancan consists of several phases, beginning with the truly amateur, spontaneous and disorganised affair of the early years, followed by several decades in which first male, then female solo dancers began to give the dance some recognisable form, and ending with the all-women, choreographed 'chorus lines' which really only appeared in the early twentieth century.

The early cancan was more a *form* of dancing, based on the galop, than a separate dance, and was usually danced by couples in a quadrille.[1] Wild improvisation, often incorporating high kicks, was the order of the day, and it was these exaggerated gestures, together with the apparent Bacchanalian frenzy that seemed to overcome the dancers, which gave this original cancan its bad reputation. It had as its basis the athletic dancing of the working classes in the eighteenth century, when such diversions had been generally a male preserve.[2] One of the first places the cancan appeared was in an establishment called the Grande Chaumière in the Montparnasse district of Paris. In the early years of the nineteenth century, the Chaumière was frequented by reasonably well-off men, often students, who came in search of amorous encounters with the poorer local girls.[3] It must have been one of these *grisettes* who, while dancing, had the urge to kick her legs into the air, no doubt to the admiration of her male companions, and thus became the first *cancaneuse*.

Once the students' female partners began to imitate them in their antics, it was apparent how much more interesting it was when women took part. As is typical of students in any era, they were desperate to challenge the conventions of the time and were on the look out for alternatives to the more formal dancing then in vogue. In high society a few years later, the polka caused some controversy, being a lively dance, particularly popular with the young, which often resulted in more bodily contact between the dancers than had been the case with its more sedate predecessors in the ballroom. The polka and the cancan are both performed to music with a lively two beats to the bar, and there are close links between the polka's arrival in France and the development of its more outrageous cousin. It seems that the two dances evolved in parallel, with a French version of the polka eventually becoming more acceptable in the ballroom than the even less restrained cancan.[4]

Besides 'cancan', other names, such as *polka-piquée*, *Robert Macaire* and *chahut*, were used to describe the energetic forms of dancing popular in the dance halls frequented by the lower classes.[5] With the early *chahut*, high kicking was a major feature, but there was much less emphasis than in the *fin-de-siècle* cancan on skirt manipulation and on exhibiting underwear. The dancing of La Goulue in the 1880s and 1890s in the *quadrille naturaliste* was more often described as the *chahut* than the cancan, although she was a professional and the *chahut* had originally belonged very much in the realm of the true amateur.[6] If any distinction can be made between the *chahut* and the cancan it is that the former refers more properly to the original high kicking dance of proletarian dance halls, whereas the word 'cancan' has been used more generally to describe both the early high kicking dancing and the later sophisticated forms also featuring skirt manipulation. 'Cancan' was in vogue to describe the dance in the Second Empire, and in post-1870 Paris was felt to be an unacceptable reminder of the former regime, hence the readoption of *chahut*; but 'cancan' continued to have a more international usage, simply because it was easier to pronounce.

The etymology of the French word *cancan* is shrouded in mystery. Some dictionaries say that it comes from the Latin *quamquam*, the pronunciation of which caused fierce argument in French schools—hence, presumably, the development of the original meaning of *cancan*: 'chatter' or 'gossip'. Others say that it approximates to a child's word for a duck (in French, *canard*), and they suggest that the dance imitates a duck's movements.[7] They surely cannot ever have seen a performance of the cancan, or perhaps they are unaware that ducks do not usually indulge in high kicks and the splits. Having said that, the early cancan was not quite as athletic as it was later to become, and some of its features do suggest the waddling of a duck. A more plausible theory claims that the word came from the Old French *caquehan*, 'a noisy assembly'.[8] What is certain is that cancan also means 'scandal' in French, and it does not take much imagination to work out how it may have come to describe the dance. The alternative word, *chahut*, means 'noise' or 'uproar', and seems appropriate to describe the effect that the dance had when it first appeared in the Parisian dance halls.

The cancan contains elements of earlier dances, and is sometimes compared to the Andalusian *fandango*, a flamenco-style dance in which the female performers make much use of their colourful skirts and petticoats.[9] Curt Sachs maintained that the trick of knocking off the hat of a spectator was copied from the Catalonian *sardana*, but he attributed the cancan's high kicks to an even earlier period, as part of fertility rites in ancient Egypt and among primitive peoples of Brittany.[10] The *triori* of southern Brittany in the sixteenth century, for example, featured high kicking and the lifting of skirts in a women-only dance.[11] In another part of France, Metz, in 1505, a certain Henry Daunoult is recorded as having indulged in some acrobatic dancing, during which he hopped about on one leg, holding the other one almost vertical. He had apparently invented the *port d'armes*, an activity which eventually became part of the cancan.[12]

It is doubtful, to say the least, whether the first exponents of the cancan in Paris had any knowledge of these apparent precursors. There were, however, some more direct influences. Castil-Blaze refers to a *fricassée* performed by the ballerina Marie-Madeleine Guimard in the 1770s for invited guests at her home in Paris. Writing in the 1850s, he claims that the most disorderly cancans are pale imitations of the dancing of Mlle Guimard and her company.[13] F. de Ménil in his *Histoire de la Danse* refers to the "vulgar *fricassée*, famous during the Revolution", coming together with the quadrille in the early decades of the nineteenth century. He also mentions that the galop began to be adopted by the *bals publics* at this time and that it was the galop that formed the bridge between the quadrille and the cancan.[14]

Perhaps even more significant were the performances of the phenomenal Charles Mazurier at the Théâtre de la Porte St-Martin in 1825. Starring in the melodramatic role of Jocko the monkey, this extremely agile dancer—one critic described him as *désossé* (boneless)—demonstrated the *grand écart* (leaping in the air and landing in the splits) and other movements later characteristic of the cancan. It is quite possible that Mazurier had observed the athletic dancing of the working classes and incorporated their antics into his performances. In doing so he was the first to present the dance as an entertainment and gave the *chahut* wider publicity. He had originally thrilled audiences with his *grands écarts* in his home city of Lyons as Polichinelle in a ballet called *La Carnaval de Venise*, which was well received. *Jocko* or *Le Singe de Brésil* proved to be just as popular in Paris. According to Ivor Guest, Mazurier bridged the gap between fairground acrobatics and classical ballet. Unfortunately, his career was tragically cut short by the onset of tuberculosis, and he died in 1828.[15]

Some of the students at the Chaumière may have seen Mazurier perform and imitated him on the dance floor. Another theory has it that soldiers on tours of duty in Algeria had witnessed something similar there, and imported it into France.[16] This may, however, be a suggestion put forward by some critics of such immodest displays in order to place blame for the dance's origins outside their cultured homeland and firmly in the lands of 'barbarians'. Reactionary objections to the cancan may have had a more concrete political motivation. It seems too much of a coincidence that the cancan appeared in the same year as the revolution of 1830 and it seems fair to say that there are links between the cancan and the *carmagnole* of 1789, in so far as each was stimulated by the general upheavals in society and an urge to demonstrate *liberté*.

The cancan may have had its direct influences, but it was as much a spontaneous development among the working classes, which was largely a way of letting off steam at the end of a hard day. The dancing at the *guinguettes* like the Chaumière in the 1830s was usually formalised in a quadrille or square dance with several figures, some of them slow and sedate, others more lively, like the galop which often formed the final figure. The galop simulated the galloping of horses and gave the opportunity for exaggerated gestures, like the high kick, which ultimately resulted in its transformation into the cancan.

One of the first descriptions we have of the cancan describes it as "the French *Cachucha*", yet another Spanish dance. Gaston Vuillier quotes "a little

CONSERVATOIRE DE DANSE MODERNE.

N° 3.

Attention , Fifine , des mœurs dans la pose, si
c'est possible ! j'aperçois le père Lahire .

Deux bahuteuse et un étudiant pur sang .

l'Etudiant de 18.° année, a passé tous ses examens
à la Chaumière.—Il est bachelier ès-cancan . Le père
Lahire ose à peine modérer ses avant-bras .

Permets-moi de te serrer sur mon cœur
d'homme ! _ Tu me fais mal, Jobard .

FIG. 14. Some of the earliest known pictures of the cancan, from *La Conservatoire de Danse Moderne* by Charles
Marie de Sarcus, published in Paris in 1845. The high kicks were not very high and one of the most shocking
aspects of the dance was the bodily contact between participants. *New York Public Library for the Performing Arts.*

book of the period" which gives a vivid picture of the cancan at the Chaumière:

The invasion of France by the Castilian Cachucha will prove a no less momentous historical fact than the first importation of the potato. Someday folks will say: A Duke of Orléans succeeded to the throne during the reign of the Cachucha. I am not here to chronicle Petitpa or Mabille, nor any of those ballet-dancers who follow mechanically geometrical figures chalked on a stage: nor am I here to eulogize the Taglionis, the Fanny Elsslers, the Grisis [famous dancers of the time], who obey cast-iron regulations, who permit themselves no pirouette, no gesture, no step, which is not measured and calculated beforehand. I celebrate the free and buoyant student, who follows his own inspiration, and the grisette whose unstudied movements speak frankly of pleasure and love.

As the music strikes up, the student falls academically into position—left foot forward, hand on one side, back curved, right arm around his partner. She, her left hand on his shoulder, clings to him like an amaranth to a palm-tree. With the right hand she pulls forward a fold of her dress, while her scarf, drawn tightly round her figure, defines its contours with provocative exactness.

They are off! It is a helter-skelter of bewildering dash, of electrifying enthusiasm. One dancer leans languidly over, straightening himself again with vivacity; another races the length of the ballroom, stamping with pleasure. The girl darts by as if inviting a fall, winding up with a saucy, coquettish skip; that other passes and repasses languidly, as if melancholy and exhausted; but a cunning bound now and then, and a febrile quiver, testify to the keenness of her sensations and the voluptuousness of her movements. They mingle, cross, part, meet again, with a swiftness and fire that must have been felt to be described.

Plutarch defined the dancing of his time as silent assembly, a speaking picture; what then shall we call the cancan? It is a total dislocation of the human body, by which the soul expresses an extreme energy of sensation. The French Cachucha is a superhuman language, not of this world, learnt assuredly from angels or from demons.[17]

At some stage, the dance worked its way into higher society, and there are interesting theories about how this may have happened. One of the more persuasive comes in *Les Dandies* by Jacques Boulenger. Charles de la Battut, a rich young man of mixed French and English parentage who styled himself 'Comte', was an aspiring dandy in French society. He apparently presented the cancan to the unsuspecting revellers at an annual Carnival ball at the Variétés theatre in 1832. Such balls were notorious for surprises sprung by guests as the hour grew later and more drink had been consumed. La Battut, who had friends both in society and in the *demi-monde*, was the ideal candidate for populariser of the cancan. When he and his companions began the dance, it was not long before the entire hall joined in, and as a result the police intervened to stop the proceedings. Despite being ejected by them, Le Battut was undeterred and returned to the Variétés only ten minutes later to resume the dance. The manager of the theatre apparently contacted him afterwards and requested that he repeat his entertainment in future years.[18]

A scandalised eye-witness to the cancan at the Variétés, the German traveller Rellstab, wrote a colourful description of it:

The couples dance it indecently close together, so close that even involuntary movements are almost inevitably improper . . . but when one sees with what gestures and movements of the body the masked men approach the masked women, press close to them, and actually throw them backwards and forwards between themselves to the accompaniment of continual acclamation and laughter and ribald jokes, one can only be filled with disgust. . . . The beat of the music is hastened, the dancers' movements become more rapid, more animated, more aggressive, and finally the contredanse evolves into a great galop, in which the dancers form into double pairs, four in a row, and galop madly round the floor . . . . [O]ne finally sees masked women, like ecstatic maenads, with flushed cheeks, breathlessly heaving breasts, parched lips, and half-undone, flying hair, careering round the room, less on their feet than being dragged along bodily, until with the last chord they collapse breathlessly on the nearest seat.[19]

The Carnival balls at the Variétés and the success of the new dance encouraged similar events elsewhere, and in 1836 the first in a new series of *bals dansants et costumés* was given at the Paris Opéra. The Opéra balls had had a long history, stretching back to the early 1700s, but by the 1830s they had deteriorated into rather dull affairs, with little or no dancing. The new Carnival balls that began in 1836 were quite different: under the direction of the enthusiastic Philippe Musard, the orchestra played for the dancers until six in the morning, almost without a break. The balls were such a success that in later years the organisers encouraged the attendance of well-known dancers from the *bals publics* to provide entertainment for the increasing numbers of revellers. These dancers, mostly female, but some with male partners, were admitted free, on the understanding that they performed polkas and cancans for the assembled crowds.[20]

Inevitably, there were a number of people, popular entertainers of the day, who became associated with the cancan, and have been credited with 'inventing' it. Among these was Chicard, who was a leather wholesaler by day, but at night became transformed into a dancer of suggestive quadrilles. Many legends exist about the eccentric Chicard: according to one of them, for a bet he once leapt from the balcony at the Opéra into the orchestra pit.[21] A jovial character, rosy cheeked with an ever-present smile, he was fond of eccentric costume, exaggerated gestures and flowery language. It seems that he was a popular performer who delighted in leading the most disorderly dances at the *bals publics*.[22] The Larousse *Grande Encyclopédie* regards him as "without doubt" the creator of the cancan.[23]

In a sense, controversy about the cancan's origins has little point, as there is a good chance that all the theories about the dance are correct to some extent. It obviously developed from several sources, and once semi-professional entertainers adopted it they imbued it with something of their own individual styles. Its form in the early years was not rigid, and many of the first stars had their own distinctive ways of dancing. In addition to Chicard,

Étude de paysage historique faite à Cremorn-Garden, ce jardin Mabile de l'endroit. — Une jeune Française de qualité, la princesse Valentino, donne quelques leçons de désinvolture parisienne à des gentlemen enthousiastes.

FIG. 15. Even when women participants began to high kick, the cancan remained a dance for couples. Here a French visitor to London shows her delighted partner how it is done. The Valentino was one of the dance halls in Paris. JOURNAL POUR RIRE, *13 February 1852, by permission of the British Library, F.117.*

there were several other male performers, including one nicknamed Mister Pritchard, after the English clergyman who supported Queen Pomaré of Tahiti against the French. He was the antithesis of Chicard, being a somewhat taciturn figure, given to wearing sombre black, while nevertheless throwing himself into the dance in an apparently insane manner. He was a well-built, muscular dancer, around whom many legends developed: some said he was a doctor, an apothecary or even a real Protestant vicar. He was reputed to have only ever spoken once at length—in court, while claiming damages from the police who had expelled him from an Opéra ball for an over-suggestive dance. He was credited with great kindness, often asking the less attractive girls in the hall to dance when he noticed they were being left out of the fun.[24]

These male dancers clearly had a major role in the development of the cancan, but the women soon became the real stars. One of these was Pavillon, who was described by Gaston Robert as the most colourful of the 'mad women' of the Bal Bullier. Little else is known about her, although it seems that she was given her name by a musician who taught her to play the horn— and to drink absinthe. She also had a lover who was a student of pharmacy, and who wrote poetry about her.[25] Another dancer, who became famous at the Chaumière and later at the Bullier and the celebrated Bal Mabille, was Elise Sergent, known as La Reine Pomaré. Her jet-black hair and olive skin, contrasting with her white dress, made her a striking figure. Her dance was completely improvised and attracted a crowd around her, who cheered and applauded at the end. They immediately coined her nickname, which seemed appropriate in view of her exotic appearance and because she wore a number of beads and bracelets. She was soon famous for the grace and originality of her dancing, which was really a polka with elements of the cancan.[26] She performed with a partner named Brididi, perhaps the most famous of the male dancers at this time. He was double-jointed, and his antics brought gasps of amazement from the audience. He was known for his *moulinets*, in which he would revolve his arms wildly, like the sails of a windmill.[27]

Pomaré's early life is an illustration of the Victorian moral hypocrisy that existed even in supposedly more liberal France. She became pregnant by a young man with whom she had eloped from boarding school at sixteen, and, despite the fact that her child died after twenty-six days, she was disowned by her family and forced to find work as a waitress. Luckily, she escaped this dismal existence when she was introduced by a student to the joys of dancing at the Mabille.

We know a little about Pomaré's career, because she wrote a small volume of memoirs. She used to like shocking people and visited the Opéra ball dressed in male attire. This was something that was to become increasingly common at these events, but in the 1840s Pomaré was ahead of her time. She also sang crude songs at the Café de Paris, causing the easily offended to walk out in protest.[28] Her fame unfortunately went to her head, and she found herself booed when she attempted to conquer the Palais-Royal with her polka.[29] She died in 1845 at the age of just twenty-one, after contracting tuberculosis.[30]

Alphonsine Plessis, whose fictionalised life provides the basis for *La Dame aux Camélias* and who suffered the same end as Pomaré, was also to be seen dancing the cancan at the Mabille in the 1840s. One of her partners was her lover and the author of the novel, Alexandre Dumas.[31] Many of her fellow dancers were similarly immortalised in prose or poetry, in newspaper columns, pamphlets and books. The women who found success as *cancaneuses* or *polkistes* were of mixed origins. Mariette was reputed to have had a private income and Léonie-la-Désossée was also thought to have had a high-class background. Clara Fontaine was supposedly once a novice in a convent, later becoming a teacher, before finding her true *métier* as a dancer and finally opening a dancing school.[32] She probably thereby managed to combine all her previous experiences in one activity (although one hopes she was not too strict as a mother superior). Some of the queens of the cancan had interesting lives after they had finished as dancers. Sophie Ponton took the opposite career route to that of Clara Fontaine and turned to religion when she became tired of entertaining the crowds at the Bullier.[33] Léonie-la-Désossée, it was said, ended her life the mistress of a château, while Gabrielle-la-Grêlée was seduced by an English lord, who abandoned her, and she opened a pub in Piccadilly in London.[34]

Perhaps the most famous dancer of the 1840s was Céleste Mogador, whose real name was Elisabeth-Céleste Vénard. The illegitimate daughter of a courtesan, she was forced to run away from home at fifteen after being nearly raped by one of her mother's lovers. She spent some time in prison, for her own protection, where she came into contact with a number of prostitutes. One of them advised her to enter the profession in order to gain some independence and, at sixteen, she joined a brothel near the rue des Moulins in

FIG. 16. Céleste Mogador, a high-class courtesan and the most well known of the early cancan dancers, only had a short career as an entertainer before marrying the Comte de Chabrillan. After he died, she made a living through writing and also worked in the theatre. *Private Collection.*

Paris. She found life in the brothel almost unbearable, but gained some relief from the regime on her one day off, when she learned to dance at dancing gardens like the Mabille.[35] She desperately wanted to escape from prostitution, but could not leave because she was heavily in debt to the madame. Eventually, a rich client took pity on her when she told him how much she really wanted to become an actress, and he paid off her debts and took her to live in his apartment.[36]

Mogador proved to be a very talented dancer, and the great Brididi was very impressed. He was looking for a replacement for Pomaré, now suffering from tuberculosis, and invited Mogador to be his new partner. He spent hours teaching her the steps of the dances currently in vogue, including the cancan and the polka. She proved to be a rewarding pupil. Her nickname arose one evening when Brididi proudly announced to friends at the dancing gardens that "it would be easier to defend Mogador than my partner". Mogador was a port in Morocco which had just been captured by France, and Brididi was joking that his new dancing partner was now so much in demand that he had difficulty keeping her to himself.[37]

Céleste Mogador was a beautiful young woman who captured the hearts of all who saw her dance. Her biographer, Françoise Moser, describes her as having had a "wonderful, classically proportioned body". For her début, she wore a lace-trimmed black dress, whose simplicity she disguised with an array of ornamentation. She was even more successful than Pomaré, with whom she had a close but difficult relationship until her death. According to Moser: "Her sensual charm contrasted with the enigma of her long, virginal face."[38]

Mogador is credited with inventing the *quadrille naturaliste*, which was so popular in the 1890s when danced by La Goulue and Valentin-le-Désossé.[39] This was a dance in set figures, with couples dancing together, as in the traditional quadrille; but in the final figure, each girl had the opportunity to improvise, while her partner danced separately, acting as her foil. When the women came into their own, as the cancan developed towards the dance as we know it today, the men in the quadrille became fewer, and they were usually outnumbered three to one.

Céleste Mogador and Pomaré were both high-class prostitutes of the kind who were acceptable in fashionable society. When Mogador gave up the cancan, in the same year that Pomaré died, there was apparently no risk involved, because she thought she would be supported by her lovers, one of whom was the novelist Alphonse Karr. However, when she was injured after falling from a horse, she was deserted by them. Fortunately, soon afterwards she met the Comte de Chabrillan, who fell in love with her and they married, much against his family's wishes. Although de Chabrillan was later ruined through unwise speculation and died not long after, his widow managed to make a living, partly through writing, and she lived to the age of eighty-five.[40]

Most famous of the next generation of *cancaneuses* was Rose Pompon, an attractive blonde who claimed that her father had been the illegitimate son of the deposed King Charles X. She developed and improved the *quadrille naturaliste*, and with it took the cancan to new heights of popularity in the 1850s.[41]

The acrobatic Nini-la-Belle-en-Cuisse (Nini with the beautiful thighs) was also one of the stars of the 1850s. She gained her nickname at the Reine Blanche by walking the length of the dance floor on her hands, showing to everyone that she was wearing no drawers. A policeman watching was so overcome by this spectacle that instead of arresting her he exclaimed: "Cré Dié! Les belles cuisses!" and Nini's future was assured.[42]

During the Second Empire, the cancan became much more widely known, both in France and abroad. From the late 1850s onwards, Rigolboche, whose real name was Marguerite Badel, built up her reputation at the Casino Cadet on rue Cadet in Paris. A somewhat unattractive woman, she made up for her lack of looks with a spirited but graceful rendering of the dance. She said that she was attacked by a form of madness when she danced, and that the music affected her so much that she became drunk, as if on champagne.

FIG. 17. Rigolboche in her favourite carnival costume, that of a Neapolitan fisherman. She was the first true cancan star and was frequently mentioned in the gossip columns. Pamphlets about her and photographs and cartoons of her were also widely circulated. *Collection of Ivor Guest.*

According to Charles Dolph, "Never were such *moulinets*, such *déhanchements* seen. Crowds gathered round her to watch that whirling mass of limbs and lingerie". [43]

Rigolboche was a *cocodette*, who counted members of the aristocracy amongst her lovers. One of these, the Duc de Gramont-Caderousse, who was a friend of the Prince of Wales, once persuaded her to walk naked from the Maison Dorée restaurant, across the boulevard des Italiens, to the Café Anglais. She performed the feat without being arrested, the duc having bribed the police to look the other way.[44] She also appeared on stage: in 1859, for example, she took part in a revue at the Théâtre des Délassements-Comiques called *Folichons et Folichonettes*.[45]

This unlikely candidate for stardom was the talk of Paris in her heyday. She was often photographed, and two journalists wrote some 'memoirs' on her behalf. It was also possible to buy pamphlets about her and cartoons. Rigolboche was, in short, a phenomenal success, as a dancer, a *cocodette* and an actress. Although she was not very astute in her business, and given to smoking cigars and drinking rum and absinthe to excess, she managed to make enough money to retire and end her days in comparative luxury in the suburbs of Paris. As with many cancan dancers, her career had been curtailed by her tendency to put on weight. *Le Figaro* reported in 1865: "The diva of Mabille has returned in an anatomical condition that gives no cause for worry about her health, but which must hinder her very much when she raises her leg to its customary height. So much the better for our noses!"[46]

Rigolboche's memoirs, whether or not they can be accepted as a true expression of her views, contain some interesting observations. She praised the dancing of another star of the *bal publics*, Rosalba: "a charming girl who dances the said cancan like no one—except Marguerite la Huguenote, who is its queen". Marguerite la Huguenote was another of Rigolboche's nicknames, so modesty was not her strong point. Her main rival, Finette, she dismisses contemptuously: "She believes she is my equal, but she is merely my disciple."[47]

Shortly after her memoirs appeared, another little book appeared in response, entitled *A bas Rigolboche* (*Down with Rigolboche*). This was an attack on the decadence and immorality that Rigolboche supposedly represented. A vicious diatribe against the cancan star and her milieu, it sought to undermine any claims to an artistic quality in the dance. Clearly, not everyone was enthralled by or even tolerant of the pre-eminence of the *cocodettes* on the dance floors. Rigolboche and her circle were viewed by the author as a highly distasteful replacement for the *grisettes* of earlier decades:

> *L'artiste—folle de passion;*
> *La grisette—folle d'amour;*
> *La lorette—folle de plaisir;*
> *Rigolboche—folle de vice!*[48]

Finette, known as 'la Bordelaise' because she had lived much of her earlier life in Bordeaux, was a Creole originally from Réunion, whose real name

FIG. 18. The apparently demure Finette was a wild cancan dancer, known at the Bal Mabille for her *grand écart* (jump splits) and for kicking the hats off male spectators. She also appeared on stage abroad in Germany and Britain. *Private Collection.*

was Joséphine Durwend. She was far prettier than Rigolboche, and the two often fought in public. Her good looks and her charm were of great advantage in her career as a *cocodette*, and one of her clients/lovers was the artist Whistler. She was in the *corps de ballet* of the Paris Opéra before becoming a *cancaneuse*, and her dance training helped her become a fine exponent of her art. She achieved great fame for her high kicks, and was particularly adept at knocking off the hats of gentlemen spectators, once winning fifteen hundred francs for this trick at an Opéra ball. She also claimed to have invented the *grand écart* or jump splits, and while this may have been an exaggeration she was certainly amongst the first to incorporate it in the cancan at the *bals publics*.[49] A more restrained version of the splits had become part of the cancan some years earlier, when a certain Marie-Louise had performed the feat in the gardens of Montparnasse.[50]

Finette had the opportunity to confirm the image of French naughtiness in the minds of the English by being one of the first to dance the cancan on the London stage.[51] She was brought to England by the theatre director John Hollingshead after she had completed a successful tour of Germany. She arrived with a small troupe of dancers, and made her debut on 26 December 1867 in a pantomime written by W. S. Gilbert for the Lyceum Theatre, where the Prince of Wales saw her more than once.[52] Gilbert watched her troupe rehearsing:

They looked white—a dirty white—after the Channel crossing. . . . Hats, cloaks, wraps were cast off—and eventually, I am bound to add—their dresses also, and in their petticoats they went through their business with extraordinary spirit. The rehearsals were a wild scramble.[53]

In the event, Finette danced an appropriately restrained version of the cancan for her British audiences and dressed as a boy in breeches, much as she might have done at the Carnival balls. Hollingshead, who had seen her perform in Paris, engaged her at the Alhambra in 1868 for a ballet entitled *Mabille in London*, and years afterwards he expressed pride that his show had had none of the "offensiveness of the cancan in petticoats. The most that could be said against it was that it was not a hornpipe."[54] Finette appeared in Edinburgh in the summer of 1870, and she was no doubt glad to be away from Paris because of the onset of war.[55] Sadly, she died not long afterwards in Constantinople "in pain and poverty", according to Hollingshead.[56]

The cancan had been seen in England at least as early as 1842, when *The Era* had had occasion to report on a 'masquerade' at the English Opera where among the "Kaleidoscopean groups there were *Débardeurs*, who danced the 'Cancan' with great zest". Also mentioned was a gentleman "whose name did not appear, but who was unquestionably formed of *caoutchouc*". He went through "sundry evolutions, to the evident wonderment of several 'flower-girls' and gazing 'goddesses'". The newspaper had no criticism of the performances, but merely observed: "The supper was good, the wines excellent, the music delightful, and the dancing spirited. The mirth was wild, and the fun glorious".[57] Charles Morton presented the cancan at his Oxford music hall in the early 1860s, where a quartet of Hungarian dancers called the Kiralfys gave their version of the quintessentially French dance. Morton is credited with devising the term 'French Cancan', later adopted by the Parisian cabarets. According to W. MacQueen-Pope, patrons of his theatre could not get enough of the "dainty but exciting high-kicking of Aniola Kiralfy". Emily Soldene, the operetta prima donna, used to watch Kiralfy limbering up, holding on to a door while her brothers worked her legs up and down.

On the bill at the Oxford at the same time as the Kiralfys was a juvenile ballet company, one member of which was a young girl named Sarah Wright.[58] No doubt she watched and was inspired by Aniola Kiralfy, because she was later to become the most well-known exponent of the cancan in the London music halls. Known as Sarah the Kicker or Wiry Sal, her unrestrained interpretations of the naughty spectacle were enough to cause the Alhambra to lose its magistrates' licence in 1870. A drawing of the troupe that she appeared with was published in *The Days' Doings*, and the police used it in evidence when the theatre's licence came up for renewal. A description in the police report indicates that again it was not really the Parisian spectacle that audiences had flocked to see, but apparently something of a pseudo-balletic interpretation.

FIG. 19. The Colonna troupe, featuring Wiry Sal, in the ballet *Les Nations* at the Alhambra music hall in London. This picture was used as justification for the refusal by magistrates to renew the theatre's licence in 1870. THE DAYS' DOINGS, *8 October 1870, by permission of the British Library.*

Of the four women performers, two were dressed as men with flesh-coloured tights, while the other two were dressed in ordinary ballet costumes, though with shorter knickers which revealed more of their thighs. The high kicks of their performances were described as "indecent" in the police report.[59]

The Days' Doings reacted to the controversy by hitting out at what it considered to be the hypocrisy of those involved. Frederick Strange, the proprietor of the Alhambra, had written to several newspapers complaining that the drawing had been "a highly overdrawn and exaggerated representation of a dance performed here in the ballet of 'Les Nations'". The magazine reprinted his letter and carried a sarcastic reply from the publisher, claiming that the drawing had been executed under the sanction of the Alhambra's management and that "they ordered, and purchased, for the purposes of advertising the performance, upwards of 80 copies of that week's issue". The magazine also pointed out that in the offending issue it had been stressed that the artist had "represented the actual action of the dance" without exaggeration. An editorial condemned the magistrates' action, saying that: "We have no doubt that some of the worthy magistrates have visited . . . Mabile [sic], the Sal Valentino, Maison Rouge, Asnières, or Wauxhall." According to *The Days' Doings*, the cancan at the Alhambra was no different from that witnessed by the magistrates in Paris, and it advised that "if you attempt hypocritically, or indeed honestly, to tell people what they ought to like, and what they ought not to like, you will merely follow in the wake of those who, by attempting to repress in one quarter, succeed in forcing out in another direction. The tight-lacing system will not succeed in matters of taste and entertainment." The editorial also highlighted the absurdity of the criteria for acceptability, which relied particularly on estimating the height of the raised leg.[60]

John Hollingshead later compared Wiry Sal unfavourably with Finette, whom he described as a "very handsome Spanish gypsy-looking lady"; he referred to Wiry Sal's cancan as a "Roast Beef and Plum Pudding Version".[61] Emily Soldene recalled that Sarah Wright "who had shorter skirts and longer legs than most girls, to the great delight and satisfaction of herself and London—kicked up her agile heels a little higher than had previously been deemed possible, and was equally successful in dusting the floor with her back hair". Soldene was responsible for employing Wright to perform in operetta at the Philharmonic Music Hall while the Alhambra was closed.[62]

It is interesting to note at this point that stage dance in general had acquired a dubious reputation in Victorian England, where any show of leg by a woman was considered shocking. Hence ballet was confined to the music halls, which of course provided entertainment for the masses and often aimed for sensation rather than true art. This did not mean that serious works were never staged, but that they were often embellished with special effects to prevent boredom. The scandalous reputation of the cancan meant, inevitably, that it was included in a number of ballets that were staged by the Alhambra and Empire music halls. It was also incorporated in many operettas, often without any relevance to the plot. Perhaps unsurprisingly, the small matter of losing its licence in 1870 had little effect on the Alhambra's long-term entertainment policy, and within months of it regaining a licence in April the following year, the "Quadrille du Grand Opéra de Paris" was once again delighting audiences there.[63]

The cancan might have been banned in England altogether, but fate intervened. Stage censorship at this time was in the hands of the infamous Lord Chamberlain's office, later vilified for its ridiculous pronouncements on erotic displays in the theatre. In 1874 the office received so many complaints about the cancan being performed at St James's Theatre that the Lord Chamberlain decided to go and see for himself. As luck would have it, although he strongly disapproved, he did not put a stop to the show, as its run came to an end very shortly in any case.[64]

The cancan was also performed in other countries of Europe from the 1840s onwards. It appeared in various contexts and was received with differing degrees of disapproval. It spread even as far as Russia, and here, according to *The Era*, it provoked a particularly extreme reaction. Two pretty French actresses, Mesdames Esther and Page, journeyed to the Russian capital in 1845 "in the intention of initiating the inhabitants of St Petersburg in all the improvements of the most advanced and Parisian civilisation". They were received enthusiastically, and the "Boyards deposed at their feet their homages and their roubles, and the chevaliers of the Guard were constant in their attentions". The ladies were apparently flattered, and the newspaper observed, not without a touch of irony, that "they determined on not delaying a single day their work of civilisation, and they determined on exhibiting to these Tartars all they were capable of teaching them, especially the cancan. A *Grande Soirée Dansante* was immediately organised, and the Russians were able to contemplate this marvellous dance, which fame with its hundred trumpets had so often told them of before." Eventually news of these events reached the ears of Tsar Nicolas, who unfortunately had "no taste for the cancan" and the two artistes were escorted out of the country by armed Cossacks. Those responsible for organising the performances of Esther and Page were arrested, together with the spectators, and taken to prison.[65]

In addition to Rigolboche and Finette la Bordelaise, a number of other dancers in 1860s Paris were highly regarded. Well worth noting was the aforementioned Rosalba, or Rosalba Cancan, who echoed the dance's supposed Spanish influences in her version. She attended the classes of Markowski, a dancing master, who found her impossible to teach because of her continual

FIGS. 20 and 21. Alice la Provençale, here showing her high kick and splits, was once banned from the Bal Mabille for dancing in too sensual a manner. Her costume seems to have been specially designed for dancing, possibly for paid performances. *Private Collection.*

FIG. 22. Rosalba was complimented on her dancing even by the conceited Rigolboche and the
dancing master Markowski once despaired of
teaching her because of her constant improvisation, a tendency which was ideal for the cancan.
Collection of Ivor Guest.

improvisation. Another pupil of Markowski, Alice la Provençale, was banned
from the Bal Mabille because her dancing was thought to be too sensual,
although she achieved success elsewhere. Fille de l'Air, named after a famous
racehorse, rose to prominence at the Bal Mabille around the time that Rigolboche began her decline. She was tall and slim, unlike Rigolboche, and was
compared favourably by Arsène Houssaye to some of the prima ballerinas at
the Opéra.[66]

Something of the atmosphere of the Mabille in the latter years of the Second Empire is provided by an American observer, who noted that any sem-
blance of order in the dancing was soon abandoned as the dancers "launched
into their own and almost indescribable extravagances". After relating the
antics of a twenty-five year old man, who indulged in some solo acrobatics to
the delight of the crowd, the American gave a wonderful account of the performances of the female participants:

A young girl, brown-eyed and with long masses of chestnut hair, then bounded to the centre of the circle, and commenced to throw herself into the wildest and most inde-cent positions, in which exhibition she was soon joined by another of the group, older and darker than herself. Each fresh pose was more pronounced than those which had preceded it, and called down lively applause from the spectators. One of the women suddenly sprang into the air and then came down to the ground with both legs at right angles to her body. A shout of laughter hailed this exploit, and a dozen hands were held out to help her from the ground; but disdaining all such aid, she sprang lightly to her feet, and both she and her companion took their places for their final effort. Delib-erately gathering up their long skirts, they threw them over their shoulders and thus left themselves unencumbered and exposed to the public view from their waists to their feet. In this condition they executed all manner of capers, with the utmost ease and coolness. One of the spectators venturing to thrust his face too close, the younger girl suddenly threw up her leg and with her foot sent his hat rolling into the circle amidst the yells and laughter of the lookers-on, and without pausing a moment went hopping around the circle with her foot higher than her head. The other, seizing her left foot in her left hand, raised to a level with her head, and holding it there, executed a remarkable dance with the other leg, never lowering her foot until she regained her place. . . .

Suddenly there is a pause in the music, and the dancers take their places again, and bursts forth the rich, voluptuous cadences of the cancan, against which French nature is powerless. The dancers seem inspired with new life, and plunge into the pas-sionate dance with a fury that fairly astonishes you. Such dancing, such embracings and coquetry, such utter abandonment of everything like individuality, such entire surrender to the sensuous influence of the music, can be seen nowhere but in this gar-den. The applause grows more enthusiastic, and what little modesty is left to the dancers is thrown aside, and they tread the thrilling measures with a zest only to be seen in Parisian women of their class. The brown-haired girl has closed her eyes, and has gathered her drapery under her arms. She sees nothing of the scene around her, but hears only the music and the applause. She is pale and panting, but she keeps on and on in the wild dance, until her strength is utterly exhausted.[67]

The cancan at this time was not exactly approved of by the *haut-monde*, but it was accepted as part of the same phenomenon as that of the courte-sans—admired for its daring and the subject of much excited gossip. In some quarters, it was viewed as potentially a revitalising element for ballroom dancing, which had lost much of its popularity.[68] Formal balls had become social events at which conversation was the prime activity, and dancing was decidedly secondary. Any proposal to introduce elements of the cancan into such gatherings was always likely to be rejected, however, due to the dance's salacious reputation. This was not helped by the coarser versions of the dance that featured in the less than salubrious surroundings of the brothels. The aim was to provide an aphrodisiac entertainment, and the dancers had little need for skill. These brothel cancans were always presented *sans-dessous* (i.e. with-out knickers).[69] There is some evidence to suggest that experienced quadrille troupes occasionally took what were lucrative engagements to dance *sans-*

FIG. 23. The all-male Quadrille des Clodoches were popular at the Paris Opéra balls in the 1860s and later turned professional, appearing several times at London music halls. Clodoche himself is kneeling, dressed as a 'Scotsman'. *Collection of Ivor Guest.*

dessous at private parties, but this was the exception, rather than the rule.[70] It is a myth that the cancan was often danced without knickers in public, once it had become established as a professional or semi-professional activity. But in the early days, when it was still solely an amateur pastime, drawers had not become a standard item of underwear.

By the 1860s, the Carnival balls at the Paris Opéra had become occasions for scenes of unparalleled gaiety and revelry, at which extravagant dancing was encouraged by drink and the anonymity of wearing masks. Exhibitions were put on by the stars of the Mabille and other dancing gardens. Both Rigolboche and Finette appeared at such events and pushed the cancan to the limits of respectability, apparently unconcerned that they might offend against the penal code. Numerous other dancers joined them in their antics, and although there may have been some arrests, these did not prevent the development of the dance into something like the cancan of the 1890s.[71]

Despite the attractiveness of the dancing by the Mabille stars, the highlight of an evening for many at the Opéra ball was a grotesque cancan performed by four men known as the Quadrille des Clodoches. These characters reputedly worked as undertakers' assistants, but no matter how solemn they were in the daytime, they certainly knew how to enjoy themselves in the evening. Clodoche himself dressed as a Scotsman in a kilt for the performance, his friend Flageolet as a fireman, and the other two, La Normande and La Comète, wore women's attire.[72] They later turned professional and were performing in London when Wiry Sal caused the Alhambra to lose its licence. No doubt the appearances by the Quadrille des Clodoches were also a matter for concern to the magistrates, who took the opportunity of the Alhambra's licence renewal application to state their general displeasure with the cancan.[73]

The apparently carefree Carnival balls, so symbolic of the Second Empire in Paris, were reflected in the lightly satirical operettas of Jacques Offenbach such as *Orpheus in the Underworld* and *La Vie Parisienne*, both of which featured a cancan or galop. Offenbach is said to have been inspired to write *La Vie Parisienne* after seeing Rigolboche dance.[74] The gaiety and confidence characteristic of this period were sadly to come to an abrupt end in 1870 with the French defeat by Prussia at the Battle of Sedan, the arrival of the German army in Paris and the crushing of the Commune. This tragic, but possibly inevitable consequence of an apparently overblown sense of national importance was symbolised by Zola with the death of the beautiful courtesan, Nana. Early in her 'career' she had performed the cancan with a full measure of gaiety and *joie de vivre* reflecting the spirit of the age—when she died, still young, on the eve of the war, her beautiful face was destroyed by the ravages of disease.[75]

CHAPTER 2 / FRILLS AND SPILLS IN THE MODERN AGE
From the 1880s to the 1990s

THE BEGINNINGS OF THE THIRD REPUBLIC WERE MORE STABLE POLITICALLY, BUT French pride had been severely dented and a more pessimistic era was ushered in. In the 1870s, the cancan all but disappeared. It survived as an amateur dance in the places in which it had begun—the bars and dance halls frequented by working men and women.[1] The dancing at such places had nothing of the glamour associated with that of the *cocodettes* who had entertained pleasure seekers at the Bal Mabille. The Goncourts described the scene at the Boule Noire in their novel *Germinie Lacerteux*:

There was not a collar to frame the youthfulness of the faces, not a scrap of a light petticoat fluttering out of the whirlwind of the dance, not a touch of white among these women, sad-coloured to the toes of their dull boots, and wholly clad in the hues of wretchedness. . . . The women dancers threw themselves about and capered, animated, clumsy and riotous beneath the lash of bestial joy.[2]

The period of gloom eased in the 1880s and the middle and upper classes began to search for new diversions to help forget the uncertainties of the time. As if in answer to their dreams, there appeared a precocious teenage girl named Louise Weber, who began to frequent the popular dance halls such as the Elysée-Montmartre and the Moulin de la Galette and—as La Goulue—played a major part in the cancan's revival and redefinition.

Born in 1866 in Clichy la Garenne, near Paris, young Louise Weber was brought up by her mother, a laundress. She was educated by nuns, and retained a certain respect for the Church, even though it is said that she offended the priest on the day of her first communion by dressing in a tutu and ballet shoes.[3] While helping her mother at work she came across all kinds of elaborate underwear left for cleaning by the rich women of Paris. When she started work as a laundress in her own right, she was able to borrow some of this exciting lingerie and dance with wild abandon in the amusement palaces of Montmartre, showing it off to admirers.[4] She quickly acquired a formidable reputation as an entertainer and was able to make the transition from amateur performer to professional in a few years.

There is some doubt as to the exact location of her début, but La Goulue's mother's business was situated close to the Moulin de la Galette, and it seems likely that she would have performed there first. Her first amorous encounter was at the Moulin, with a young artilleryman from whom she also learnt dancing. She had affairs with other men, but it soon became clear that she preferred women, and she later lived with another dancer known as La Môme Fromage.[5]

La Goulue was made aware of the potential of a career in entertainment when friends from the Moulin de la Galette took her to a more upmarket establishment, the Grand Véfour, where well-dressed gentlemen were evidently more than willing to pay to see her dance.[6] Soon afterwards she appeared at the Elysée-Montmartre, whose management also recognised her undoubted talents and encouraged her attendance by granting her free entry. In the years before the opening of the Moulin Rouge, the Elysée-Montmartre was the main venue in Paris where members of the upper and lower classes could mix. La Goulue's down-to-earth and cheeky rendition of the dance and her general lack of sophistication proved to be a great attraction for the idle rich clientele.[7]

Her cancan was described by Eugène Rodrigues in 1892:

From the start, her cheeks glow like ripe peaches, her wild hair flies about like gossamer fibres. No method, no order, but a sure sense of rhythm and an undeniable openness and gaiety. She lifts her arms, careless of the strap taking the place of a sleeve; her legs bend, sway about, hitting the air and threatening hats. . . . She constantly looks for the risqué gesture of the hand, the foot, the whole body; she finds it, she imposes it and the audience applauds. La Goulue is an enchantress.[8]

Although not regarded as pretty, La Goulue had impudent good looks, which her audiences found irresistible. She was also an object of fascination for the artist Toulouse-Lautrec and for photographers. Numerous photographs exist

FIG. 24. La Goulue with her rival Grille d'Egout in the early days of their appearances at the Moulin de la Galette and elsewhere. Their styles contrasted markedly, La Goulue being decidedly more suggestive and provocative in her gestures. *Carnavalet/Photothèque des Musées de la Ville de Paris.*

of her, either in the familiar role of *cancaneuse* or in various erotic poses, sometimes completely naked. Unfortunately she could not be photographed actually performing the cancan, owing to the fact that a camera's need for a lengthy exposure would have resulted in a blurred image. She was clearly proud of her body, and sometimes she appeared bare-breasted in tableaux at the Moulin Rouge. Although she seemed willing to be portrayed as a dissolute woman, she clearly considered herself morally superior to many of the other girls, whom she referred to as "tarts".[9]

La Goulue is also renowned for her amiable disrespect towards Edward, Prince of Wales, who was busy promoting *entente cordiale* at the Moulin Rouge and other cabarets in Paris in the 1890s. He was captivated by her, like many others, and did not take offence when she asked him if his old mother was still alive, and whether it was she or the prince himself that now ruled. La Goulue also once demanded that the prince pay for champagne at the Jardin de Paris, saluting him in her inimitable fashion with one leg raised to her forehead. He was glad to oblige.[10]

At the Elysée-Montmartre and the Moulin Rouge La Goulue's partner was Valentin-le-Désossé—'Valentin the boneless'. It is he who appears in grotesque silhouette in Toulouse-Lautrec's first poster commission for the Moulin Rouge, with La Goulue herself in the centre. It seems that Renaudin, for that was his real name, deserved his nickname even more than Léonie-la-Désossée had done in the 1840s, his limbs appearing as if made from rubber as he pranced and pirouetted across the floor.[11] Valentin helped train the new dancers at the Moulin Rouge and is shown doing so in Toulouse-Lautrec's *Dressage des Nouvelles, par Valentin-le-Désossé (Moulin Rouge)*. He played a major part in La Goulue's meteoric rise; having 'discovered' her, probably at the Moulin de la Galette, he then partnered her at various venues before her triumphant début with him at the Moulin Rouge.[12]

Valentin was born in 1843, and in his teens began to frequent the *bals publics* where he became acquainted with the dancing of Rigolboche, Finette and Alice la Provençale.[13] He soon gained a formidable reputation as a performer in his own right, although it must be said that by the time of the Second Empire the women had eclipsed the men as exponents of the cancan. It is therefore to his credit, and a reflection of his ability and appeal, that he is the only male dancer to be remembered from the *fin-de-siècle quadrille naturaliste*.

By day, Valentin was an apparently respectable member of Parisian society, often to be seen driving in the Bois de Boulogne. His father had been a notary, and Valentin continued to work in the family practice (his brother was also a notary).[14] He also at one time owned a wine shop. At night, in his guise of the slippery, elongated partner of La Goulue and others in the *quadrille naturaliste*, he was transformed into an eccentric genius of almost acrobatic ability. He always wore a top hat, which never became dislodged even while executing the most dramatic and daring manoeuvres, and he also often frequently danced while smoking a large cigar. He was a 'perfect gentleman' between dances, although his private life was subject to endless speculation.[15]

The *quadrille naturaliste* at the Elysée-Montmartre was a popular amateur pastime, but La Goulue, Valentin-le-Désossé and their fellow performers developed it into an artistic tour de force. Their complex steps and sheer physical superiority soon alienated amateur performers from the dance and ensured the *quadrille*'s future as a spectacular entertainment, danced by professionals for an audience. The opening of the Moulin Rouge gave these new stars the opportunity to move into a purpose-built cabaret.[16]

The *quadrille* at the Moulin Rouge was usually danced by three women and one man. It was choreographed in set figures, but each of the performers had the opportunity to improvise in the solos which were a major feature of the spectacle, and which caused the greatest excitement among the audience. It was during these improvisations that the famous trick of knocking off the hat of an admiring male onlooker took place, not always with absolute accuracy.[17]

The women's brightly coloured skirts were as much as twelve metres in circumference, and underneath they wore gorgeous frothy, lacy petticoats, frilly knickers and black silk stockings held up with ribbon garters. The excitement of the dance grew from graceful beginnings, when the *danseuses* first lifted their skirts and carried out subtle balletic movements in time to the

FIG. 25. La Goulue may not have been the first to perform this trick in the cancan, but somehow its insolence so perfectly summed up her personality that it became her trademark. She is pictured with her partner, Valentin-le-Désossé at the Jardin de Paris. LE COURRIER FRANÇAIS, *29 June 1890, by permission of the British Library,* M.F.*85*.

music, and gradually accelerated in pace until all were involved in a frenzy of high kicks and rhythmic gestures with their skirts. La Goulue's treat for the audience came when she bent forward to toss her skirts over her head and reveal an embroidered heart on the seat of her drawers.[18] The *quadrille naturaliste*—or *quadrille réaliste*, as it was also known—was not usually referred to as the cancan by contemporary writers, who regarded the Moulin Rouge frolics as something distinct from the dances that had appeared at the Carnival balls fifty years earlier. As previously mentioned, the word 'cancan' also had undesirable associations with the Second Empire, of which few in the Third Republic wished to be reminded. Hence, the writer Gaston Vuillier described La Goulue and her fellows as "professional celebrities of the *chahut* and the *grand écart*".[19]

One star of the Moulin Rouge in its early years who was not required to join in with the *quadrille* was Jane Avril. She was allowed this concession by the director of the cabaret, Charles Zidler, who always singled her out for special attention, recognising in her charm and refinement not found in most of the other girls.[20] She was Toulouse-Lautrec's favourite model, and the slim beauty who appears in his paintings and lithographs received little of the caricature treatment sometimes found in his work. She eschewed the absurd nicknames adopted by her fellows, although she was sometimes referred to as 'Mélinite', a type of explosive, because of the exuberance of her dancing.[21] She appears to have had wit and intelligence, which set her apart from many of the dancers at the Moulin Rouge, and several writers were among her acquaintances, including Oscar Wilde and Verlaine.[22] Unfortunately, she came to be referred to by her colleagues as 'Jane la Folle' ('Crazy Jane'), which was appropriate because it described her sometimes wild individuality, but which for Jane herself recalled a sad episode of her teenage years.[23]

Jane's Avril's background was more bourgeois than that of La Goulue, but she had a very difficult early life. Her mother, Elise Richepin, a Second Empire *cocotte*, at first wanted little to do with her baby and left her with her grandparents in the country. When they died, the young girl was taken in by sisters at a convent, where she lived happily until taken away by her mother and brought to Paris to live with her in an unpleasant, dark and smelly flat.

Her mother had by now lost her looks and her money and was showing signs of madness. She still had some male clients, and one of these actually paid for her daughter's education until the age of thirteen. Avril learnt both singing and dancing at school, but the enjoyment of her lessons was severely undermined by her home life, where her mother frequently beat her, and eventually she was forced to run away from home.[24]

She was taken in by another of her mother's former clients, who found her to be ill and called a doctor. Diagnosed as having St Vitus's Dance, she became an inmate of the Salpétrière hospital—under the renowned Dr Charcot, who treated unbalanced women in the Grandes Hystériques ward. These women were often suffering from repressed lusts and desires, and the ward and its doctors acquired some notoriety in late-nineteenth-century Paris. For Avril, the spell in hospital was a blessing in disguise. She was able to attend school again. She also had gymnastics lessons and was taught classical dance by one of the patients who had been on the stage.[25]

When she had finally recovered from the illness, she attended a costume ball at the hospital and it was here, in front of other patients, doctors and nurses, that she gave her first performance as an individual dancer. She was apparently carried away by some of the music, and, having no partner for that dance, indulged in a solo which brought her a round of applause, kisses and hugs from both friends and strangers. An indication of the impression that she must have made is that the floor completely cleared of other dancers while she performed, the other guests at the ball being totally captivated by the sixteen-year-old girl.[26]

FIG. 26. The enigmatic Jane Avril, whose style was different from other dancers at the Moulin Rouge. Although she did perform the cancan, her solo performances seem to have been more akin to skirt dancing, with graceful movements carried out to a waltz tune. *Musée de Montmartre.*

She was released almost immediately afterwards, but her troubles were not over. Her mother now felt Avril was ripe for being exploited and tried several times to force her into prostitution. She knew that her daughter's good looks were far more likely to attract clients than her own fading allure. During one of these attempts, Avril was nearly raped and then was beaten when she returned home for having failed to earn any money. This time, she left home for good.[27]

The first appearance by Jane Avril at a public dance hall came when she visited the Bal Bullier with some friends. These friends were prostitutes who had looked after her since her final escape from her mother's control. She never joined their profession, but she found their company enjoyable, and their protection very necessary. She did have liaisons with men, but insisted that she was never a common courtesan. The first of these developed after her performances at the Bullier, where she again danced alone, to the great admiration of spectators.[28]

Her lovers, who were mostly artists of one kind or another—poets, painters, etc.—provided her with a home and security while she was still essentially an amateur performer. The bohemian life on the left bank suited her perfectly, but she soon found the Bal Bullier too limiting for her and she moved to dancing at the more elegant *bals* of Montmartre, including the Elysée-Montmartre.[29]

In 1889, she briefly gave up dancing to earn her living as a cashier at the Great Exhibition.[30] After the exhibition closed, she joined an equestrian show, but soon tired of this and returned to the dance. She always insisted that she performed purely for her own pleasure, and it certainly seems that she was totally absorbed in her art. Nevertheless she became a professional dancer for the first time at the Moulin Rouge, which first opened its doors on 6 October 1889 and soon established its continuing reputation. When Jane Avril appeared there, Zidler was so taken with her that he offered her a contract on the spot. Her dancing was quite a contrast with that of La Goulue, and universally considered to be more artistic and subtle.[31]

While at the Moulin Rouge, Avril became a model for one of its most famous customers, the painter Toulouse-Lautrec. Something of the paradoxical nature of her personality comes out in his paintings and in contemporary photographs of her. She can appear demure, soberly dressed, even dowdy, while at other times she looks smart, sophisticated and elegant; she can be like an innocent little girl with a cheeky smile, or a sensual dancer, carried away by the music. Arthur Symons summed up her appearance thus: "Everything about her suggested a kind of dark and morbid depraved virginity, a mixture of corruption and innocence."[32]

Avril usually danced solo, often to a waltz tune, and had a number of 'trademarks' which set her apart from all the other dancers. Zidler was always anxious to please her, as he was determined to keep her at his theatre, and he allowed her to wear coloured undergarments while insisting on white for the other girls. She took advantage of this concession to design many beautiful colour schemes for her outfits: her dresses, of silk and chiffon, contrasted—

sometimes slightly, sometimes dramatically—with her petticoats and knickers. Her biographer, José Shercliff described them: "Her first gown was scar-
let and underneath it tiers of skirts shaded down the whole gamut of reds to
the palest shell pink. Another was cherry-coloured silk, the petticoats fading
through tones of heliotrope and lavender. Under a flame-coloured gown that
made her hair look almost platinum blonde, she wore tulip green, ice-blue
under cyclamen, primrose under green."[33]

Zidler allowed Avril not to take part in the *quadrille* with the other *cancaneuses* so that she could develop her specialities without distractions. One of
these was known as the 'the fan' and involved leaning backwards until her
shoulders touched the floor, while she held her leg up vertically.[34] Clearly her
gymnastics training came in very useful. She occasionally joined in with the
quadrille, but Zidler never demanded that she did so. Other dancers inevitably
became jealous, but she never suffered any serious attacks, possibly because
Zidler protected her, but also because she commanded considerable respect as
a truly outstanding exponent of her art.[35]

The Moulin Rouge had many other stars at this time, some of whom
approached the fame of La Goulue or Jane Avril for brief periods, but are less
well known because they were never immortalised in paint by the "little
genius of Montmartre", Toulouse-Lautrec. Nini-Patte-en-l'Air actually opened
her own cancan school in the rue Frochet. This was a shrewd move, as dancers
of the cancan were now much in demand in many European and North American cities.[36] Among her pupils was Eglantine, whose troupe was featured on a
famous poster that Toulouse-Lautrec designed for their tour of England.[37] Nini
charged high fees for instruction and earned more money and an unfortunate
reputation by admitting elderly and (most importantly) rich gentlemen to
practice sessions—supposedly to offer advice and encouragement to the bud-
ding *cancaneuses*, but giving rise to inevitable misinterpretation by the general
public.[38]

As a performer at the Moulin Rouge, Nini-Patte-en-l'Air had many admirers, some of whom preferred her style to that of La Goulue. Her high kicks
were dazzling, apparently executed with little effort, her legs seeming to act
independently of her body. She whirled around the floor in a frenzy, her face
convulsed with delirious excitement.[39] It was Rigolboche, in her memoirs,
who described how the cancan infected her with a kind of madness, that she
forgot everything around her. Nini's behaviour on the dance floor seemed to
bear out perfectly what her illustrious predecessor had said.

Nini took her dancers to other venues besides the Moulin Rouge, and
even to other countries, including Germany and England. In 1894, they gave
several performances at the Trafalgar and Palace Theatres in London, where
they were billed as "Nini-Patte-en-l'Air and Troupe in their Celebrated
Parisian Quadrilles".[40] When they appeared at the Casino de Paris, Nini must
have been proud that her dancers were described on posters as *ses élèves* (her
pupils). She became rich, but her school was soon closed, partly because of
scandal surrounding it which had been promoted by newspapers. She eventually retired to the country, where she married.[41]

FIG. 27. Nini-Patte-en-l'Air and some of the pupils at her cancan school visited other countries to present their version of the quadrille naturaliste. The school was eventually closed after it had been suggested that it was a front for less salubrious activities. *Roger-Viollet*.

La Môme Fromage (the cheese kid) was La Goulue's lover, but this did not mean that they always saw eye to eye on the dance floor. They frequently had loud arguments and fights, which added to the entertainment value of the performance for many.[42] Her rather odd nickname derived from a slang term for the youngest person in a workshop, and originated in her case from the time when she was a dressmaker's apprentice.[43] She was not regarded as attractive, except by La Goulue, and a contemporary observer described her as "nothing but an ignoble, ugly woman".[44]

Grille d'Egout was La Goulue's greatest rival, but their performances were quite different. La Goulue's earthy sexuality was in great contrast to Grille d'Egout's much more light-hearted treatment of the cancan, which was sexy but not vulgar. Her appearances in the *quadrille naturaliste* at the Moulin Rouge were much admired for their artistry and grace. Eugène Rodrigues wrote that she had raised the *chahut* to the level of a gavotte.[45] André Warnod described her cancan as being "elegant, witty and delicate".[46]

LEFT, FIG. 28. Réjane was a highly popular comedy actress in 1890s Paris. Grille d'Egout's humorous nature made her an appropriate coach for Réjane's role in *Ma Cousine*, during which she was required to perform a cancan. *Theatre Museum, V&A Picture Library.*

RIGHT, FIG. 29. Rayon d'Or and La Sauterelle. This pose was held with some help from a table, discreetly positioned but not hidden; before the advent of fast film it was not possible to photograph the cancan actually in progress. *Carnavalet/Photothèque des Musées de la Ville de Paris.*

Grille d'Egout was slightly built, but hardly beautiful, with her jutting chin and misshapen teeth. She was reputedly more intelligent than most of the dancers and sought out sophisticated company, which may have aroused jealousy in some quarters. She became friends with the actress Réjane and taught her to dance the cancan for performances of *Ma Cousine* by Meilhac at the Variétés. This was a great success, and the pretty comedienne surprised and delighted those in the orchestra stalls when she lifted her skirts and exhibited her shapely legs in an extremely proficient version of the dance. Réjane's performance was a credit to her tutor, who was disappointed when this did not lead to a new career. Incidentally, the nickname Grille d'Egout means 'drainage grille', and referred to the gaps between her teeth.[47]

One of the most experienced dancers at the Moulin Rouge was Rayon d'Or. She was a big, strong woman who wore a red wig to accentuate her dark eyebrows. Despite her large frame, she was an extremely nimble dancer who was much admired for her skill, particularly by the younger girls. According to Rodrigues, when resting she had the disciplined appearance of a soldier, but in action the capriciousness of a street urchin. Rayon d'Or was the usual partner of Grille d'Egout, whose dancing she complemented with suppleness and grace, the fruit of her long experience in a career which had begun at the Bal Mabille. She had no resort to the ungraceful acrobatics of some of her successors, who tended to sacrifice the more attractive features of the cancan in exchange for providing sensation.[48]

A hiatus occurred in her career when she left Paris in the 1890s with an American she had met at the Moulin Rouge. They travelled to Alaska together where they made their fortunes prospecting for gold. It is not known whether she was tempted to demonstrate the 'genuine' cancan in the dance halls of the Klondike, where the dance was to become the equivalent of traditional folk entertainment.[49]

Of the numerous other *cancaneuses* of the 1890s, worth mentioning are La Glu, whose appearance was attractive although her language was coarse; Georgette Macarona, who also competed with La Goulue as a belly dancer; and La Sauterelle, who, as her name suggests, used to leap about like a grasshopper. Each of these struggled to gain recognition while being outclassed in personality, skill or both by the real stars of the Moulin Rouge. They were all competent performers, but their careers only spanned a very few years.[50]

Throughout the sixty or so years in which the cancan was chiefly the preserve of individual female performers, the nicknames given to these women were important in increasing their notoriety. In the early years these nicknames were often descriptive: Finette, for example, was known as 'la Bordelaise' because she had lived in Bordeaux or 'la Créole' because she was indeed a Creole. Similarly, there existed Alexandrine aux Cheveux d'Or (Alexandrine with the golden hair), Bébé de Cherbourg, Elise Belle-Jambe (Elise with the beautiful legs), Pauline la Blonde, Marie la Polkeuse and many others.[51] Some nicknames had rather obscure origins, like those of Céleste Mogador and La Reine Pomaré, and some were distinctly exotic. In almost all cases they were attractive and rarely uncomplimentary, in contrast to some of those of the 1890s. Grille d'Egout may have had ugly teeth, but such a feature would not have been highlighted in the Second Empire, when Nini Belles-Dents (Nini with the *beautiful* teeth) was a famous dancer. Even Jane Avril had to suffer the title 'Crazy Jane', as well as the more attractive 'Silken Thread' and 'Mélinite'. By no means all of the nicknames in the 1890s were unpleasant, and in fact some were quite charming, like Rayon d'Or, meaning 'ray of gold' and la Sauterelle, 'grasshopper'. Then there were Eglantine (wild rose), Gazelle, Hirondelle (swallow), and many more. Attempts to revive the tradition of nicknames at the Moulin Rouge in the 1920s were doomed to failure, as the dancers were no longer recognisable as individual personalities.[52]

The cancan dancers of the 1890s were kept in order by a strange character known as Père la Pudeur, whose real name was Durocher. A former photographer and friend of Toulouse-Lautrec, he had been employed at the Elysée-Montmartre to make sure that little improprieties between clients did not occur in public.[53] At the Moulin Rouge he was responsible for making sure 'the forbidden zone' was not seen during the cancan—quite a problem when drawers were often still of the open type. Revealing knickers would certainly have transgressed the penal code, and so Durocher made sure they were sewn up. Some girls, however, deliberately kept them open, and he had to close them personally with safety pins.[54] La Goulue and her contemporaries were not subject to such strict control when dancing as 'amateurs' at the Moulin de la Galette and elsewhere, and an article in *Gil Blas* in 1891 described how La Goulue drew the eyes of spectators beneath her skirts in search of glimpses of naked flesh and "her most intimate efflorescence, revealed at a certain point by a dark patch".[55]

Georges Montorgueil wrote that La Goulue tried

every possible way of showing what she should not, and worse. She provokes by displaying her bare flesh as far as it can be seen amongst the magnificent jumble of her underwear, intentionally allowing a liberal amount of naked skin to be visible between her garter and the first flounce of her knickers, which slide up when she extends her leg. The transparent material barely covers the rest. She observes the fascination this provokes, gradually stirring it up through movements each more risqué than the last, and encouraging unhealthy curiosity to stretch to frantic searching, making the most of the effects of shadows in the pink areas glimpsed through gaps in the lace.[56]

This certainly contrasted with the position of Grille d'Egout who declared that a woman who showed her skin in the cancan was *"sale"* (dirty).[57] Montorgueil commented that Grille d'Egout performed all the high kicks of the cancan and knocked the hats from the heads of spectators, but "without unseemly provocation, without ribald immodesty, without deliberate indecency".[58] Clodoche, star of the Second Empire Opéra balls, witnessed the *quadrille naturaliste* in the 1890s and was not impressed. Interviewed at the time, he also declared the dance to be *"sale"*.[59]

Although the 'private parts' were generally not seen by the public, the small area of flesh between stocking top and knickers, emphasised in the late nineteenth century by the prevailing fashion of black stockings, became, despite Grille d'Egout's exhortations, an enduring feature of the cancan. This was even more the case when suspenders were introduced and the long bloomers were replaced by shorter 'French' knickers. Many men who witnessed the cancan at this time waxed lyrical about what James Laver was to describe as the "thigh eroticism" demonstrated in the dance.[60] Black stockings became *de rigueur* for the costume, providing a contrast with the white or pale-coloured underwear and, as Jane Avril pointed out, emphasising the shape of the legs.[61]

There *were* nightclubs in 1890s Paris where it was possible to see a knickerless cancan, although these appear to have been more like brothels than public dance halls, but rumours reaching other countries naturally exaggerated the situation and foreigners coming to Paris hoped to catch La Goulue in such a state, by accident or design. Warnod claims that she and others would sometimes 'forget' their knickers for a bet, and that Père la Pudeur was known to turn his back when this happened.[62] Such events could not have taken place very often; contemporary photographs and paintings show the dancers all properly dressed, and it is worth bearing in mind that nude photographs of La Goulue, Nini-Patte-en-l'Air, Rayon d'Or and others also exist, so they would not have been reluctant to pose without knickers if it had been customary in the cancan.

The Moulin Rouge has become known as the home of the cancan, but this is misleading as it was by no means the only venue which presented this exciting spectacle. Jane Avril continued to entertain a less well-heeled audience at the Bal Bullier in the Latin Quarter for a few years, and amateur performers gained inspiration from her and kept the dance hall alive as a place to find the cancan until the early 1900s.[63] Avril also regularly appeared at the fashionable Jardin de Paris after the Moulin Rouge closed for the evening. The proprietor of both establishments, Joseph Oller, used to bring his other well-known dancers, including La Goulue, Grille d'Egout, Rayon d'Or and Nini Patte-en-l'Air, to the Jardin by horse-drawn coach from the Moulin Rouge. Each night the drivers of the vehicle dressed in ceremonial uniform for the journey, in order to emphasise the theatrical nature of the exercise and to create a carnival atmosphere. Some enthusiastic customers also travelled the same route in order to see the cancan once again.[64] The Moulin de la Galette was another dance hall which continued to encourage the cancan, and both Jane Avril and La Goulue were still reliving their past triumphs there as late as 1892.[65]

The reputation of the cancan spread all over the Western world during the last decade of the nineteenth century, and each country produced its own exponents of this dance, which somehow encapsulated the spirit of the age. A memorable version was performed by the British artiste Lottie Collins while she sang 'Ta-ra-ra-boom-de-ay' in the music halls and variety theatres of Great Britain and the United States. She first presented her fast and furious act in October 1891 at the Tivoli music hall in London. On a trip to America, she had heard the song and recognised its potential: she would begin quietly and sweetly with the verse, and in the chorus throw caution to the wind in her

FIG. 30. Lottie Collins's performance was so frenetic that it often left her fainting in the wings and doctors later suggested that it had shortened her life. It certainly appears that she was severely corseted which would have affected her breathing. *Theatre Museum, V&A Picture Library.*

wild cancan-style extravaganza, which for many in England was an enduring symbol of the naughty nineties.[66] Collins gave three low kicks with the first three syllables 'Ta-ra-ra' and then a dramatic high kick on the 'boom'.[67] According to Ernest Short, "Lottie wore a Gainsborough hat and a short frock of red silk, which readily displayed the wealth of white petticoat, and the excitement began with a clash of cymbals which accompanied the opening 'Boom'".[68] The chorus could be repeated as often as Collins and her audiences liked—she was usually called on to give several encores. One contemporary critic commented on Collins's performance: "It is part of a modern liberal education to see it once at least."[69]

George Bernard Shaw admired Lottie Collins and contrasted her style with inferior imitators, of which there were many. According to Shaw, her act was "a most instructive example of the value of artistic method in music-hall singing". He described another performer's rendition of 'Ta-ra-ra-boom-de-ay' as "a complete failure", mainly because it was too rushed and unrefined. He said that Collins took the song "at an exceedingly restrained tempo" and clearly articulated the words.[70] This was evidently very important and the act relied heavily on the combination of song and dance, something that was unique in the history of the cancan at this stage. There was something distinctly suggestive about Collins's performance, and the way she teased her admirers through the innocent verse and then rewarded them for their 'patience' in the chorus was a delight.

Lottie Collins took her act to music halls throughout Great Britain and the United States, where she toured for seven months. American audiences liked her act as much those in Britain, and a critic in Kansas City appeared astonished by her stamina:

Lottie Collins has the stage all to herself and she bounces and dances and races all over it in the most reckless and irresponsible way, precisely as if she was a happy child so full of health and spirits that she couldn't keep still if she wanted to. . . . She is invariably in motion except when she stops to chant the gibberish that passes for verses, but the wonder is that she has breath enough to sing after the first cyclonic interlude.[71]

She remained in America for a further three years, appearing with the 'Lottie Collins Troubadours', and then returned to Britain. She was never allowed to forget 'Ta-ra-ra-boom-de-ay', and wherever she went it was requested.[72] She became quite rich on the basis of just this one song, receiving £150 per week to perform during a pantomime at the Gaiety in 1892, and £200 a week in the United States when she appeared between the acts of a musical show called *June*. When she died at the relatively early age of forty-four in 1910, doctors suggested that her heart disease was a direct result of the extraordinary gyrations which accompanied her song.[73]

It may seem surprising, but in the days before mass communications the fame of some of the Paris-based *cancaneuses* was widespread abroad and they were often invited to perform in other countries, although no doubt they had to tone down their acts much in the way Finette had in the 1860s. Nini-Patte-en-l'Air's dancers and the Troupe de Mademoiselle Eglantine, which included Jane Avril, received a number of such engagements, but they did not always live up to their audiences' expectations. Avril had been offered work in cities as far afield as New York and St Petersburg, but she turned them all down in favour of a trip to London with the beautiful and accomplished Eglantine and two other girls of more limited talent. Her biographer, José Shercliff, maintains that she was the driving force behind the *quadrille* troupe, rather than Eglantine, and it was certainly Avril who asked Toulouse-Lautrec to design the poster for their show.[74]

Although Eglantine had had the experience of visiting London as part of Nini's troupe in 1894, this time the French girls had mixed fortunes during their engagement at the Palace Theatre. Gazelle and Cléopatre had difficulty in coping with the audience's clear preference for their more gifted fellow dancers and they made their feelings obvious during serious quarrels backstage. In addition, the English critics found the show unimpressive, being used to the more witty, unrefined home-grown performers and being intolerant of the artistic treatment of the cancan provided by the visitors from across the Channel.[75] Despite the problems, audiences were generally favourable—Shercliff goes as far as to say that the tour was a "riotous success".[76]

The cancan had now become more recognisable as the dance that still persists today. Not only were the high kicks and other energetic movements a major element, but also the skirt manipulation and display of erotic underwear. The dancers of the 1860s had lifted their skirts when performing, but primarily to give themselves freedom of leg movement. With the coming of layers of lace, embroidery and ribbons on the petticoats and knickers, and black stockings, the *cancaneuses* of the nineties had much more to offer by showing their *dessous*. Here the cancan borrowed something from the more erotic versions of the skirt dancing that was also in vogue at the end of the nineteenth century.

The skirt dance was essentially a solo dance performed by a woman in a long dress who manipulated the material of the skirt while executing graceful movements with her feet. It was popularised in Britain by Kate Vaughan, who had ballet training and was able to provide a more aesthetic alternative to Wiry Sal in the music halls of 1870s London. In its original form it was not very revealing, but some of the less accomplished dancers who followed Kate Vaughan relied on the enticing nature of the latest underwear fashions, together with flashes of leg, to guarantee success with their audiences. They also danced in a considerably more energetic fashion, and inevitably high

FIG. 31. The much-photographed Kate Vaughan was an actress as well as a dancer, but her early success was in developing the skirt dance into an attractive and artistic phenomenon. She was later copied by less accomplished performers. *Theatre Museum, V&A Picture Library.*

kicks crept into their performances. Shaw, who had been so complimentary about Lottie Collins, was scathing about the inexpert skirt dancers whose only real attraction was "their variegated underclothing".

Who has not seen a musical comedy or comic farce interrupted for five minutes, whilst a young woman without muscle or practice enough to stand safely on one foot—one who, after a volley of kicks with the right leg has, on turning to the other side of the stage, had to confess herself ignominiously unable to get beyond a stumble with her left, and, in short, could not, one would think, be mistaken by her most infatuated adorer for anything but an object-lesson in saltatory incompetence—clumsily waves the inevitable petticoats at the public as silken censers of that odor di femina *which is the real staple of five-sixths of our theatrical commerce?*[77]

Kate Vaughan had given the skirt dance a reputation of having some artistic merit, while the cancan was viewed as merely outrageous and provocative. By claiming to skirt dance, while really cancanning, many young women in the music halls of the late nineteenth century caused something of the reputation of one to stick to the other, and vice versa. Lifting skirts right up and shaking them from side to side in time with the music is certainly much more revealing and suggestive than anything the first skirt dancers were prepared to do, but it only really became a fundamental part of the cancan towards the turn of the century, after the skirt dancers had shown how fascinating it was to employ petticoats to erotic effect.

Jane Avril, Eglantine and their fellow dancers appeared in London wearing very long dresses with layers of petticoats. As was observed at the time in the journal *St. Paul's*, this was as they were costumed at the Jardin de Paris or the Moulin Rouge, whereas Nini-Patte-en-l'Air's troupe had worn comparatively short skirts during their visit in 1894. Perhaps it had been felt that Britain was not ready for the cancan in its full splendour at that time. Whatever the reason, the cancan was still felt to have more erotic content than the increasingly popular *tableaux vivants* which employed nude 'statues' (the nudity was only apparent, as the performers invariably wore a form of flesh-coloured body stocking). As a writer in *St. Paul's* pointed out,

there is much more that is suggestive about the average skirt dance, with its profusive exhibition of lingerie *and things than in all the living pictures in the world. . . . There was a deal more suggestiveness in the dances of the Eglantine Troupe at the Palace, and of the Nini Patti en L'Air [sic] combination . . . than in all the undraped living pictures put together.*

The writer added that he did not disapprove of mild suggestiveness at all, but was merely recording these comments for the benefit of prudes.[78] As if to emphasise the innocuousness of the *tableaux vivants*, *The Times* went as far as to describe those of Diane de Fontenoy (who played Eve, Lady Godiva and a number of other historical nudes) as elegant and providing a "harmonious and pleasant effect".[79]

The Troupe Eglantine, as rendered by Toulouse-Lautrec, is dancing in a line facing the audience. This 'chorus-line' image of the cancan, which most people are familiar with, was rare in France in the 1880s and 1890s, because the performers at the Elysée-Montmartre, the Moulin de la Galette or the Moulin Rouge usually danced in a *quadrille* on the dance floor, rather than on a stage. The chorus line also implies a degree of coordinated choreography, and less of the spontaneity that remained in the dance halls as a surviving feature of the amateur versions of the dance from earlier decades. Lona Barrison and her 'sisters', who travelled from America to appear on the Folies Bergère stage in the 1890s, gave Paris its first taste of the chorus line. This was regimented, precision-style dancing of a kind unfamiliar to Paris audiences. *La Revue illustré* tried to analyse the Barrison sisters' success:

Their gallant exercises performed each evening at the Folies Bergère attract the crowd. What do people most like about them? The pale gold of their hair, the litheness of their bodies, the whiteness of their teeth, the carmine of their smile, the slightly acid freshness of their voices, their mechanical toy waddle, the gracefulness of their slender legs, the sensuous seething of their frilly and beribboned underwear—this kind of charm cannot be explained—it has to be experienced.[80]

The chorus-line form of choreography almost certainly first appeared in the United States, where Lydia Thompson and her British Blondes had established the 'girlie' show in the early 1870s. They had begun their career typically with a 'classical' show, *Ixion*, modelled on the Offenbach style, and with plenty of opportunity for exhibiting the Blondes' legs, and in which Venus showed a penchant for the cancan. Before long the company dispensed with paying lip-service to the classics, but continued to appear scantily clad, and in 1873 concluded their performance in the now familiar, high-kicking line-up. A woman critic of the time observed icily that "It doesn't look pretty to see a lady kick."[81]

The cancan was as phenomenally popular in America as elsewhere. When Offenbach visited the country in the 1870s to conduct *Orpheus in the Underworld*, the first-night audience were disappointed when he did not dance the cancan himself. When Marie Aimée, who had popularised his operettas in the United States, suggested a revival of *La Vie Parisienne*, he decided to reward his American fans. While Aimée danced the cancan on the stage, he pranced about in the orchestra pit, and the show was a huge success.[82] Within a few years, the dance had become a favourite in burlesque shows, which were widespread in the latter part of the century. M. B. Leavitt, a successful American producer, was behind many of the troupes that visited American cities, providing a package of female sexuality for the mostly male audiences. A stagehand with Leavitt's 'Mme. Rentz-Santley Burlesque Troupe' remembered the ecstatic reaction to a presentation of the cancan in San Francisco: Mabel Santley's dance was advertised well in advance, and she apparently only had to lift her foot twelve inches from the floor and the audience went wild! The prop-boy later commented: "It sent them crazy. . . . It became the talk of the town. The theatre was jammed, as a result, for three full weeks."[83]

Offenbach's influence on popular culture was also felt in Russia, where it was not universally welcomed. In fact undesirable Western influences were condemned in some quarters, especially by radical political figures. The populist writer, Nikolay Mikhailovskiy, saw Offenbach's operettas as signs of decadence and moral bankruptcy brought on by liberal 'social Darwinian' ideas. He said: "In earlier times people feared hell. Now the souls of the greatest sinners are doing the cancan." He was dismayed that the cancan was gaining popularity in St Petersburg, especially at the dance hall known as the Khutorok (little farmstead). Mikhailovskiy's friend, Vasiliy Kurochkin wrote a poem complaining that young people were abandoning the study of revolutionary texts in favour of this decadent pursuit:

> *Young woman, are you reading* Chto delat'?
> *That book is full of every kind of filth and evil*
> *Throw away the debauchery and vice in that evil book*
> *And come with me to dance the cancan at the Khutorok.*[84]

It may seem extraordinary just how much the cancan has been attacked for its corrupting influence over the years. This attitude remained ingrained in certain areas of Russian political thinking and was to gain worldwide publicity when Khrushchev was Soviet leader in the 1950s.[85]

The coming of the new century brought a feeling of change: in 1900 Jane Avril performed with her *quadrille* troupe in several French cities, but generally the era of the individual cancan star was over. La Goulue, for example, was by now well in decline. In 1895 she had dramatically announced that she was quitting the Moulin Rouge to organise her own show. She had been fighting a losing battle with her weight, but surprisingly it seems that she had also become pregnant and was unable to indulge in such a strenuous activity as the cancan.[86] But she was now rich enough to take time off to have the baby and then invest in a venture of her own, and she decided to present the belly dance in a fairground booth. Unfortunately, her fame from the Moulin Rouge was not enough to compensate for the lack of appeal that her new show had for the general public, and within a few years her wealth had disappeared.[87]

She had no chance of returning to her former glory, as her size now prevented any thoughts of dancing, and she even resorted to lion taming as a method of earning money. She took to the bottle and degenerated further. In 1914, a Toulouse-Lautrec retrospective was being organised in Paris, and she was invited to a meeting to discuss the possibility of setting up a replica of her fairground booth, in which the organising committee hoped she might perform her original programme. Unfortunately, her general appearance was by now so unattractive, that the idea was abandoned.[88] La Goulue ended her days selling matches in Montmartre outside the Moulin Rouge, an ironic twist

FIG. 32. The 'Théâtre de la Goulue' towards the end of the nineteenth century. La Goulue's original fairground booth was decorated with panels painted by Toulouse-Lautrec, but they were soon sold, presumably because her new venture was not a financial success. *Getty Images.*

of fate and a sad end to a legendary life. After earning enough at the Moulin Rouge to amass a small fortune and invest it in her own venture at the Foire du Trône, now, in 1929, she was to die in poverty.[89]

An interesting postscript to the story of La Goulue came in March 1992, at the time of the large-scale Toulouse-Lautrec retrospective exhibition in Paris. It was announced that his famous model's ashes were to be transferred to the cemetery in Montmartre, a stone's throw from the site of her greatest triumphs, the Moulin Rouge. The Association of the Friends of La Goulue had campaigned for some time for her remains to be transferred to this most appropriate resting place. It was almost a hundred years to the day since the famous poster advertising the dancer's appearances *tous les soirs* at the nightclub had first appeared on the streets of Paris.[90]

In sharp contrast to La Goulue, Jane Avril kept her slim figure and continued to dance the cancan well into the twentieth century. She had experienced some difficulty when Joseph Oller, the proprietor of the Moulin Rouge, had persuaded her to join in the *quadrille* each night in exchange for a regular wage. This was after Zidler had departed, and without him to protect her, Avril had felt obliged to agree. Her creativity was somewhat stifled by this new arrangement, but ultimately Oller had shown flexibility. He was very

FIG. 33. La Goulue in 1929, near the end of her life, on the steps of her squalid caravan at the Porte de Clignancourt in Paris. A sad figure, perhaps recalling her all too brief period of fame and fortune at the Moulin Rouge. *Roger-Viollet.*

understanding when she had to leave the show for many months to have a baby, and in 1901 did not stand in her way when she wished to go to America to be with her lover Maurice Biais.[91] She was soon back again, however, and dancing to great acclaim as before at the Moulin Rouge.

Jane Avril appeared at many different theatres and cabarets from the mid-1890s through to the end of the first decade of the twentieth century, including the Chat Noir, the Décadents, the Casino de Paris and the Bal Tabarin. Her career diversified into musical comedy and plays, and she had the distinction of creating the role of Anitra in *Peer Gynt* at the Folies Bergère. When she took a *quadrille* troupe to Madrid towards the end of her career, the audience was initially extremely hostile to the dancers, but Avril showed she had lost none of her artistry and succeeded in winning over the Spanish with her individual performances.[92]

In an effort to revitalise her dancing after Oller had turned her into a salaried performer, Avril had accepted charity engagements at which she still felt the thrill of being a true amateur, performing for her own pleasure. During the First World War, she had a similar experience when she decided to entertain for the benefit of wounded and sick servicemen, munitions factory employees and Red Cross workers. Rich society ladies even paid for her to dance for them in their drawing rooms in aid of the war effort. Shercliff described these occasions thus: "In a *frou-frou* of silk and lace, dug out of her old trunks, she kicked a breath of the fanciful 'nineties into the grim present of the war-ridden twentieth century."[93] Although she had effectively retired when she married Biais in 1910, she had clearly continued to practise.

During her later life she found herself periodically sought after by nostalgia seekers. In 1935, a Toulouse-Lautrec ball was organised at the Moulin de la Galette and Avril was invited as one of the few stars of 1890s who was still alive and whose fame was still recalled by many. Although now well into her sixties, she danced a few steps for the assembled luminaries and received a standing ovation.[94] Her last appearance in public came in 1941 when a gala evening was held in her honour in Paris.[95] She died in 1943, in relative obscurity in a retirement home on the outskirts of the city, having always retained her grace and dignity.[96]

The first decades of the new century ultimately produced the definitive cancan which still continues to be copied today. Music halls throughout the Western world offered chorus lines of pretty dancers performing the famous French dance and operettas such as *The Merry Widow* ensured that the dance would be remembered forever as being symbolic of the era.

Throughout the twentieth century the cancan has been performed in Paris, although no dancer since the 1890s has ever built her reputation solely on her expertise at this one dance. When the Moulin Rouge reopened in 1921 after fire had destroyed the original building, André Warnod remarked that the lovers of the *quadrille* had not been forgotten in the new cabaret. However, he complained that it bore little resemblance to the dance of La Goulue and Grille d'Egout and described the modern *danseuses* as executing a veritable ballet based on the steps of their predecessors.[97] Warnod was really describing how the dance had developed, being now the cleverly choreographed 'French Cancan' rather than the wild, exuberant *chahut* of La Goulue and her associates. Some people naturally desired this more outrageous evocation of the 1890s, but in a sense it is the refinement of Jane Avril which has survived in the more successful of the later versions. The choreographer at the Moulin

Rouge at this time was Pierre Sandrini, the son of a famous dancer at the Opéra. He was also a classically trained dancer, and in devising the French Cancan he gave the dance a kind of gracefulness and subtlety quite unlike the wild dancing of La Goulue.

The new name for the dance had first been used by London music-hall proprietor Charles Morton in the 1860s. The cancan on stage had always required a degree of choreography, because it was essentially a performance for an audience, whereas the dance of the Paris *bals* relied on a great deal of improvisation, reflecting its roots as an amateur participatory activity. In using Morton's term, Sandrini was acknowledging that his choreographed spectacle owed much to the development of the cancan as a stage dance outside France.

Sandrini's dancers were highly competent ballet-trained professionals, and they brought the Moulin Rouge new fame as the home of the French Cancan. The famous dance hall had lost any right to such a title to the Bal Tabarin in 1904, after the management had decided that the era of the popularity of the *quadrille naturaliste* was over and had converted the establishment into a music hall, though with a ballroom attached.[98] The Tabarin was opened by an accomplished orchestra conductor, Auguste Bosc, who recognised that the cancan still had great potential, with as much appeal for the French as for foreign tourists.[99] (See colour illustration no. 1.)

For almost twenty years, the Tabarin saw great success as a venue for the dance, but when Sandrini arrived at the Moulin Rouge, Bosc's business inevitably suffered. Within a few years, the situation had changed, as Sandrini, together with Pierre Dubout, took over the management of the Tabarin and built a new show around Sandrini's magnificent French Cancan. Bosc's establishment had attempted to follow the tradition of the Moulin Rouge, with grand parades and *fêtes de nuit*, as well as the *quadrilles naturalistes*. Sandrini created something completely original by introducing the *cancaneuses* in spectacular and ingenious tableaux. Each new season he came up with something new, with the girls perhaps entering the hall in a balloon or appearing riding on a merry-go-round. Such devices added to the excitement of the anticipation of the dance, and Pierre Sandrini's establishment was soon noted for the quality of its cabaret and its exceptional French Cancan.[100]

In the 1930s, the Tabarin had a corps de ballet of thirty-four professionally trained dancers. Each girl had to have at least three years' experience in ballet companies, and be at least five feet eight inches tall. They nearly all appeared in the earlier part of the show in various other dance numbers, but the undoubted highlight was the cancan, performed by eight of the very best dancers. Four of these would perform specialities—individual feats of acrobatic brilliance, incorporating the well-known cancan movements: the high kick or *battement*, the *rond de jambes* (quick rotary movement of lower leg with knee raised, and skirt held up), the *port d'armes* (turning on one leg while grasping the other leg by the ankle and holding it almost vertical), the cartwheel and the *grand écart*. Perhaps the feat that drew the most gasps from the audience was the *grand écart*. No doubt many an untrained dancer had injured herself (or himself) while executing this difficult movement since Finette had claimed it as her invention in the 1860s. At the Tabarin, the dancers learnt to perform this manoeuvre very carefully, and no girl would try the jump splits until she was quite ready for it.[101]

Pierre Sandrini's French Cancan was an exquisite interpretation of the dance. The individual specialities, which each girl was encouraged to develop during rehearsals and make her own, were an important link with the solo exponents of the dance that had been witnessed in *fin-de-siècle* Montmartre.

FIG. 34. The French Cancan performed during a gala evening at the Moulin Rouge in 1954, led by a successor to Valentin-le-Désossé, Jean-Louis Bert. Many of the Paris cabarets presented their own versions of the dance in the 1950s. *Roger-Viollet.*

The Tabarin cancan had the best of both worlds—dazzling choreography and individual talent.

Other nightclubs in Paris copied the Bal Tabarin and produced their own elaborately choreographed French Cancans, often lasting ten to fifteen minutes, far longer than had been envisaged by Offenbach when he was writing his music for the dance in *Orpheus in the Underworld*. Several different pieces of music were therefore used, usually culminating in his famous *galop infernal*. It was generally assumed that a three-minute cancan would not be satisfactory, and would merely leave the audience hungry for more. Certainly, three minutes was nothing like long enough to give scope for the improvisation, or rather the rehearsed solos of the French Cancan. A large-scale French Cancan can be seen in the film of the same name, supposedly set on the opening night of the Moulin Rouge, but the film was made in the 1950s and clearly owed more to the development and consolidation of the dance as manifested at the Tabarin.

Another film, made in Hollywood, and based on the Cole Porter musical about the cancan, had the dubious distinction of leading to an international incident. During Nikita Khrushchev's visit to the United States in 1959, he was treated to a trip out to the Twentieth Century Fox studios where shooting for the finale of the film was taking place. Shirley Maclaine, Juliet Prowse and the company gave the Soviet leader a full performance, and afterwards he met the dancers. The atmosphere was warm and friendly, and Khrushchev expressed his pleasure at meeting the stars.[102] But the following day he had a meeting with trade union leaders at which he surprised everyone by prancing around the room, playing with his jacket in imitation of a cancan-dancer's skirt and declaring that the dance was immoral: "This is a dance in which the girls pull up their skirts. You're going to see that—we're not. This is what you call freedom. Freedom for the girls to show their backsides to us is pornography, the culture of a people who want pornography. It's capitalism that makes the girls that way." As Shirley Maclaine said later: "You would never think that a few pantaloons and some petticoats would cause such a furore." Certainly the US State Department was acutely embarrassed about the whole affair. *Dance Magazine*'s editor commented that those responsible for arranging Khrushchev's visit "have still to learn that dance is a language that communicates, and it is not 'just entertainment'".[103]

The cabarets of Paris have not been equalled in any other country, but attempts have been made to copy their style, even to the point of giving a theatre the same name as one in the French capital (there was Moulin Rouge in New York, for example). One phenomenon that occurred in more restrained Britain in the 1930s and 1940s was that of the 'French revue', associated with the Windmill Theatre in London and with the striptease artiste Phyllis Dixey. She was famous for her 'peek-a-boo' fan dance, which relied on the audience thinking they saw more than they actually did. Her shows, and those of her imitators, contained a certain amount of coy nudity, and always a troupe of cancan dancers. The Windmill's shows were a successful revival of the music-hall tradition of the nineteenth century, and provided London audiences with *tableaux vivants* and a cancan to rival that of the Tabarin in Paris. Like the dancers at the Tabarin, the Windmill's girls were ballet trained, and they wore very attractive traditional costumes with Victorian-style underwear. Such revues were very popular throughout Britain, but Phyllis Dixey gave up in the 1950s in the face of increasingly crude and less artistic competition, and the Windmill also closed its doors in the early 1960s, having suffered from competition with television.[104]

FIG. 35. The cancan at the Windmill Theatre in London in the 1950s. The Windmill's attempt to reproduce for British audiences something like the Paris cabarets was restricted by stage censorship, but evidently not in the case of the cancan. *Theatre Museum, V & A Picture Library.*

With the establishment of a recognised form for the cancan in Paris, the French Cancan, the only changes that tended to be made were to the costumes, sometimes for the worse, unfortunately. Attempts to 'modernise' the skirts and underwear or introduce gimmicks such as blonde wigs for the performers took away some of the spirit of the naughty nineties, which the cancan needs for its vitality and a feeling of abandoned gaiety. Another undesirable tendency was the increasing speed with which the dancers hurtled around the floor at some venues, quite undermining the sensation of subtle sexiness and the illusion of spontaneity which is the cancan's *raison d'être*. Despite such problems, the cancan remains largely unscathed, and is still performed at many nightclubs and theatres in Paris and around the world.

The cancan has had a varied history, and has always caused controversy. That it is still capable of doing so today is illustrated by the experience of the former Gold Rush town of Whitehorse in western Canada in March 1992. A local newspaper editor tried to provoke discussion about the town's resident cancan troupe (and sell more newspapers) by accusing them of not being 'politically correct', and saying that it was time, in his words, to "can the cancanners". The man's own politically correct credentials seemed severely flawed, as he described the dancers as "heifers" and "strumpets" in his article.[105] In any case, he found that he had bitten off rather more than he could chew, because he not only provoked discussion, but also angry demonstrations in the streets. Some people, proud of the Whitehorse traditions and determined that the cancan should continue to be a highlight of the local theatre's Gold Rush revue, demanded that the hapless editor be hounded out of town![106]

CHAPTER 3 / THEATRES, MUSIC HALLS AND DANCING GARDENS
The Many 'Homes' of the Cancan

AN ASTONISHING VARIETY OF MUSIC HALLS, THEATRES, DANCE HALLS, OUTDOOR dancing gardens and other open-air venues such as fairgrounds have been associated with the cancan in its long history. After the early years in Paris the dance spread to other cities in France, Europe, North America and throughout the Western world. Music-hall and variety shows regularly featured the cancan from the mid-nineteenth century onwards, although not without some difficulties if municipal officials believed the dance offended public decency. Small-scale venues, such as country fairs in England and elsewhere, began to include steam organs, which were used to accompany troupes of dancing girls, often to the disapproval of local village moralists. In the American West, saloons in small towns set up makeshift stages on which to organise entertainment for the cowboys, and the cancan was foremost in the fare on offer, usually inexpertly performed by women from the brothel. Later in the century, when the cancan was becoming more professional, proprietors and impresarios strove to provide their audiences with a quality performance, as near as possible to the 'genuine' article found in Paris. The venues themselves became more luxurious and attractive, in recognition of the fact that audiences were now drawn from all sections of society. Artistes were becoming more mobile, and French dancers occasionally visited other countries to show them the real *quadrille naturaliste*.

The theatre in Paris that is often described as 'the home of the French Cancan' is the Moulin Rouge, which first offered its attractions to the Paris public in 1889, a few years after La Goulue's and Jane Avril's débuts in Montmartre. As with many dance halls, the Moulin Rouge has undergone a number of changes. It was originally the site of the Reine Blanche, where Nini-la-Belle-en-Cuisse gave her revealing display. When the Spanish theatre manager Joseph Oller built his new establishment in the year of the *Exposition Universelle* he calculated that the *quadrille naturaliste* would pull in the crowds. Paris was a cosmopolitan centre long before this exhibition—Offenbach had recognised this in 1866 with his operetta *La Vie Parisienne*—and the new dance hall was designed and decorated with images and motifs which reflected styles from different parts of France and Europe.[1] Oller's enterprise was probably the first example of Paris nightlife deliberately catering for foreign tourists, a tradition that continues today in the major cabaret venues.

To say that the Moulin Rouge was a dance hall is misleading. People did come to dance, but they also expected much more than that. Zidler, the manager of the establishment in its early years, was eager to oblige and employed singers, acrobats, conjurers and a number of other entertainers to keep the crowds amused. He invited the best dancers in Paris to appear in his shows, having been aware of La Goulue, Valentin-le-Désossé, Jane Avril and others from their appearances at the nearby Moulin de la Galette.

Le Figaro illustré, describing the Moulin Rouge's attractions in 1890, made it

Paris, le

Le Moulin Rouge

FIG. 36. As this turn-of-the-century postcard shows, the Moulin Rouge had already become part of the Paris tourist industry. The picture is a drawing with the heads of La Goulue, Nini-Patte-en-l'Air and others superimposed. *Private collection.*

clear that Oller's original conception was a masterful combination of the traditional dancing gardens with the modern cabaret theatre. According to the paper, the Moulin had a "magnificent garden which can accommodate more than 600 people, shaded by large trees". In the garden there was a stage on which was presented "a *concert-spectacle* from 8.30 until 10 p.m. before the dancing". The garden was overlooked by a huge cardboard elephant, in which the belly dancer Zélaska performed for men only, a stage and an orchestra, and elsewhere in the grounds were to be found "donkey races, merry-go-rounds, shooting-galleries and various games".[2] *Le Figaro illustré* also promised seasonal masked balls and other attractions and claimed, without exaggerating, that the establishment was attended by painters, sculptors, writers and other members of the Parisian artistic community.[3]

The dance hall itself, on the Place Blanche, was entered via a red-walled foyer decorated with posters and photographs. Before you reached the ballroom there was a small stage presenting an almost continuous cabaret as an alternative to the entertainment on offer in the main hall and outside. Lesser-known performers took their chances here, hoping that they would achieve success and eventual fame either in the Moulin Rouge *bal* itself or in other venues. Inside, below the orchestra gallery, where there were huge mirrors let into the wall to give the illusion of extra space, aspiring *quadrille* dancers were often to be seen practising their steps. Around the dance floor were galleries, where members of the public could drink and socialise.[4]

Apart from the delights of the *quadrille naturaliste* and the skirt dancing of Jane Avril, the audience was also offered a variety of other entertainers, including exotic dancers 'from the mystic Orient', and singers both of sentimental love songs and those of the *réaliste* variety.[5] Included among the latter was the remarkable Yvette Guilbert, who later had a successful international career. Among the more eccentric performers at the Moulin Rouge was the famous Le Pétomane, who specialised in breaking wind to music.[6]

Journals such as *Le Courrier français* gave the Moulin Rouge and its artistes welcome publicity, guaranteed to make the venue highly fashionable. It attracted a varied clientele, including members of the bourgeoisie from Paris and the provinces, foreigners (particularly from Russia and England), as well as society figures, including, of course, the Prince of Wales. The dance hall also acquired a reputation as a market for prostitution, of high and low class varieties. Toulouse-Lautrec's painting of the interior of the Moulin Rouge, *Dressage des Nouvelles, par Valentin-le-Désossé*, shows a high-class courtesan in the foreground.[7]

Crucial in establishing the new entertainment venue as the most famous of all Parisian dance halls were the choice of location, on the busy Place Blanche below the Butte Montmartre, and the inspired decision to erect the

FIG. 37. The exterior of the Moulin Rouge today superficially resembles the original building, with the famous red windmill still dominating the scene, but much has changed on the inside and the garden has also disappeared. *Private collection.*

FIG. 38. One of the bizarre acts presented in the Moulin Rouge garden, Les Ecossais, seems to be have been quite a hit with female audiences if this cartoon is anything to go by—or were they shocked? It is difficult to tell. LE COURRIER FRANÇAIS, *27 October 1889, by permission of the British Library, M.F.85.*

Les Ecossais au Moulin-Rouge.   Dessin de F. Lunel.

magnificent red windmill above the entrance. The latter has become internationally known as a landmark in the French capital, along with Notre Dame, the Arc de Triomphe, the Eiffel Tower and the Sacré Coeur. Real windmills were a common sight in Montmartre until the late nineteenth century, and even at the time of the opening of the Moulin Rouge the area was still regarded by many as a village beyond the boundaries of the city proper.

The initial success of the Moulin Rouge was short-lived, and the excitement that it generated in the Parisian nights had dissipated by the middle of the 1890s. La Goulue's departure was certainly a factor which caused this, but Zidler's public quarrel with Oller and the increasing competition from other venues were probably more significant. One way in which the Moulin Rouge tried to attract more customers was by presenting gala nights featuring parades or processions. Several of the stars of the *quadrille* took part in these shows, known as *redoutes*, which were effectively a revival of the masked carnival balls of the Second Empire, only this time packaged primarily as entertainment. The first took place in December 1894, and each had a theme, usually historical and often associated with decadence and debauchery. The first evening presented the procession of Bacchus, Greek god of wine, a theme that was often repeated in later years. Another popular subject was spring and fertility; other parades covered 'love' in many different forms and there were a number of appearances by the Roman goddess of love herself, Venus.[8]

Unsurprisingly, many of the processions contained naked or semi-clothed women, which at first caused some friction with the authorities, but was soon accepted. Nudity in the theatre was at this time usually only illusory and body stockings were used in *tableaux vivants* to give the impression of nakedness. Oller had experienced the moral censure of Senator Béranger's 'Society of Protest Against Public Licentiousness' as early as 1893, when its members objected to a parade during the *Bal des Quat'z' Arts*. It seems that a young woman named Sarah Brown had portrayed Cleopatra wearing a very revealing fishnet costume. She and one her 'handmaidens', who had been similarly attired, together with the organiser of the event were taken to court. La Goulue, who had also been present at the ball, was upset because she had been virtually ignored despite her own diaphanous Indian costume and took her revenge by appearing as a witness for the prosecution. According to Georges Montorgueil, she adopted the attitude of an innocent in court, claiming that she had been shocked to see the dance floor invaded by a troupe of such improperly dressed women.[9]

In the event, the organiser of the show and two of the participants were found guilty, but received such low fines that it was almost as if they had been cleared of their 'crimes'. Strangely, the case prompted violence in the Latin Quarter after police arrived to remove effigies of Senator Béranger that had appeared hanging from lamp-posts. One innocent young man was killed, and the riots that followed led to the prefect of police being dismissed.[10] It all seems to have been a regrettable storm in a teacup, especially as nudity, or semi-nudity, was soon to be an intrinsic part of Paris revues, with few people raising objections to it.

Oller's other popular establishment was the Jardin de Paris, near the Champs-Elysées. There was a dance floor, but visitors to the Jardin could also amuse themselves at rifle ranges, watch circus performers and slide shows, see belly dancers perform in their booths, have their fortunes told, take rides on a rollercoaster, and enjoy seeing singers and other entertainers in all manner of variety shows. Some of the latter had a geographical theme, and others were in the form of short plays or mimes.[11] The climax of the evening, and a master stroke by an experienced showman, was the arrival by coach of the dancers from the Moulin Rouge, which closed its doors much earlier in the evening than the Jardin de Paris.[12] Charles Zidler, who managed both establishments for Oller, no doubt saw the Jardin de Paris as a modern version of the Bal Mabille, whose memories it certainly evoked, not least because of its location.[13]

Zidler's ability accurately to assess the needs of his audiences led many to identify him, rather than Oller, as the real genius behind the two cabarets. It was Zidler, after all, who discovered such diverse talents as Yvette Guilbert and Le Pétomane, and he also commissioned Toulouse-Lautrec to design the famous poster of La Goulue in 1891.[14] He appears to have had a very good relationship with the artistes in his shows, and when he left Oller's employment in September 1892, Guilbert said he would be irreplaceable.[15] The two men's much-publicised disagreement, which led to their parting company for good, has never been satisfactorily explained, although it was most likely a familiar conflict over demarcation of roles in management. Zidler may have resented too much interference by Oller in the running of the two operations, but after his departure Oller continued to have success with both the Moulin Rouge and the Jardin de Paris.

By the early 1900s, the management of the Moulin Rouge had decided that the time of the cancan had passed, and the establishment was turned into a variety theatre, where lavish revues and operettas were staged. In 1908, the aggressive *apache* dance or *valse chaloupée* made its first appearance in a revue, performed by Max Dearly and Mistinguett. The latter became known as the 'queen of the music hall' and starred in many shows at the Moulin Rouge and the Folies Bergère. In the basement of the new theatre there was a restaurant with Tyrolean orchestra playing, and boxing matches were also presented as a secondary attraction.[16] Fortunately for the survival of the cancan in Paris, the Bal Tabarin was opened in 1904 and it took over much of the Moulin's former activities, including the *quadrille naturaliste* and the *redoutes*.[17]

In 1915, a fire destroyed much of the building of the Moulin Rouge, and it was allowed to stand empty for a number of years until it was reopened as a music hall in 1924 with a revue entitled 'New York–Montmartre'.[18] This was a successful attempt by the creator of the 'Parisian revue', Jacques-Charles, to cultivate a 'transatlantic' image for the theatre, recognising the increasing interest of American visitors to Paris. In the basement dance hall, Pierre Sandrini presented his thrilling French Cancan to the delight of both French and foreign customers. The *quadrille naturaliste* had continued to be featured spasmodically at the Moulin Rouge, but only as a relatively minor attraction. The fact that the cancan was now presented only as an alternative to the main event in the theatre suggests that the management still had a somewhat ambivalent view of its value.

The new Moulin Rouge lasted as a theatre only until 1929, when the management turned it into a cinema. Cabaret continued at the venue only on an occasional basis. During the Second World War, live entertainment was provided in the dance hall and in the 1950s international artistes were invited to give performances. The interior was enlarged and refurbished in the early 1950s, with a dance floor both for dancing by customers and for entertainment. Images of La Goulue, Valentin-le-Désossé and Jane Avril adorned the walls, together with frescoes of other entertainers and people historically associated with the dance hall, including Toulouse-Lautrec.[19]

The tradition of the dinner show only began in 1959, with the French Cancan as the climax of the evening. At this time, the nightclub became known as the cancan's 'home', although it was by no means the only location where it could be enjoyed.[20] The Moulin Rouge could rely on the historical associations with the cancan provided through the well-known posters and paintings of Toulouse-Lautrec from the 1890s, but the fact that the theatre almost abandoned the dance at times in the first five decades of this century, and indeed on occasions ceased to provide live entertainment of any sort, makes one question the validity of the title 'home of the cancan'. However, the French Cancan of Pierre Sandrini did certainly originate here, although he only stayed for a few years before moving to the Tabarin.

FIG. 39. The Grande Chaumière in its early days, as recalled by the *Journal pour rire* in 1852, with a mazurka in progress rather than a cancan, no doubt meeting with the approval of the formidable Père La Hire. JOURNAL POUR RIRE, *6 November 1852, by permission of the British Library, F.117.*

Purists would claim that the cancan's real, original home was the now long-gone Grande Chaumière, which was to be found in the southern outskirts of Paris in the first half of the nineteenth century. It was here, most historians agree, that the cancan first came to prominence, although, of course at this time it was a very different dance from the French Cancan or even the *quadrille naturaliste* of La Goulue and Valentin-le-Désossé. The word *chaumière* means 'thatched cottage', and indeed the gardens where the students and *grisettes* met to indulge in innocent pleasures were dominated by a building resembling a country cottage, where drinks were sold. Albert Vandamm, who visited the Chaumière in its early years, described it as a "simple enough place" which was open all day, with a skittle alley, a primitive shooting gallery and other similar attractions. The students came in fine weather to seek "their 'lady-loves' sitting at work demurely under the trees". The refreshments on offer were inexpensive, and the customers would pass the time chatting and singing or merely strolling about.[21]

The Chaumière in fact dated from just before the French Revolution of 1789, and was originally built by an Englishman named Tinkson. He had acquired a piece of land in the then village of Montparnasse just outside Paris, and he decided to establish gardens where ordinary people could come to drink and dance. Unfortunately he had to flee Paris in 1793 after being denounced during the Terror, but within a few years he returned and resolved to expand his enterprise. He teamed up with a restaurateur and they demolished the original Chaumière and replaced it with a larger, two-storey building.[22] The extensive gardens were beautifully laid out, and the new *guinguette*, as such suburban dancing gardens were called, was soon very popular, not only with the working classes, but also with members of the petite bourgeoisie, soldiers and, of course, students at the nearby university. The latter often came from prominent French families, and hence were quite rich and willing to buy drinks both for themselves and for the local girls who had little money. The students tended to be tribal in outlook, and each table was occupied by young men exclusively from a particular town or region of France. This competitive nature probably encouraged the development of the cancan, as each group tried to outdo the other in their dancing. For this they had a loud orchestra to help them.[23]

Tinkson must have been pleased with the amount of business generated in his establishment, which was soon extremely popular and well known throughout Paris. The reputation of the Chaumière grew further under the somewhat strict 'Père' La Hire from the late 1830s onwards, and it also became notorious for offending public decency with its dancing displays. A larger than life character in many ways, La Hire tried to keep firm control over his customers, personally ejecting any who indulged in any form of immodesty. He once had occasion to deal in this way with La Reine Pomaré when she dared to kick her legs in the air for an admiring crowd of students.[24] It has been argued that La Hire's attitude had a stifling effect on the cancan's development, but in general he was fighting a losing battle. The cancan had arrived, and nothing he was able to do could make it disappear.[25] The *grisettes* who danced at the Chaumière often acquired rich husbands from among the students. Many of the latter failed to complete their courses because they spent too much time enjoying themselves at La Hire's establishment. The proprietor himself, despite his fierce reputation regarding behaviour on the dance floor, was generally benevolent towards his regular customers, although no doubt it paid him to be so.[26]

The Chaumière was only a summer venue and it closed every year in September, at which time its place was taken by the Prado, a dance hall that was founded in 1810 and was to be found in the passage de Flore, near Notre Dame cathedral. It had two rooms, one of which was known as the *Rotonde* and which catered for the students and their *grisette* partners. The other dance floor, in the *Grand Salon*, was occupied by the celebrities of the time, including Céleste Mogador, Rose Pompon, Clara Fontaine, Louise la Balocheuse, Jeanne la Juive and many others, who performed wild dances to entertain the customers. Bullier, the manager of the Prado, had a much more relaxed attitude to the behaviour of the dancers and even encouraged the cancan, stressing that they need not be restrained like they were at the Chaumière. La Hire, in turn, was known to bellow at Chaumière regulars on occasions that the way they were behaving one might think that they were at the Prado![27]

The Chaumière in summer and the Prado in winter were where the students came to "learn the ways of the world", as the *Journal pour rire* described it.[28] Both establishments closed their doors for the last time at the end of the 1850s. The Chaumière had been eclipsed by Bullier's new venture, also in the Montparnasse district. This was the Closerie des Lilas, which, under its later name of the Bal Bullier, was to retain its high reputation as an amateur dancing venue until the early 1900s. It was developed in 1846 on the site of a dance hall known as the Chartreuse (commemorating the Carthusian friary that used to be situated there), close to the boulevard St Michel, and hence nearer to the university than the Chaumière. Bullier, incidentally, had been a lamp cleaner at the Chaumière, and was now responsible for putting his former employers out of business. It was soon clear that the new *guinguette* was becoming more popular by far than the Chaumière. This was probably partly due to a considerably more liberal atmosphere, and a cleverly contructed series of rooms for different customers: the least experienced dancers occupying the 'kitchen', whence they graduated to the 'anteroom', then to the 'salon' and finally to the *'préfecture'*. The latter was frequented by stars of the cancan and polka such as Pavillon and La Reine Pomaré, the latter no doubt happy to be able to dance as she pleased without suffering the ignominy meted out by La Hire.[29]

Bullier's dancing gardens were eulogised in a book by Gaston Robert entitled *Mystères du Bal Bullier*. According to Robert, at the centre of the "enchanted" gardens was found a dancing salon decorated in Moorish style, with paintings recalling "some glowing oriental paradise". The dance floor, which was open to the sky, was illuminated by thousands of gas lamps, and a cool fountain brought relief from the heat.[30] Not everyone was as impressed as Robert, however. A brochure on the *bals* of Paris said that it was clear that Bullier had "wanted to recall the marvels of the Alhambra, but between wanting and being able there are more Pyrenees than he believes, as his Alhambra is a failure".[31] Perhaps—but the design for the building was pure fantasy, and no doubt pleased the majority of the clientele.

An article in the *Journal pour rire*, written in 1848, a year of revolution in France and throughout Europe, praised the Closerie des Lilas for providing an escape from misery, hunger and unemployment. Despite these problems and the long journey required to reach Montparnasse, the *bal* was always full of fine young men and beautiful girls. "The Closerie des Lilas, this forest of flowers in the middle of Paris . . . seems to have been invented expressly to preserve the pleasant mysteries of youth." The most severe troubles were effaced by a quadrille danced with Camille at Bullier's garden, according to the *Journal*.[32] Alfred Delvau, writing in 1864, found that some of the innocence evident in the early years of the dance hall's existence had been supplanted by sophistication in the form of the *cocodettes* who now reigned supreme in such establishments. Resplendent in the latest fashions, these girls—Finette la Bordelaise, Henriette Zouzou, Anita l'Espagnole, Isabelle l'Aztèque, Peau de Satin, Bouffe Toujours, Nini Belles-Dents, Canard, Emma Cabriole—spoke a form of *argot* (slang) that

FIG. 40. The Bal Bullier in ferment, fancifully portrayed on the cover of the London magazine *The Days' Doings* in 1870 during the Prussian invasion of France. The gardens are referred to as the Closerie des Lilas, their original name. THE DAYS' DOINGS, *13 August 1870, by permission of the British Library.*

Delvau found astonishing.[33] It is quite probable, however, that he was suffering from the effects of the generation gap, and was simply out of touch with the youth of the day.

The Bal Bullier continued to preserve its amateur reputation for many years, and it was still functioning largely unaltered in the early 1900s. The tradition of solo performances of the cancan was perpetuated in these gardens, and the professionals of Montmartre in the 1890s rarely appeared here. Jane Avril was one exception, but this was because she always resisted becoming professional and enjoyed the easygoing atmosphere of the Bullier. At the end of the century, the clientele were generally better off, and the *grisettes* had been replaced by fashionable women, wearing petticoats of silk and lace and extravagant hats rather than cotton skirts and simple caps. The *Guide des Plaisirs à Paris*, published in 1907, still nostalgically refers to them as *grisettes* and says that the Latin Quarter remained the place to find beautiful twenty-year-old girls and young men engaged in their studies of life.[34]

A revamped Bullier opened in 1921 and continued to attract the same classes of customer, but now the era of the amateur cancan was over, and other popular dances of earlier decades such as the polka and the waltz had been replaced by the Charleston and the foxtrot.[35]

FIG. 41. The Bullier dancing gardens may have gone but they are recalled in the name of this brasserie on the site in Montparnasse. A short distance away, the Grande Chaumière is commemorated in a street name. *Private Collection.*

The most famous dancing gardens of the Second Empire, the Bal Mabille, at first provided relatively simple entertainment for its uncultured patrons and was certainly no competition for the Grande Chaumière in the early 1840s. Household servants from the surrounding district came to Charles Mabille's establishment to dance by the light of oil lamps to music provided by a small group of instrumentalists. The gardens surrounded an inn, originally opened in 1813, on the Allée des Veuves (now the Avenue Montaigne) off the Champs-Elysées. The area was not as attractive or recherché as it is today; in fact, the upper classes tended to avoid the area because it had the reputation of being dangerous, a den of thieves.[36] All this was soon to change, and the Bal Mabille played a major part in altering perceptions.

The proprietor's sons, recognising the potential of the gardens, persuaded their father to allow them to develop the site into a much more attractive enterprise. Half a million francs were reputedly spent in transforming the Mabille into a place of real beauty, with sanded paths, hedges and an enchanted grotto. Gas lighting replaced the smelly oil lamps, and a full orchestra now played for the dancing. The huge outlay was rapidly recouped through some shrewd business operations: a publicity campaign was mounted, with posters appearing all over Paris next to advertisements for theatres; and the admission price was also raised to two francs from fifty centimes.[37]

The intention of the Mabille brothers was to move very definitely upmarket, and they succeeded admirably, soon attracting local, national and foreign celebrities. Over the years, the poet Baudelaire, Gustave Doré the illustrator, Arsène Houssaye the theatre director and other members of artistic professions were joined in the revelry by bankers, industrialists, journalists and men from the upper classes with private incomes. Amongst the tourists, Edward, Prince of Wales, was the most distinguished visitor, surprisingly often travelling to Paris just for the day. Despite the long journey—over twelve hours—he must have felt it was all worth it to have the chance of spending a few hours in the Mabille gardens and seeing the famous cancan.[38]

The Bal Mabille's major attraction for these customers was the opportunity to watch and possibly meet the beautiful *demi-mondaines* who frequented the establishment. The arrival of each of the high-class courtesans—at different times Alphonsine Plessis, Cora Pearl, Adèle Courtois, Blanche d'Antigny and many others were seen at the Mabille—was one of the highlights of the evening, each woman sweeping on to the dance floor with an unerring sense of decorum, each wearing the most sumptuous gowns, adorned with magnificent jewellery.[39] On a slightly lower level in the social order were the *cocodettes*, a number of whom were highly regarded for their dancing. Among the most famous were Finette (la Bordelaise) and Alice la Provençale. Some of the more talented dancers were paid by the management to give exhibitions of the polka and the cancan for the customers.[40]

The Mabille family had soon earned so much from their new venture that they were able to open another, the Château des Fleurs, not far away near the Arc de Triomphe, where their customers could go on nights when the Mabille itself was closed.[41] Both establishments were only open in summer and the

Casino Cadet, on rue Cadet, became the dancers' winter 'residence'. This dance hall, which was opened in 1858, was where Rigolboche made her notable début. It had two orchestras, a *promenoir*, galleries where customers could drink and chat, and a foyer for smoking. Here could be seen portraits of the celebrated ladies of the day.[42]

As with the other dancing gardens, the main dance floor of the Mabille was well lit, but the surrounding lawns and shrubberies gave plenty of oppor-

FIG. 42. The impressive entrance to the Bal Mabille dancing gardens, close to the Champs-Elysées, frequented by the *grandes cocottes* and their lovers and the cancan-dancing *cocodettes*, including Finette and Alice la Provençale. *Private Collection.*

tunity for secret rendezvous for lovers. Inevitably this gave the Bal Mabille a certain reputation, which the proprietors wisely made no attempt to efface. The gardens were a place for pure enjoyment, for dancing, drinking and conducting love affairs.[43] They were also a symbol of the prosperity and confidence that prevailed in France under Napoléon III, and defeat in the Franco-Prussian War, together with the very visible social unrest which reached its climax in the Commune, brought to an end the Second Empire and signalled the demise of the glittering dancing gardens. Although the Mabille struggled on for a number of years after 1871, it was never the same either in quality or popularity. The great era of the *grande cocotte* was over, as was the time of carefree hedonism which supported the *bals publics* like the Mabille.[44]

Perhaps even more redolent of the supposed decadence of the Second Empire were the Carnival balls which took place every year in the major theatres of Paris. The cancan's development owed as much to these as to the dancing gardens and dance halls described above. The most renowned of these was

ARME AU BRAS!...

Le plus fier mouvement de la danse nationale française. (Traduction anglaise de ce qu'à Mabille on nomme tout bonnement le cancan) SHOKING! et « Pas de début » pour toute femme qui veut se poser un peu bien dans le monde.

FIG. 43. A cartoon by Jules Pelocq in the *Journal amusant* shows English visitors to the Mabille finding the '*danse nationale française*' rather 'shoking' (*sic*). The magazine delighted in portraying the English as somewhat stuffy. JOURNAL AMUSANT, *12 September 1868, by permission of the British Library, F.117.*

BATTA, violoncelliste, comme Bériot est violoniste. Belges tous deux. Exécution admirable; composition un peu au-dessous, bien que très-estimée. La preuve en est que l'éditeur Bernard Latte n'y a jamais perdu et qu'il en demande toujours. ———— GRISAR, Sarah la Folle, l'An mille, les Travestissements, Lady Melvil, le Spectacle à la cour, l'Eau merveilleuse, Gilles le ravisseur, les Porcherons, Bonsoir, monsieur Pantalon! le Carillonneur de Bruges. — Si j'en oublie, c'est peut-être des meilleurs. Voilà la glorieuse couronne de ce compositeur charmant. Le feu roi Louis-Philippe, qui avait, dit-on, meilleur goût en musique qu'en peinture, appréciait beaucoup la musique de Grisar; — et le public, donc! ———— Le génie du quadrille, MUSARD. Plus actif qu'impresario au monde, plus fécond que tous les compositeurs réunis, plus inventif dans ses Arrangements que les mélodistes dont il se sert, Musard s'est fait un nom européen. Il a fini, dans toute la force de l'âge et du talent, par laisser le sceptre des bals de l'Opéra à ———— son fils. Musard père n'est pas mort! mais vive MUSARD fils! Il lui a donné aussi la flamme intérieure et le talent. Entendez plutôt les quadrilles sur l'Enfant prodigue, le Prophète et le Moulin des Tilleuls. Bon sang ne saurait mentir, dit d'une part la sagesse des nations, comme elle a dit de l'autre: Bon chef d'orchestre conduit de race. ———— De BERIOT, le premier violoniste du monde. M. de Bériot, qui ne joue plus du violon que pour se divertir, se repose sur ses fils, ses élèves, et il a raison. Belge. ———— Frédéric BRISSON, auteur de l'Arabesque, de la Pluie d'or, de l'Ondine, de la Chasse et des Etudes de mécanisme du 4e doigt adoptées par le Conservatoire. Du talent et de l'étude.

FIG. 44. Musard and son, caricatured with other musicians by Nadar in the *Journal pour rire*. Both conductors were highly regarded but at the Opéra balls they were almost required to be entertainers, sustaining the revelry until daybreak. JOURNAL POUR RIRE, *13 November 1852, by permission of the British Library, F.117.*

the one held at the Paris Opéra, continuing a tradition that had been established in the reign of Louis XV. The original idea was that a huge ball held in one place would be easier for the *garde militaire* to police than the number of disparate celebrations that had been customary each year until then.[45] Masked balls as a concept had arrived from Italy and had spread to most countries of Europe. They were once banned in England for a year because they were seen as encouraging debauchery, and the great earthquake of Lisbon in 1855 was attributed to God's judgement on the town for its masquerades. In general they were condemned by moralists for allowing the mixing of classes and for inciting indecency. The masks ensured a certain amount of anonymity, and thus freedom to indulge pleasure to excess, and the costumes worn were often quite revealing, certainly of women's legs. A considerable amount of cross-dressing was also common.[46]

In Paris of the 1830s other theatres had usurped the position of the Opéra as a location of unbridled revelry during the Carnival season, and the famous occasion of the introduction of the cancan at one of the balls occurred not at the Opéra but at the Variétés in around 1832. In truth, the masquerades at the Opéra had lost much of their former brilliance, being tainted with associations with the aristocracy from before the 1789 Revolution, and by this time having become balls in name only, with no dancing for the 'guests'.[47] The organiser provided entertainments of varying quality, but came to realise that the exciting dancing at the Variétés and other theatres was liable to make such evenings a poor attraction in comparison. The cancan had really captured the Carnival spirit and bore some responsibility for a complete reorientation of the Opéra balls.

Towards the end of the decade, permission was given for a *bal dansant et costumé* at the Opéra following the style of the original balls from the eighteenth century.[48] The new Opéra ball was a resounding success, lasting through the night until six in the morning. After it had finished, the dancing continued in the streets. The orchestra's conductor that night, Philippe Musard, had been directing the music at the Variétés when the cancan had made its memorable first appearance there, and so was well used to providing inspirational dance tunes for the revellers. At one point in the evening they enthusiastically transported him around the dance floor on their shoulders. Musard's pock-marked face with deadpan expression and his sober style of dress seemed completely incongruous with the occasion, and only added to the fun. His orchestra, with its loud brass section and with pistol shots adding to the general noise, created an thrilling atmosphere.[49]

The Opéra masquerades were immediately and hugely popular, but the public who attended them demanded more than simply to dance—they wanted entertainment. The women who danced at the *bals publics*, together with their male partners, were accordingly invited to provide expert displays of waltzing, the new polka and, of course, the cancan galop. In exchange, they

LE GALOP INFERNAL, — par GUSTAVE DORÉ.

Gravé par Dumont.

FIG. 45. The *'Galop Infernal'*, an illustration of the Carnival ball at the Opéra by Gustave Doré. Offenbach used this title eight years later for his famous cancan music in *Orpheus in the Underworld*, but he clearly did not invent the term. JOURNAL POUR RIRE, *9 March 1850, by permission of the British Library, F.117.*

were admitted free of charge, or at a very low admission fee. This policy of the organisers was viewed with some dismay in some quarters, particularly by women of the upper classes, who thought it would encourage the baser elements of society to attend. To some extent, this was true, and the balls soon acquired some notoriety. It was a little difficult to tell what type of person was present, due to their disguises, but an English visitor was probably near the mark in 1867 in stating that the women there were "exclusively of the Aspasian sisterhood" (i.e. prostitutes) and that the men were "a mixture of butchers' boys, linendrapers, shopmen, hairdressers' assistants, and persons of apparently respectable social position, but these latter were a smaller minority than ever before".[50] By the end of the 1860s, few members of the upper classes were attending the functions, which had become more licentious affairs while the cancan as performed by Rigolboche and Finette had developed into a more ribald entertainment, anticipating the style of La Goulue in the 1880s. The quadrille of Clodoche and his troupe was viewed as the highspot of the evening.[51]

The glory of the Opéra balls was fading fast towards the end of the Second Empire. Musard was long gone, as was his son, who succeeded him for a few years as conductor of the orchestra, and perhaps the lack of a really charismatic figure to lead the dancing was a significant factor.[52] As fewer members of the *haut-monde* now felt inclined to take part in the Carnival gaiety at the Opéra there was less mixing of the classes and less for moralists to find offensive. This no doubt also diminished the appeal of the balls in the eyes of many. The English visitor quoted above referred to the shabbiness of the costumes worn, and if this was not simply a jaundiced viewpoint (much of his commentary certainly indicates that it might be) then it suggests that the occasion had lost some of its earlier glittering aspect.[53] Perhaps more than anything else, the falling prestige of Napoléon III and his notion of empire certainly meant that the Opéra balls could no longer be seen as symbolising the gaiety and confidence that had epitomised the early years of his reign. Any gaiety that was left by 1870 was somewhat forced, and it is doubtful whether the emperor would have survived many more years even had he not suffered defeat at the Battle of Sedan.

Carnival balls limped on as an institution in the closing decades of the nineteenth century, but they never regained anything like the status that the Opéra balls had enjoyed from the late 1830s to the reign of Napoléon III. They were a relic of a former time, and the growth of the *café-concert*, as the small-scale cabaret venues were called, as well as the larger music halls and cabarets indicated a demand for more sophisticated forms of entertainment.

The more proletarian dance halls and gardens survived the revolution in 1870–71, and these were mostly found on the outskirts of Paris. The Bal Bullier in Montparnasse has already been described, but another area of the city was also beginning to attract increased attention as a place to go for cheap entertainment and refreshments. This was the village of Montmartre to the north, where a number of small inns and gardens providing dancing had already been in existence for a number of years, some even pre-dating the Bullier and the Mabille. Perhaps the oldest was the Moulin de la Galette, which as a mill was actually built in the seventeenth century, but which was converted into dancing gardens early in the nineteenth century. Montmartre failed to acquire as high a reputation as other centres of pleasure in Paris for a number of reasons: it was too far away from the Latin Quarter to be a draw for students; it was too working class for the courtesans; and it also was thought to be a haven for criminals. The Elysée-Montmartre did attract some of the cancan stars of the early years, but the real growth in the area's popularity began from the 1870s onwards.[54]

Working-class dance halls such as the Boule Noire and the Reine Blanche contrasted sharply in appearance with the Bal Mabille or the Casino Cadet. Their basic facilities were sometimes disguised by incongruous decorative features, which only served to emphasise the poverty of the majority of their clients, as the Goncourts illustrated in their description of the Boule Noire in *Germinie Lacerteux*:

The room had the modern character of the pleasure resorts of the people. It glittered with false riches and poor luxury. There were paintings and wine-sellers' tables to be seen; gilded gas-apparatus and glasses for drinking a quarter of brandy, velvet and wooden benches, the wretchedness and rusticity of a country inn amid the embellishment of a palace of cardboard. Crimson velvet valances with a gold-lace stripe hung at the windows, and were economically repeated in paint under the looking-glasses, which were lit by triple-branched sconces. On the walls, in large white panels, pastorals by Boucher, surrounded by painted frames, alternated with Prud'hon's Seasons *astonished to find themselves there, and over the windows and doors hydropic loves played among fine roses that had been taken off the pomatum-pot of some suburban hairdresser. Square posts, spotted with sorry arabesques, supported the middle of the room in the centre of which was a small octagonal gallery for the orchestra. An oaken barrier, breast-high and serving as a back to a red, meagre bench, enclosed the dancers. And against this barrier on the outside, green-painted tables with wooden benches were crowded together in two rows, thus surrounding the ball with a café.*[55]

The heroine of the novel is the object of hatred when she visits the dance hall because, although she is from the same class as the other customers, she is the maid to a 'respectable' woman and is conspicuous in her bonnet, gold brooch and white petticoat.[56]

The appointment of the respected Olivier Métra, a former conductor at the Mabille, to direct the orchestra at the Elysée-Montmartre was a turning point in the fortunes of Montmartre. This dance hall had originally been founded early in the century, but had remained a humble establishment, very much associated with the working class. Nevertheless, some of the well-known dancers of the day were seen here, including Céleste Mogador and Rose Pompon. It was considerably renovated in the 1850s, with the addition of gilded stucco and velvet wall hangings, in time for the official incorporation of Montmartre as a district of Paris. With Métra conducting, the dance hall soon attracted customers from fashionable circles. The courtesans Cora Pearl and Blanche d'Antigny visited in the 1860s, giving the establishment their seal of approval.[57]

The success of the Elysée-Montmartre meant that the whole area was revitalised, but the defeat in the Franco-Prussian war led to the declaration of the Paris Commune and its tragic consequences. The Elysée became a political club, and its name was changed briefly to the 'Club de la Révolution'.[58] But surprisingly soon after the crushing of the revolt the dance hall was revived and by 1875 it had become more upmarket and indeed was even seen as fashionable again.[59] In 1879, Emile Zola chose the venue for the organisation of *"une grande fête à l'occasion de la centième de l'Assommoir"*, at which the guests were dressed as characters from his famous novel, the men as labourers and the women as laundresses. The cancan was danced at this event in the traditional amateur fashion, by both male and female participants for their own enjoyment. This was a case of the bourgeoisie 'slumming it', and was an increasingly familiar pattern in the final decades of the nineteenth century.[60]

In the 1880s, the cancan's revival as entertainment had begun to accelerate after the first appearance of La Goulue at the Moulin de la Galette, and the Elysée-Montmartre took advantage of the dance's new popularity by inviting a number of the most accomplished dancers to appear there. For a time the

FIG. 46. This two-page picture in *Le Courrier français* of the dancing at the Elysée-Montmartre appears to show La Goulue and Valentin-le-Désossé, with possibly Grille d'Egout. The magazine held its regular costume balls at the dance-hall. LE COURRIER FRANÇAIS, *1 December 1889, by permission of the British Library,* M.F.85.

dance hall's fortunes seemed to have really improved, and the attentions of *Le Courrier français* and artists such as Toulouse-Lautrec only helped publicity. Unfortunately, the opening of the Moulin Rouge in close proximity in 1889 caused a rapid falling away in attendances, and the Elysée-Montmartre was eventually transformed into a *café-concert* and renamed the Trianon.[61]

According to Georges Montorgueil, the professionalising of the cancan in the 1880s and 1890s ended the pre-eminence of the dance hall in Paris because ordinary people were too embarrassed to dance in the presence of the stars.[62] But to say that spectacle and *café-concert* had completely replaced participatory dancing as an attraction in Montmartre would be incorrect, as the Moulin de la Galette continued to provide the opportunity for this for several years after the opening of the Moulin Rouge and the many other cabaret venues that proliferated in this period. Professional stars would often put in an appearance at these traditional dancing gardens, but they were not paid to do so. They apparently enjoyed the atmosphere there as much as the ordinary people who were the Moulin de la Galette's main customers.

In its original concept as a *guinguette*, owned by the Debray family, the Moulin de la Galette appears to have been a charming place, with simple amusements such as swings and merry-go-rounds, as well as arbours where

FIG. 47. Despite attractive posters like this one in 1890 by Adolphe Willette, reproduced in *Le Courrier français*, the Elysée-Montmartre was already losing customers to the recently opened Moulin Rouge, situated a relatively short distance away. LE COUR-RIER FRANÇAIS, *2 November 1890, by permission of the British Library*, M.F.85.

La nouvelle Affiche du Bal de l'Elysée-Montmartre

one could consume the delicious *galettes* (small cakes) from which the establishment gained its name. However, it began to attract customers from the rougher suburbs of Paris and became the setting for violence and the seedier forms of prostitution, in common with much of Montmartre.[63]

While painters, followed by the bourgeoisie, were beginning to 'discover' Montmartre in the 1880s, many of the great attractions of future years at the Moulin Rouge—La Goulue, Valentin-le-Désossé, Grille d'Egout and others— were appearing at the humble Moulin de la Galette.[64] With the growth of the area as an attraction for the *bons vivants* of Paris, the proprietor, one of the next generation of Debrays (the *guinguette* was alternatively called the Maison Debray), made some attempt to discourage the more violent element. He provided more luxurious surroundings for his customers, and as a result they felt obliged to dress appropriately. Some of the bourgeoisie began to attend along with the establishment's traditional working-class clientele, and the less desirable amongst the latter soon transferred elsewhere.[65] The Moulin retained its essential simplicity well into the 1890s, and there was no attempt to move with the times and provide entertainments designed to shock the customers; instead,

FIG. 48. One of the entrances to the Moulin de la Galette *guinguette* after Montmartre had been officially incorporated as part of the city of Paris, but while it still retained a strong village appearance with its genuine windmills. *Private Collection.*

it continued to be a place simply for dancing, where young people would come to dance the polka or the waltz and sometimes try to imitate La Goulue or Grille d'Egout in their high-kicking displays, much to the proprietor's amusement. The interest shown by painters in this *guinguette*, and the delicacy with which they treated it as a subject, are ample evidence of its innocent charm.[66]

Another category of dance hall still surviving in the 1890s was the *bal musette*, found on the fringes of the city and named after the accordions that used to provide the music in such places. They were regarded as dangerous, certainly not the place for the bourgeoisie to visit. Along with the poorer dance halls of Montmartre, they were responsible for the cancan's survival in the gloomy years after the fall of the Second Empire. The working classes were not affected by the defeat of Napoléon: their lives had not been changed in any way, neither for the worse nor for the better.[67]

The cancan in Paris in the nineteenth century was usually regarded as a ballroom dance, no matter how much it had developed into an form of entertainment by the 1890s. In other countries it had been presented as a stage dance, part of the music-hall programme and later included in operetta and ballet. The

FIG. 49. The Moulin de la Galette today, with renovations in progress in the gardens. The mill remains intact, the only one left today in Montmartre—apart from the false red windmill down the hill at the Moulin Rouge. *Private Collection.*

music hall was essentially a development from the fairground tradition, and as such featured acrobats, jugglers and animal acts, as well as musical items. The first music halls were very small—city taverns and inns with a small stage, but from the mid-nineteenth century much larger theatres came to feature music-hall programmes, and some were purpose-built. This was particularly the case in Great Britain and the United States, where music hall, variety, burlesque or vaudeville forms of entertainment were extremely popular from the 1850s until the early decades of the twentieth century. Dancing of various kinds was often on the bill, as were other displays of female sexuality such as the *tableau vivant*.

The first recorded instances of the cancan being performed on stage in Britain were at the Oxford, Alhambra, Princess's and Lyceum theatres in the 1860s, but no doubt there had been other occasions previously. The Oxford's proprietor, Charles Morton, often described as the 'father of music hall', also had the Canterbury, and later other music halls, under his control and was responsible for providing his customers with varied and exciting fare. The

FIG. 50. The Alhambra music hall in Leicester Square, London, which once had its licence refused following a performance of the cancan. It later became a respected venue for ballet, including the première of *La Boutique Fantasque*—featuring the cancan! *Theatre Museum, V&A Picture Library.*

famous courtesan, Cora Pearl, appeared at the Canterbury, and Emily Soldene, the singer and operetta producer (who employed British cancan star Wiry Sal after the Alhambra had lost its licence), sang at the Oxford. The cancan at the Oxford was a great draw for the 1860s audiences, and tables near the front of the auditorium were much in demand. To help those who could not get close enough to see the naughty French dancing, Morton imported opera glasses from Germany which could be hired at sixpence a time. [68]

The appearance of the cancan on the London stage in the 1860s bolstered in Anglo-Saxon minds the image of Paris as the centre of licentiousness. Wiry Sal's appearance with her fellow-dancers at the Alhambra, which caused so much controversy, would, however, probably have seemed tame in comparison with the activities of Rigolboche and Finette in France. It seems that the licensing authorities felt that the cancan was in danger of undermining British society. It was certainly becoming widespread in music-hall programmes: Finette visited London in the 1860s, as did Clodoche, the star of the Paris Opéra balls, and his now-professional troupe. In fact Clodoche was appearing at Morton's Philharmonic Hall in 1870 at the same time as Wiry Sal and the Colonna troupe were performing in *Les Nations* at the Alhambra, and, as *The Observer* newspaper pointed out on 16 October 1870, the refusal of licences in some cases did not prevent cancan performances elsewhere:[69]

British morality—always successful in hitting the happy mean—has drawn the line at the cancan, and we confess that it was certainly high time that the line should be drawn somewhere. At the same time the refusal of the Middlesex Magistrates to relicense the Alhambra and the Highbury Barn [dancing gardens in east London where the cancan had been performed] is not altogether satisfactory. . . . it would perhaps have been fairer—seeing that the cancan is allowed in 'Orphée aux Enfers' at the St James's and prohibited at Leicester Square—that some sort of notice should have been given of the intention to appeal against a renewal [of music hall licences].[70]

The authorities in Victorian London may have overreacted in this case, but they unwittingly helped to further the cancan's reputation as a challenge to conventional morality. In any case, the cancan in various forms was destined to become staple fare in the British music-hall tradition.

Although the smaller local music halls, away from the centre of cities, catered for family parties, audiences at the halls tended mostly to be composed of young males.[71] They visited the music hall expecting to see attractive young women performing on stage, and also because of other attractions that the theatre offered. Both the Alhambra and the Empire music halls had promenades at the back of the circle, where high-class prostitutes plied their trade. These women were allowed in for a minimal entrance fee, as the proprietors knew that some of their custom would come from men who were aware that the music halls were places at which to find an attractive girl for the night. This symbiotic relationship was added to by the dancing girls on stage, who supposedly provided an aphrodisiac effect and encouraged male spectators to engage one of the prostitutes. A certain etiquette was observed, and a woman would rarely solicit trade directly, but would wait until invited by a man to his table for a drink—and discussion of terms. The music halls in this way became almost like gentlemen's clubs—many of the prostitutes had regular clients—and respectable women were discouraged from attending.[72]

It was only a matter of time before moralists made their presence felt over this (to them) highly objectionable state of affairs. A certain Mrs Ormiston Chant conducted a campaign against the promenade at the Empire that was so successful that the London County Council ordered the management to abolish it. Mrs Chant claimed, with some justification, that some prostitutes on the promenade *did* accost men when looking for business. She had learned this from two "less than worldly" American acquaintances who had suffered the experience when they had visited the theatre merely to see the show. George Edwardes, the theatre's proprietor, maintained somewhat disingenuously that a sergeant and a detective were always present to ensure that such incidents did not take place. According to Edwardes, prostitutes were not allowed to solicit, and neither were men allowed to approach prostitutes.[73] This of course begs the question of why the promenade was so popular with the ladies and their potential clients.

In October 1894 the theatre closed for a month, and when it reopened the promenade was blocked off from the rest of the auditorium by screens. This destroyed the symbiosis—the stage was no longer visible from the promenade—but it also meant that some of the relaxed atmosphere of the theatre was lost. It was now not possible to stroll along or stand in the promenade and watch the acts on the stage, whether you were interested in the prostitutes or not. The problem was solved by a group of young men who took matters into their own hands and tore the screen down. The future prime minister, Winston Churchill, described the event in his autobiography *My Early Life* and may have been directly involved.[74] The Empire's promenade was only closed finally in 1916, after which the theatre never recovered financial stability. In 1923 it made a loss of £20,000 and the decision was soon made to cease variety performances. In contrast, the Alhambra, which also closed its promenade in 1916, continued to be profitable as a music hall, providing "clean and wholesome" family entertainment.[75] So it seems that bad management at the Empire was responsible for its demise, rather than the lack of prostitutes.

Music hall in Britain and America relied on programmes comprising a whole series of acts, which were sometimes repeated during the day, during which members of the audience drifted in and out, not necessarily staying for the whole show. They were as much places to socialise as to be entertained, and indifference was as much a worry for the performers as heckling. Nevertheless, some artists managed to achieve great fame in the halls—Lottie Collins, for example, whose cancan-style dancing caused a sensation on both sides of the Atlantic. She was an exception, however, with regard to the cancan, whose exponents were rarely well known, unlike in France. Even when Nini-Patte-en-l'Air and her pupils or the Eglantine Troupe visited the Palace Theatre in the 1890s, they had an obscure position on the bill. However, it must be said that home-grown troupes were beginning to make their presence felt as serious competition for the genuine French article. Later in 1896 the Eglantine troupe were emulated by the Tiller troupe, who presented their "'Fin de Siècle' Quadrille with entirely new dresses designed for and executed by Madame and Mons. Alias".[76] The cancan was increasingly popular in ballet and operettas produced in music halls towards the end of the century, but it was generally performed by anonymous dancing girls. The earliest presentations of the cancan in London gave its exponents some degree of personal fame, but British audiences were generally prepared to give such recognition to singers or comedians, and seldom to dancers. Some of the skirt dancers, Kate Vaughan in particular, were regarded highly, but there seems little doubt that Lottie Collins would not have experienced her fantastic success if she had been unable to sing.

American variety theatres presented a similar style of entertainment to the music halls of Britain, and indeed there were many cases of successful acts crossing the Atlantic. The theatres themselves in America were as varied as in any country, ranging from the very small and simple to the grand and elegant. Some were distinctly sleazy and violent, but even in those that were not the audiences for variety shows certainly tended to be predominantly male, with women suffering from the same harsh morality as found in Britain. The theatre was not for respectable women, neither on the stage nor in the audience, and it was only when vaudeville, which aimed at a family audience, became more widespread that things began to change.[77] The fare on offer at variety theatres ranged from the usual individual acts involving singers, comedians, magicians, acrobats and dancers, to fully staged plays, operettas and ballets. One major difference in America, compared to Britain, was that away from the 'civilised' large cities in the East, around the Great Lakes and in California, much of the country had a lawless reputation in the nineteenth century. The prosperous new towns in the 'Wild West' grew fast and attracted settlers from the East, but some were slow to change. Stages were often set up in saloons or dance halls for the entertainment of hard-drinking cowboys, who tended to be even more intolerant than audiences in the cities if they thought the performers were unsatisfactory. The dance-hall girls, who generally were also prostitutes, sometimes danced a kind of cancan, which, even if they had little skill, no doubt pleased the customers, especially if they performed without knickers, as they often did. It was an unedifying spectacle, and hardly helped the reputation of the dance.

Visits by travelling theatre and opera groups became more common as the West opened up with the spread of the railways, and especially when towns grew large enough to warrant having a proper theatre. The quality of performance was accordingly improved, and dancing began to be taken more seriously in shows. Even when dancers were not included in the show itself, they would perhaps appear in the intervals between acts, along with a number of other entertainers, mostly local talent, in an olio. This word, derived from the Spanish *olla* (stew), came to describe the miscellany of items in variety performances provided as a prelude to the main event or as light relief in the interval.[78]

The new settlers from the large cities, such as businessmen who had arrived with the aim of making money in the cattle trade, were used to quality in the theatre, and so the performers made efforts to provide a higher standard of entertainment. Thus the disreputable shows of saloon and dance hall were increasingly replaced by sophisticated 'concert halls' or 'opera houses', to which performers from New York, Boston and San Francisco were attracted. The names of the theatres rarely included the word 'theatre' itself, as this was tainted with notions of immorality as far as many people were concerned. While it was not acceptable to visit a theatre, it was thought perfectly proper to see a show in the concert hall. [79]

In the big cities themselves, vaudeville and burlesque were very popular and some of the theatres were very ornate, as in Britain. Audiences were of a similar social mix, with middle-class women only gradually acquiring approval for visits to such places. Vaudeville as a name for the American music hall was also euphemistic, and had grown out of variety, a title that was now associated with the lowest forms of burlesque. Vaudeville was a name adopted primarily to attract more middle-class audiences, and the acts were similar to many that were found on the burlesque circuit—many performers graduated from one to the other—but were felt to be distinctly superior in quality and taste.[80] The first vaudeville theatre was opened by Tony Pastor in Paterson, New Jersey in 1865 and he deliberately aimed to attract women and children with a policy of having no bar in the theatre and not allowing suggestive performances on the stage.[81] Clearly the cancan had no place in vaudeville, but burlesque was another matter.

Burlesque had developed from its earliest appearance as a form of parody of respected entertainments, usually performed by women provocatively dressed in men's clothing, to a form dedicated to pushing the boundaries of what was permissible as far as the amount of women's bodies on display. In America, as in France, major political upheaval seemed to signal fundamental change with regard to moral standards. Thus it is that the first 'living statuaries' first appeared in the period after the Civil War. As in the *tableaux vivants* in other countries, the women only *appeared* to be naked, being mostly enclosed in body stockings. The subjects were similar to those found elsewhere: Psyche entering her bath, Aphrodite rising from the sea, the Sultan's favourite—classical myths and the exotic used to treat men in the audience to a sight of the undraped female form.[82]

The format of burlesque was established in 1866 with *The Black Crook*, an extravaganza sometimes referred to as 'the first musical', in so far as it combined sometimes irrelevant dance routines with traditional melodrama. *The Black Crook* came into existence by accident, when a French ballet company were stranded in America without a place to perform, after the theatre which had booked them burnt down. It so happened that Niblo's Garden Theatre in New York City had commissioned a melodrama which seemed unpromising to its director until he was offered the chance to enliven it with the addition of the French dancers, who numbered more than one hundred. The result was a spectacular show, lasting more than five-and-a-half hours, which was a critical success and a hit with audiences, although moralists were extremely offended by some of the dancing and the revealing costumes. It was revived in different

FIG. 51. The 'French quadrille' from an 1890s production *of The Black Crook*, sometimes described as the first 'musical'. It also represented the beginnings of the burlesque 'girlie' show and was revived many times until the late 1920s. *New York Public Library for the Performing Arts.*

forms several times until 1929.[83] One of the popular dance numbers, certainly in later incarnations of the show, was the famous Parisian Quadrille.

Burlesque became more and more associated with pushing the bounds of what was morally acceptable, and eventually in the twentieth century was associated almost exclusively with striptease revues, whereas vaudeville gave audiences very similar fare to that provided by the British music halls, without the more risqué elements: singers, comedians, short plays, operettas, ballets, animal acts, acrobats and dancers. One of the most well-known groups of dancers on the burlesque circuit was the Rentz-Santley troupe who presented, according to the posters, "The sensational scene 'Gay Life in Paris', introducing the famous Jardine [sic] Mabille Dance".[84] The troupe was arrested in San Francisco in 1878 for a performance which a policeman described as the "most indecent he had ever witnessed". The manager of the troupe, one M. B. Leavitt, presumably feeling that the cancan deserved a more sympathetic response, offered the jury free tickets to see the show and make up their own minds. They did—they found the dancers guilty. [85]

Burlesque variations on the cancan or skirt dance in the early twentieth century included the 'cootch-dancing' of Millie De Leon, who performed a kind of belly dance fully clothed, during which she lifted her skirts to reveal her stocking tops. She delighted in removing her garters and throwing them into the audience. Sometimes she would invite a man up onto the stage and allow him to fumble under her skirts to remove the garters himself. This may have sounded an attractive proposition for a full-blooded male, but De Leon was not in the business of being exploited, and she took pleasure in humiliating her 'victims'.[86]

As in Britain, operetta and ballet and later musical comedy were presented at American variety and vaudeville theatres. Travelling companies entertained the citizens of far-flung towns of the West as well as those of the big cities with the latest Offenbach or Gilbert and Sullivan to have arrived in America. Presenting the cancan in such a context probably helped to give the dance more respectability. However, when Lydia Thompson and her British Blondes gave a performance of *Ixion* in New York in 1868, the critics were not fooled into believing it was great art. One said that the show's success depended on "dressing up all the above-named good-looking young ladies as immortals lavish in display of person—and setting them to dance in the most reckless and burlesque manner". *Ixion* was a crude imitation of the Offenbach-style updated Classical myth and had little to commend it, according to the critics. "To present Minerva with a fan and whiskey flask, Jupiter as a jig-dancer, Venus with a taste for the cancan, is all done we suppose in a laudable spirit of burlesque, but we could almost hate Miss Thompson and her assistants for spoiling this pretty story." Another said: "It [*Ixion*] resembles an Irish stew, as one minute they are dancing a cancan and the next singing a psalm tune."[87] Offenbach himself visited the U.S.A. to present his own genuine operettas for the American public, which may have pleased the critics, but audiences were not satisfied until the composer himself was seen dancing the cancan in the orchestra pit along with the performers on stage.[88] Emily Soldene's English Opéra Comique also travelled to the United States in the 1870s and included the cancan in presentations of popular operettas.[89]

Music hall staged something of a revival in the 1930s in Britain with the opening of the Windmill Theatre. Strictly speaking this was a revue theatre, in deliberate imitation of the Parisian style of show, with non-stop entertainment employing mostly British artistes. Entitled 'Revudeville' (a contraction of *revue de ville*), the first variety bill at the Windmill was presented in February 1932. It proved to be a very successful format and continued for three decades, proudly proclaiming "We never closed" despite the bombing of London during the Second World War.[90]

The Windmill's triumph in overcoming the opposition—there were a number of other variety theatres in London at this time—was surprising because neither the owner nor the manager had any experience of presenting this type of show. The owner of the theatre, Mrs Laura Henderson, who was nearly seventy when she took it over, had never visited a theatre until after she was married. At twenty-two, her husband had taken her to the Gaiety and she had been shocked at the sight of the chorus girls' legs.[91] Nevertheless, she had visions of presenting live shows at the Windmill. Unfortunately, her manager, Vivian Van Damm, had at first played safe by showing films—because he had never produced a stage show in his life. Mrs Henderson eventually convinced him that live performances were likely to be profitable, and Van Damm luckily proved to have the creative and business capabilities to exploit a gap in the

market. His stroke of genius was the presentation of *tableaux vivants*—very similar in concept to those of the turn-of-the-century music hall, only this time the
girls were really naked, as opposed to wearing body stockings. The Lord Chamberlain's office objected to nudes moving on stage, claiming that this was indecent, whereas static, expressionless nudes in 'artistic' poses were perfectly
acceptable.[92] Another feature of an evening at the Windmill, fan dancing, was
also acceptable, because the woman performing never actually revealed her
body to the audience while performing. These rules seem absurd now, and,
probably did then, but they did at least result in good taste prevailing and a
string of amusingly ingenious ways of stretching the rules. For example, a girl
could be perfectly still standing on a plinth, but this did not mean that the
plinth could not revolve. George Bernard Shaw had often stressed the confused
nature of moral standards in British theatre, and in 1909 had commented on
"the assumption that a draped figure is decent and an undraped one indecent":

FIG. 52. A view from behind the stage at the Windmill during a dress rehearsal, with camera
club members much in evidence in the balcony. The creator of 'Revudeville', Vivian Van
Damm, can be seen in the audience, keeping an eye on proceedings. *Theatre Museum, V&A
Picture Library.*

It is useless to point to actual experience, which proves abundantly that naked or apparently naked living figures, whether exhibited as living pictures, animated statuary, or in dance, are at their best not only innocent, but refining in their effect, whereas those . . . skirt dancers who have brought the peculiar aphrodisiac effect which is objected to to the highest pitch of efficiency wear twice as many petticoats as an ordinary woman does, and seldom exhibit more than their ankles.[93]

The Windmill was certainly not restricted in other ways of producing "the peculiar aphrodisiac effect", and its cancan was stunning in its costumes and choreography. The dancers at the Windmill were highly professional, and the high kicks were sometimes performed *à pointe*. The original choreographer, Eve Bradfield, was said to have caused more of a stir with her cancan than when the dance was first performed.[94] The cancan usually came as part of musical item, a mini-operetta or ballet, with typical titles from 1955 being: 'La Vie à Paris', 'Stage Door Scandal 1894', and perhaps less obviously, 'Early Basin Street' (set in the southern United States) or 'Maiden Voyage' (on an ocean cruise). Like earlier music halls, the Windmill was responsible for creating more serious ballet sequences, and its dancers also gave performances of other classic show dances. Van Damm valued the individuality of his dancers, and said that although the precision dancing popular in the United States was beautiful and exciting to watch he would never introduce it into his shows.[95] There were six shows a day non-stop, but there were two entire troupes of girls, so they only needed to work every other day.

Mrs Henderson, it was said, had been worried about the number of variety artistes out of work during the Depression and had wanted to provide them with employment. She succeeded probably beyond expectations, and the Windmill concept was copied in variety theatres throughout Britain, though often with less style and decorum. It would be dishonest to claim that the Windmill shows were not designed to be titillating—after all, 75 per cent of the audiences were men—but their quality was much admired. Mrs Henderson used to enjoy creeping into the theatre incognito, sometimes even in disguise, to check that high standards were being maintained. [96]

In France, true music hall began in 1869 with the opening of the Folies Bergère. Prior to this, there had been no real tradition of such a form of entertainment, which explains why the term 'music hall' was borrowed from the English. On the other hand, France had its own kind of small-scale music hall in the form of the *café-concerts*. The growth of the *café-concerts* in the mid-nineteenth century gave new possibilities for solo performers, but many of these were initially formidable venues, intimate, but also intimidating for those on stage. As in other countries, audiences were not prepared to be bored, and heckling and the throwing of objects to indicate displeasure were a normal occurrence. The Parisian satirical or sentimental *chanson*, which had achieved popularity in the eighteenth century at the dancing gardens, was still the staple diet at the *café-concert* or *café-chantant*.[97]

Another form of entertainment well-established in Paris was the revue, which again developed out of fairground acts. The Théâtre de la Porte St-Martin, where Charles Mazurier presented his version of the *chahut* in 1830 in the part of Jocko the monkey, and the Théâtre des Délassements-Comiques, where Rigolboche made an appearance, may have been popular with the Parisian public, but they did not have quite the same appeal as either the *bals publics* or the *café-concerts*. This was not surprising because revue gave little opportunity for participation, and Parisians loved to dance and sing. In the late 1850s and 1860s, many theatres which had hitherto been popular were emptied because their customers now preferred the *café-concerts*.[98]

The concept of *café-concert* (or *caf'conc'*, as they were often called) developed in a similar way to the music hall in London, with the proprietors of small taverns wishing to provide some further attraction for customers with a view to selling more drink. Encouraging them to sing along with the *chansonnier* was an ideal way of achieving this. No charge was made for entrance, but consumption of refreshments was obligatory. The singers and dancers that appeared at such places were often subject to abuse from the audience if they did not come up to scratch. A performer of the cancan in such an atmosphere needed to be extremely brave, as she would inevitably experience ribald shouts from the men in the house. Generally the artists who chose to attempt to amuse the customers at the *café-concerts* on the fringes of the city succeeded best if they matched them in their vulgarity.[99]

This situation changed towards the end of the century, with more sophisticated and larger *café-concerts* being opened, some of them becoming more like the British music halls or American variety theatres. There were at one time around one hundred and fifty *café-concerts* in Paris, of varying sizes and degrees of comfort. From the 1870s, true music hall also began to establish itself.[100] The Folies Bergère, which opened, just before the fall of the Second Empire, was built in imitation of London's Alhambra theatre and sought to offer Paris a similar range of acts. It boasted a plush interior, with magnificent staircases leading up from the entrance hall to a balcony and with private boxes and stalls, behind which was the *promenoir* where the prostitutes strolled up and down, waiting for suitable clients (like in the Alhambra's promenade). There was an open garden with fountains outside, where drinks could be ordered. On stage could be seen circus acts, magicians, jugglers, illusionists, animal acts, musical entertainments of all types, operettas and musical comedies—and of course dancing girls.[101]

The latter generally provided the standard music-hall fare, with any excuse to appear scantily clad, as they were employed to please the male members of the audience. However, despite the fact that the Folies Bergère is often associated in popular myth with the cancan, it was not a major feature of the programme. On the other hand, the Folies was the first theatre in Paris to present chorus-line dancers; the five Barrison sisters regularly appeared there in the 1890s.[102] These American entertainers (who were not really sisters) set a trend at the Folies Bergère, and were followed by similar troupes in later years, notably John Tiller's Girls, the Jackson Girls and, most famously, the Bluebell

Girls. Again these dancers were a product of a tradition established outside France, this time in Britain, and they were influential in the development of the cancan into the French Cancan by Pierre Sandrini. In America, uniformity was, and is still, considered desirable: witness an American audience's reaction to the sight of chorus dancers linking arms and rhythmically high kicking as they approach the front of the stage. In Britain, this precision form of dancing was not as popular, but was more popular than in France, where the individual improvisations of the dancers at the Moulin Rouge were more highly regarded.

The other music halls of Paris have on occasions presented the French Cancan, although it would be misleading to suggest that they had any significant role in the development of the dance. Nini-Patte-en-l'Air and her pupils danced on the stage of the Casino de Paris in the 1890s, but their cancan was only really a restatement of the Moulin Rouge's *quadrille naturaliste*. Jane Avril also had a short engagement at this music hall, which the *Guide des Plaisirs à Paris* described as having "a wide variety of attractions: beautiful women, both in the hall and on the stage, magnificent ballets with battalions of dancers delightfully dressed and undressed, performances of the highest order".[103]

The smaller *café-concerts* of Montmartre were also the scene of sporadic appearances by the stars of the larger venues, even though some had stages barely large enough for a single performer. Among the most famous of these were the Chat Noir and Aristide Bruant's Mirliton. Customers of such cabarets could expect to be treated with disrespect: the waiters at the Chat Noir, who dressed in the robes of the Académie Française, were renowned for their rudeness, and Bruant himself was given to treating new arrivals with the full force of his acerbic wit.[104] Jane Avril was particularly suited to some of the smaller establishments, from the point of view of her wish to avoid being classed as a professional and because her dancing was nearly always solo. She joined the Chat Noir cabaret for several shows, performing to a violin or a piano. She also appeared at the Café du Divan Japonais, a tiny *café-concert* which was decorated, as the name implies, in the then modish Japanese style and whose waitresses were dressed in kimonos.[105] The star of this cabaret was Yvette Guilbert, who felt more at home in its intimate surroundings than in the Moulin Rouge. It was situated just off the boulevard Rochechouart, on which were to be found the Mirliton, the Elysée-Montmartre and many other small theatres such as the Alcazar, The Eldorado and the Bouffes du Nord. Their artistes sometimes graduated to the larger establishments, like the Moulin Rouge and the Jardin de Paris, where Joseph Oller was always looking for fresh talent to please his more bourgeois audiences. The audiences for the little cabarets like the Mirliton were decidedly not bourgeois, and members of the class were the butt of much of the humour in songs.[106]

The beginning of the twentieth century brought an end to the era of the cancan star. It might have also resulted in the disappearance of the dance itself in Paris if it had not been for the foresight of the orchestra conductor, Auguste Bosc. Bosc was described by André Warnod as following the example of Musard, the eccentric conductor of the orchestra at the Paris Opéra balls, in so far as he also wrote popular contemporary dance tunes. He also had much of Musard's talent for pleasing an audience. Taking advantage of the decision by Oller to abandon the *quadrille naturaliste* at the Moulin Rouge in favour of spectacular revues and operettas, Bosc opened his Bal Tabarin in February 1904 with the intention of continuing the Moulin Rouge traditions. He persuaded a few of the former stars of Oller's establishments to participate in his new venture and succeeded in attracting new audiences to see what had now become traditional Parisian entertainment.[107]

The Tabarin was conveniently situated in the rue Victor-Massé, not far from the Moulin Rouge and the Elysée-Montmartre, and so was in the heart of the city's nightlife. The highlight of the week was the Saturday evening pageant, which followed a theme from history or contemporary life. Ancient Greece and Byzantium alternated with boating at Bougival or horse racing scenes in the pleasant setting of the Tabarin's Art Nouveau interior, with its frescoes by Willette. According to Warnod, the main hall was illuminated by a thousand lights, and there were staircases leading to galleries, balconies and private boxes from which to view the spectacle.[108]

The cancan at the Tabarin remained a major draw for both French and foreign visitors for nearly twenty years, but when Pierre Sandrini revived the dance at the new Moulin Rouge in the 1920s, Bosc's business suffered dramatically. He accepted that his concept of a show had now been eclipsed by the success of his competitor at the Moulin Rouge, and he permitted Sandrini, together with Pierre Dubout, to buy his theatre.

The new owners considerably altered the interior of the Tabarin, taking away the Art Nouveau decorations and setting up a small stage.[109] The cancan was the now the main event of the evening's entertainment, and the excitement of the arrival of the girls on stage was heightened through Sandrini's considerable efforts to place the dance within different extravagant settings each year. Once the cancan was in full swing, every movement was reflected in a huge mirror, enabling spectators further away from the dance floor to obtain a good view.[110]

The Tabarin was the third claimant of the title 'home of the cancan', and indeed was worthy of the description for several years until it closed in the 1950s. Bosc's original design may have been somewhat modest in outlook, being derived from the Moulin Rouge formula in the 1890s, but under Sandrini and Dubout the Tabarin became a truly superior music hall, and Bosc was known to have much admired the productions of his successors.[111]

The success of the Tabarin prompted other Paris nightclubs to present their own versions of the French Cancan, and from the 1950s there were a number of shows available to the connoisseur. The Moulin Rouge, the Lido, the Folies Bergère, the Nouvelle Eve and the Alcazar de Paris have all excited their customers with the frills and high kicks of an expertly choreographed spectacle. The Nouvelle Eve was actually opened in 1897 as the Fantaisies Parisiennes and until the Second World War presented a series of satirical plays, music-hall and revue shows. It was refurbished in 1949 in the *fin-de-siècle* style, renamed

FIG. 53. A dramatic view of the *grand écart* at the Tabarin in its heyday. For over two decades, the night-club was known as the home of the French Cancan, and when it closed its doors for the last time in the 1950s many mourned its passing. *Popperfoto.*

the Nouvelle Eve, and began a tradition of spectacular revues incorporating the French Cancan. At this time, it became a very fashionable place to visit and attracted a sophisticated clientele. Jean Trocher described the dance at the Nouvelle Eve as a "cancan de Luxe".[112] The Alcazar, which had been operated as a music hall from the 1920s, developed a particularly inventive style of entertainment which proved remarkably popular with Parisian audiences in the 1960s. A burlesque style of revue was presented, with satire, female impersonation and extravagant dance routines. The French Cancan was the high point of the show, with sumptuous costumes evocative of the most frothy creations from the turn of the century.[113]

While some of the cabarets have now abandoned the cancan in favour of Las Vegas glitter, the tradition still persists in Paris and tourists still expect to find the most definitive performance of the dance in the city where it originated. When the most recently created major cabaret venue, the Paradis Latin, opened its doors in 1977, this demand was satisfied with an exciting show, featuring as its climax the French Cancan. This theatre, designed by Gustave Eiffel, was originally opened in 1889, but only survived as such for five years and was then turned into a warehouse. It was reopened as a cabaret venue by Jean Kriegel, who had acquired the building in the 1970s in order to convert it into flats. His change of heart when he saw the potential of the fine old theatre has been rewarded with a successful series of revues.[114]

FIG. 54. The finale of the cancan at the Paradis Latin. Men are once again taking a prominent role in the dance at this relatively new addition to Paris night life, based in a theatre designed by Gustave Eiffel. *Paradis Latin.*

CHAPTER 4 / OFFENBACH IN THE UNDERWORLD
The Cancan in Operetta, Ballet and Musicals

For many there is only one piece of music for the cancan: Offenbach's *galop infernal* from *Orpheus in the Underworld*. But in fact many composers have written cancan music, and music by others has been used for the dance in various contexts—at the *bals publics*, Carnival balls, in music halls, in ballet, operetta and musicals. The nature of the dance requires energetic music with a real sense of fun, which Offenbach had in apparently unlimited supply and few others have matched. His compositions have certainly contributed to the cancan's continuing popularity, but it must be remembered that when the dance first appeared he was still in his childhood and not even living in France. The originators of the dance would have been inspired by popular tunes of the day; unfortunately we cannot be sure which particular piece of music first encouraged the high kicks of the students and the *grisettes*, as no record of this was kept.

The cancan is a dance in a quick $\frac{2}{4}$ time, and most music written for a galop is eminently suitable. The galop's bouncy rhythm gave the young men and women who frequented the dance halls of Montparnasse the ideal opportunity to let off steam. Many dance tunes originally written for slower, more restrained movement were also often played at a faster tempo to enhance the pleasure of the dancers and help them to lose their inhibitions. The polka became increasingly popular from the 1840s, and much music written for this dance, which is also in $\frac{2}{4}$, was used for the cancan in dance halls.

Some composers wrote music specifically for the galop, and it often featured as the final figure in the quadrille, hence the link between the quadrille form and the cancan. For example, in the opera *Gustave III* by the composer Daniel-François-Esprit Auber, which had a finale set at a masked ball, the climax was a galop which was danced by a grand total of 122 people on stage at the first performance in 1833. Although *Gustave III* was set in the eighteenth century, it must have owed much to the contemporary Carnival balls. The critic Jules Janin commented that the behaviour of the guests at the ball was such that "one would think that they were there for their own pleasure and not ours". He described the galop as "wonderful". "The galop takes possession of these men and women body and soul. . . . You cannot imagine how realistic it is."[1]

Offenbach included a lively galop in his operetta *Ba-ta-clan*, which he produced in 1855, three years before *Orpheus*. Described as a *chinoiserie musicale* because of its setting in the exotic Orient, *Ba-ta-clan* was typical of Offenbach's irreverent style, with its gentle satire, undermining the current vogue for Italian opera and also lampooning the respected composer Meyerbeer, who in fact was secretly flattered.[2] At one point in the plot, a former actress and a society gentleman, far from home, reminisce about their times in Paris, as the orchestra plays waltzes and the galop. In the public dancing gardens

FIG. 55. Jacques Offenbach, the composer of numerous operettas, including *Orpheus in the Underworld*, which contains probably the most familiar tune in the operatic repertoire, the *galop infernal*, known to many simply as 'The Cancan'. *Theatre Museum, V&A Picture Library.*

of the city at this time, the galop was frequently danced as a cancan, and Offenbach was hinting that his protagonists had spent many a boisterous evening at places such as the Bal Mabille.[3] Offenbach was well acquainted with dance-hall entertainment in Paris, and it may seem strange in fact that he waited until he was in his mid-thirties before actually composing for the cancan. An explanation is probably not difficult to find.

When Offenbach first arrived in France, the cancan had only just emerged, and only by the late 1850s was it being developed by extremely gifted dancers, who all had their own individual styles. During its first twenty years, it had belonged largely in the realm of the true amateur, and, apart from Céleste Mogador and Pomaré, few performers had managed to imbue it with any real quality. According to Siegfried Kracauer, Offenbach did not like the directness of the cancan in its primitive form.[4] Subtlety and refinement appealed to him, and while the dance's raw energy and under-mining of conventional morality would not have offended him, he would have found it difficult to incorporate in a work of art. It was also a few years before he found his true forte as a composer of satirical operetta, and the inherent subversiveness of the cancan and his natural inclination to poke fun at contemporary society inevitably (and eventually) converged. Once the dance had achieved a more polished form, he clearly felt able to exploit its potential in an ingenious fashion.

Operetta as an entertainment for the masses had, like the cancan, origi-nated in the fairgrounds around Paris and had begun life by deliberately par-odying well-known operas. This had so offended the opera authorities in Paris that they had successfully managed to ban such satirical works at times during the eighteenth century.[5] When operetta first appeared on stage in the city, there were still restrictions imposed through theatre licences. Offenbach was limited by his theatre's licence to a maximum of four characters on stage for *Ba-ta-clan*, and consequently had no scope for large-scale set pieces. But from 1858, he was no longer subject to such restrictions and was able to include as many characters as he liked.[6] With *Orpheus in the Underworld* he celebrated this new freedom in fine style. It is another mildly satirical work, with a fair amount of poking fun at social mores through the medium of free adaptation of a classical legend. Subjects from Greek or Roman mythology proved popular in operetta, partly because they were such 'grand' subjects that the audiences loved to see them treated with disrespect, and partly because they gave an excuse for the appearance on stage of (relatively) scant-ily clad women.

Offenbach expertly wove into the music a number of rather risky items, including the quotation of the famous aria 'Che farò' from Gluck's revered *Orfeo ed Euridice* and a brief excerpt from the 'Marseillaise' (which was then banned because of its revolutionary connotations). The *galop infernal* itself comes at the very end of the operetta, when Eurydice and the gods and god-desses take part in a Bacchanalian romp which is clearly much more enjoy-able than the preceding, more suitably 'god-like' minuet. This contrast between the boredom of heavenly pursuits and the fun to be found in Hades is a constant theme of the libretto by Crémieux and Halévy.

The dancing in the finale in the early performances bore little resem-blance to the cancan of the dance halls of Paris. Offenbach did not entitle it 'cancan', and it was only later referred to as such, when it became the most popular music for the dance. The galop was in fact performed by both male and female performers in a variety of mock-classical costumes. The women did not wear the long skirts and petticoats normally associated with the can-can—in fact the attractive and flirtatious Lise Tautin, Eurydice in the original performance, was a great draw for the Paris public because of the *shortness* of her skirt in the final act.[7] The overall effect was more akin to the dance as it appeared at the Carnival balls than the popular entertainment of the Mabille and other pleasure palaces.

The music for the galop is frenetic, exciting and vital, and was an imme-

FIG. 56. Lise Tautin, whose flirtatious nature made her an ideal choice to play Eurydice in the first production of *Orpheus in the Underworld*. She was apparently a big draw for the Paris public because of the shortness of her costume for the part. *Private Collection.*

diate hit with the first-night audience, whereas most of the rest of the operetta was received with less enthusiasm. Its simple, three-chord harmony, the constant, driving rhythm in the bass, and an energetic melody combine to extraordinary effect. After the opening bars, there is apparently no opportunity for performers to pause for breath, the tempo is unremitting and the thrills are kept at fever pitch by the dynamics and phrasing. All in all, it is a masterful example of popular composition, guaranteed to have an audience clapping along and cheering at the end. Add to this the spectacle of a frenzied bacchanal, as in the first performances of Orpheus, or a troupe of high-kicking *cancaneuses*, as has been usual in revivals, and you have a recipe for continued success.

It is possible that the *galop infernal* of the finale ensured that *Orpheus in the Underworld* survived during its first run. The public's initial reservations about the operetta were overcome in the second act, and many who left the Bouffes Parisiens theatre after the first night in October 1858 found themselves humming the now well-known tune. Sheet music sales were very important to Offenbach and his contemporaries, which is why so many of the songs in his operettas are essentially dance tunes with popular appeal. Anyone hearing the music at the *bals publics* or sung at the *café-concerts*, or even performed by a pianist at an elegant soirée, would have been tempted to see the operetta

FIG. 57. The *galop infernal* in *Orpheus in the Underworld* as portrayed by Gustave Doré, who also designed some of the costumes. The scene is comparable to the Carnival balls at the Paris Opéra that epitomised Second Empire decadence. *Musée de Strasbourg.*

itself.[8] When *Orpheus* arrived on stage in other countries, the music was often already well known to many in the audiences in the same way.

The critics on the whole liked the work (although were somewhat offended by the treatment of the respected classics), but Offenbach nevertheless made a number of changes, removing weak passages and generally tightening up the score, adding new music and lyrics if necessary.[9] As it happened, the final guarantee of the operetta's financial success had little to do with any of the composer's tinkerings. After the presentation of the latest version in February 1859, Jules Janin unintentionally did great service to Offenbach and his theatre by denouncing *Orpheus* as sacrilege and contempt for antiquity and classical literature. It seems likely that the critic was in fact upset because the operetta was clearly ridiculing the bourgeoisie, although in the most gentle way possible. Whatever his motives, the public found this sort of bumptious comment intensely amusing, especially when Offenbach revealed to *Le Figaro* that Crémieux had actually used some of Janin's own overblown prose in one of Pluto's speeches.[10] As a result, audiences at the Bouffes Parisiens increased dramatically. The fact that tickets were often sold out only increased people's desire to see the operetta, and it rapidly achieved cult status. In March 1859, the box office was averaging receipts of 2,250 francs a night.[11]

Janin's criticism also helped to arouse interest in the music in other

FIG. 58. Offenbach's Bouffes Parisiens theatre, where his operettas are occasionally still performed. This was not his original
theatre, but was acquired when the authorities permitted him,
eventually, to have more than four characters on stage at one
time. *Private Collection.*

spheres of Parisian society. Those who could not make it to the theatre all
wanted to hear Offenbach's sparkling melodies, in particular the *galop infernal*. Dance halls and fashionable ballrooms echoed to the sounds of the new
operetta. The stars of the cancan in Second Empire Paris quickly recognised
the potential of the bacchanal for their form of outrageous dancing, and the
music has remained pre-eminent in this context ever since. It is frequently
described as 'The Cancan' without any further explanation. No doubt Offenbach had this use in mind when he wrote it, even if he was apparently reluctant to use the term.

Emperor Napoléon III gave *Orpheus* his seal of approval, despite his
court having been the brunt of much of the satire, especially in the scene on
Mount Olympus. His troops used Offenbach's music on their triumphant
march home from victory over the Austrians at Magenta, and soon afterwards the emperor personally intervened on the German-born composer's
behalf to ensure that he was granted French citizenship.[12] Perhaps the high
point of imperial patronage was the emperor's promise to attend a benefit
performance for Offenbach in April 1860 on condition that *Orpheus in the
Underworld* was included in the programme.[13]

Offenbach may not have written the first cancan music, but he made the
form his own and imbued it with a real sense of Second Empire frivolity.
Many of his operettas include a cancan or galop, but perhaps the most
famous after the one found in *Orpheus in the Underworld* is that of *La Vie Parisienne*. Here he placed it in a contemporary setting and also acknowledged the
growing interest of foreign tourists in Paris as a city of pleasure. Offenbach

FIG. 59. The urbane Urbain resists the attentions of the ladies of the chorus during the party scene in D'Oyly Carte's 1995 production of *La Vie Parisienne*. The operetta contains cancan music that rivals the *galop infernal* from *Orpheus in the Underworld*. *Alan Wood.*

was taking some risks in writing a satirical piece removed from the apparent safety of a historical or mythological setting, and there were many who believed that the operetta would fail. In the event, it has become one of his more durable compositions, which in many ways is more truly representative of his own character.

The plot is designed to reflect the many joys of contemporary Paris, and it features an array of colourful characters, typical of the visitors expected in the city for the *Exposition Universelle* of 1867 (a year after the operetta's début). The Swedish Baron de Gondremarck is after some fun with the actresses at the theatres, while his wife is interested in hearing Paris's great operatic voices. The Brazilian millionaire merely wishes to spend his money on the ladies, the less respectable the better. The Parisians are finely drawn, like Urbain, the head waiter, who is a master of diplomacy in dealing with guests, and a colonel's widow, who sings of her departed husband with clearly ambivalent affection, and who is now determined to have a good time.

The gaiety of the city is portrayed through the ebullient protagonists, and the apparent absurdity of the plot was probably not too far removed from reality. Clever devices, such as having servants dress up in their employers' clothes to masquerade as guests in a 'hotel' designed to fool the baron and his wife, delighted audiences, even if the upper classes were slightly disconcerted by the suggestion that their social inferiors could so easily change places with them. The fun and excitement of the party reaches its climax in a cancan which almost achieves the flair and finesse of the *galop infernal*.

The story of *La Vie Parisienne* implies that nothing really matters, life should not be taken seriously, and frivolity is the order of the day. The cancan so supremely embodies this feeling and provides a wonderful highlight in a glittering show. Whereas in *Orpheus in the Underworld* Offenbach was evoking the atmosphere of the Carnival balls with the final galop, in *La Vie Parisienne* he was celebrating the excitement of the Second Empire *bals publics*.

In the 1870s, Offenbach's music was as popular outside France as it was at home, where a period of gloom and self-doubt had set in after defeat by Germany had led to the collapse of the Second Empire. The composer did however continue working, after a brief period of being subject to some prejudice because of his German origins, and in 1874 presented an expanded version of *Orpheus in the Underworld* in Paris. Now in four acts, the production was an excessive reaction to the straitened times, with 120 singers and a corps de ballet of sixty, plus eight principal female dancers.[14] Revivals today also generally present a longer version of the operetta than the original, and they incorporate the revised overture arranged by Carl Binder for a production in Vienna in 1860. This ends dramatically with the *galop infernal*, which unfortunately tends to ruin the impact of the music when it appears as the climax to the final act.

Offenbach's music is used for a traditional French Cancan in Léonide Massine's ballet *Gaîté Parisienne*, whose plot is based largely on Act Three of

FIG. 60. Léonide Massine, as the Peruvian, and two 'cocodettes' in the Ballets Russes 1946 production of *Gaîté Parisienne*. The original production by the same company and also starring and choreographed by Massine was in 1938. *Theatre Museum, V&A Picture Library.*

FIG. 61. The cancan finale to *Gaîté Parisienne* by the Ballets Russes. The music for the dance is from a selection of Offenbach operettas, including *La Vie Parisienne*, *Robinson Crusoé* and of course *Orpheus in the Underworld*. *Theatre Museum, V&A Picture Library.*

La Vie Parisienne. The ballet is really a showcase for the cancan and also employs music from a number of other Offenbach compositions, including the *galop infernal*, imaginatively arranged by Manuel Rosenthal. The music is generally loud and exciting—even the Peruvian's theme is a galop. The costumes for the original were archetypes of the traditional, with nearly all the female leads wearing frilly petticoats, and the *cancaneuses* themselves provocatively flaunting their black stockings and suspenders.

The action of the ballet takes place supposedly in the 1860s at a fashionable restaurant, the Café Tortoni, a haunt of Parisian *bons vivants*. The curtains open to show waiters and young women cleaning the dining room and dance floor in preparation for the arrival of that evening's customers. Several characters enter: a flower girl, *cocodettes* with their male escorts, and a glove seller, who is the heroine of the ballet as she is of *La Vie Parisienne*. The international reputation of the café is underlined when a number of foreign visitors appear, including a Peruvian and the baron, who are both fascinated by the pretty glove seller. Some soldiers arrive in their uniforms, and distract the girls, who in turn are soon angry at being deserted by all the men when La Lionne, the famous courtesan, enters the room.

The various characters dance to Offenbach's evocative music: a polka, a mazurka, a waltz—all typical of this optimistic era. The cancan is of course anticipated, but first of all trouble erupts between the various protagonists when their jealousy gets too much for them. La Lionne's escort, the duke, is annoyed with her for taking interest in the officer in charge of the soldiers and the baron is furious when the glove seller flirts with the Peruvian. Inevitably a fight ensues. When calm is restored and the baron has settled his differences with the glove seller, the cancan dancers enter and clear the air with their spirited high kicks.

They initially perform to the galops from *La Vie Parisienne*, *Orpheus in the Underworld* and other operettas. After they have finished with a flourish by each leaping in the air and landing in a magnificent *grand écart*, the dance begins again and everybody joins in. Something of the image of Finette is introduced by the Peruvian, who encourages the girls to kick at his top hat. La Lionne also dances the cancan, as do the other women. The whole cancan sequence lasts several minutes, and is a dramatic climax to the ballet. When at last the evening draws to a close, the couples depart to the sounds of the sensuous barcarolle from *The Tales of Hoffmann*, Offenbach's last work. The Peruvian is, however, still without a partner.

This balletic version of the cancan is very beautiful. The grace of the dancers' movements, combined with the inevitable suggestiveness of the skirt manipulation and high kicks, provide a subtly erotic rendition of the dance. Massine must have been heavily influenced by Pierre Sandrini's French Cancan at the Bal Tabarin, and purists may argue that chorus-line cancans did not exist in 1860s Paris, and that the costumes were also anachronistic. But really this is irrelevant: the whole thing is fantasy, and should be enjoyed on that basis.[15]

Léonide Massine was also responsible for other ballets employing the cancan in different forms and guises. The most well known are *La Boutique Fantasque* and *Beau Danube*, first performed in 1919 and 1924 respectively. *La Boutique Fantasque* (*The Magic Toyshop*), originally performed by Diaghilev's Ballets Russes company, has music by Gioacchino Rossini, arranged by Ottorino Respighi. Rossini coined the title 'The Mozart of the Champs-Elysées' with which to describe Offenbach, and he imitated his effervescent style in a piece called 'Capriccio Offenbachique'. It forms part of a collection of short compositions which Rossini produced during his retirement, mostly for his own amusement or for friends who came to visit. They are often named after food, reflecting presumably what he and his guests ate for dinner. Hence, we have pieces entitled 'Gherkins', 'Radishes', 'Butter', 'Almonds', etc, together with 'Themes in Variations', 'Abortive Polka', and the aforementioned Offenbach tribute.[16] The whimsical humour of this music is well suited to the story portrayed in the ballet, and Respighi's orchestration is masterful.

The scene is a toyshop in Nice in the late nineteenth century, where the shopkeeper is busy demonstrating his working life-size 'dolls' to various potential customers, among them an American family and a Russian family. Italian tarantella dancers, 'court cards' dancing a mazurka, Cossacks, performing dogs—all delight the customers, and the shopkeeper finally

FIG. 62. Pamela May and Harold Turner in the 1947 Sadler's Wells Ballet production of *La Boutique Fantasque*. The costumes for this production are much the same as those for the original production at the Alhambra theatre in 1919. *Theatre Museum, V&A Picture Library.*

announces his *pièce de résistance*: a pair of cancan dancers. These are the finest dolls he has ever created, and are as beautiful as they are ingenious. The man is a suave, handsome rake, whose clothing is flamboyant and flashy; his partner is prettily dressed in a short cancan dress, with white skirt covering layers of lace petticoats, ornamented with ribbons.

After their dance, the American children are very excited. The boy tries to pull up his mother's dress, and the girl imitates the kicks of the female doll. Their father seems very interested in the female doll, and his wife clearly disapproves. However, the children demand that he buys the man, while the Russian children ask for the woman. The shopkeeper is reluctant to split the dolls up, and asks for a huge sum. Eventually, the sale is agreed, and the customers arrange to collect their purchases in the morning.

At night, the dolls come to life in the toyshop, and it is revealed that the cancan dolls are lovers. The other dolls are sad that they are to be parted. Although there is an air of despondency, the dolls dance until they are carried away by their own movements, and there is a feeling of triumph in the final cakewalk.

In the morning, the customers arrive and the shopkeeper is horrified to find the boxes containing the cancan dancers empty. He is attacked by the Russian and the American, who think they have been swindled. To his

1. This painting by Abel Truchet shows the *quadrille natural-iste* in progress at the Bal Tabarin in 1906. This cabaret took over many of the Moulin Rouge's traditions when the latter changed its policy in favour of presenting revues. *Musée d'Art Moderne/Photothèque des Musées de la Ville de Paris.*

2. Les Cancaneuses du Sud, a troupe of dancers in the south of France who re-create the atmosphere at the Moulin Rouge in the 1890s. Like their predecessors of a century ago, they have nicknames, such as 'Lily Dynamite', 'Valentine la Coquine', and even 'Eglantine' and 'Nini-patte-en-l'air'. *La Compagnie des Cancaneuses du Sud.*

3. The finale of the *galop infernal* in the English National Opera's extravagant production of *Orpheus in the Underworld* in the mid-1980s, designed by the cartoonist and caricaturist Gerald Scarfe. *Donald Cooper/Photostage.*

4. Valencienne triumphant following her performance at 'Maxim's' with the *grisettes* in the Wiener Volksoper's production of *The Merry Widow*. The operetta remains a favourite with audiences in the city of its birth, and is performed each year by the Volksoper. *Österreichischer Bundestheaterverband.*

5. The Jardin de Paris as portrayed by Adolphe Willette in Georges Montorgueil's book, *Paris Dansant*. This establishment was operated by the same management team as the Moulin Rouge, and La Goulue and her fellow cancan dancers also appeared here. *By permission of the British Library, K.T.C.6.B.1.*

6. Chorus members from D'Oyly Carte opera's production of *La Vie Parisienne* in 1995. Freely adapted and updated from the 1860s to the 1890s, this version had its finale set in a private room at the Moulin Rouge. *Private Collection.*

7 and 8. Toulouse-Lautrec's *Jane Avril dansant* shows the dancer performing one her solo routines at the Moulin Rouge. In most of his paintings of her she wears a serious, thoughtful expression, while in contemporary photographs she often appears smiling, sometimes looking girlish and cheeky. Her volatile nature was reflected in her dancing, and by one of her nicknames—Mélinite, a type of dynamite. *7. Giraudon/Bridgeman Art Library; 8. Musée de Montmartre.*

9. One of the later studies for Georges Seurat's *Le Chahut*, which depicts a chorus-line style of dancing which was never actually part of the *chahut* itself. The diagonal of the dancers' raised legs was used by the artist to symbolise happiness. *Courtauld Institute Galleries/Bridgeman Art Library.*

10. An illustration of the *quadrille naturaliste* accompanying a chapter on the subject in Georges Montorgueil's *Paris Dansant*. Willette stressed the sexuality of the women in his paintings and was not afraid to portray their sexual proclivities. *By permission of the British Library, к.т.с.6.в.1.*

11. A poster for the refurbished and relaunched Bal Tabarin in 1928 by the respected artist Paul Colin. It is an ingenious mixture of the modern day with the Victorian traditions of the cancan which the new cabaret employed to such great effect. *V&A Picture Library.*

12. The cancan dancers at the Nouvelle Eve. This cabaret celebrated its one hundredth anniversary in 1997, having originally been named the Fantaisies Parisiennes. The show is now a sophisticated mix of classical ballet and modern dance. *Nouvelle Eve.*

13. The Paradis Latin is a relatively new cabaret in Paris, but the climax of the show there is a French Cancan, performed by dancers from many different countries. *Paradis Latin*.

14. The Golden Heart cancan dancers and their cowboy partners who entertain visitors to Fairbanks, Alaska in a Gold Rush revue. One of the many amateur groups around the world who keep the traditions of the cancan alive. *Golden Heart Dancers*.

15. The dancers at Turner's Musical Merry-go-round in Northampton, England. The cancan is the finale to a cabaret on a dance floor overlooked by a traditional merry-go-round, recalling the dance's roots as fairground entertainment. *Turner's Musical Merry-go-round.*

16. One of Rosie O'Grady's 'bar-top cancan girls' in Orlando, Florida. A colourful if not very traditional rendition of the dance in one of America's most popular holiday destinations. *Rosie O'Grady's.*

surprise, the other dolls come to the shopkeeper's aid and fight off his ass-ailants, eventually chasing them from the shop. The ballet ends with all the dolls, together with the cancan dancers, congratulating the confused but happy shopkeeper.

In the original production of *La Boutique Fantasque*, Massine himself danced the part of the male cancan dancer, and Lydia Lopokova the female dancer. The London audience applauded and cheered the protagonists after their cancan, and many of the other dances were similarly well received. Lopokova was rightly praised for her performance, playing with her skirts as if to tease and entice her partner, while at the same time retaining the fixed expression of a mechanical doll on her face. Gestures with head and arms by both dancers conveyed emotions, but at no time did any show in their faces.[17] Alexandra Danilova, who later took over the part of the female doll and also played the part of the glove seller in *Gaîté Parisienne*, visited the Bal Tabarin on more than one occasion to observe the real French Cancan. She said she performed the same steps, only with a little more refinement. She com-plained that her skirt with its petticoats was heavier than normal ballet cos-tumes, and made pirouetting difficult—when she turned, the skirt followed a few seconds later.[18]

Danilova dressed in similar costume for her role as the street dancer in *Beau Danube*. This is a ballet choreographed to the music of the Strauss family, and set in Vienna in the 1860s. The action takes place in a park on a Sunday afternoon, and the array of characters who stroll by in their finery bear simi-larity to those in *Gaîté Parisienne*: dressmakers and seamstresses, salesmen, an artist, dandies, shop girls, a hussar. Polkas, waltzes and a mazurka are all danced with light-hearted gaiety as a series of encounters takes place between the various characters.

The centrepiece of the ballet is a show put on by a group of three strolling players. The street dancer begins their performance with a solo polka, mak-ing mischievous use of her red velvet skirt and white petticoats. The strong-man performs feats of weightlifting to a waltz tune, and the street dancer continues with another cheeky dance. A cancan completes the performance.

After the show the street dancer recognises the hussar as a former lover, and she insults his female companion, causing her to faint. The street dancer then collapses as well, and she has to be revived by her manager. The hussar then dances the Blue Danube waltz with her, only for his girl-friend to return and demand that he choose between them. He realises he is in love with her, and the street dancer admits defeat and later joins in their betrothal celebrations.

This a delightful ballet, with the vivacious street dancer an attractive leading character. The whole atmosphere of the piece is very similar to that of *Gaîté Parisienne*, the plot being of little consequence, and with everyone out to have a good time. Not only were both ballets choreographed by Massine, they were also both designed by Comte Etienne de Beaumont, and it seems that these men were really inspired in creating two works which so perfectly encapsulate the carefree atmosphere of the period. Alexandra Danilova's contribution to the three Massine ballets featuring the cancan was also significant. She had a natural sense of humour, which was ideal for her roles, and as the glove seller in *Gaîté Parisienne* she conveyed a coquettish charm which has not been equalled. When she died in 1997, an obituary highlighted one particular story relating to this role. She was on a tour of Japan and was observed to have tears in her eyes while talking to a Japanese man, who was clearly a great fan of hers. He had said to her that "after seeking for many years to reach a state of Nirvana, he had achieved it at the moment she lifted her famous ruffled skirts in Massine's *Gaîté Parisienne*".[19]

Massine's influence was evident in *The Bar at the Folies Bergère* of the Ballet Rambert, first produced in 1934 and created by Ninette de Valois. It was also directly inspired by Manet's well-known painting, and it began and ended with the image of the barmaid standing behind her counter. In the ballet, she is in love with the handsome waiter Valentin, but finds she has to compete for his affections with the dancers from the theatre next door. The first to arrive in the bar is none other than Grille d'Egout, whom Valentin serves with a drink, and at the same time he steals a kiss. Two other cancan dancers enter and it is evident that the handsome Valentin's attentions are much in demand.

Once all his customers are catered for, Valentin finds time for a short dance with the barmaid, but it is over far too soon, because more people come into the bar. An elderly gentleman is followed by La Goulue, the star of the show. Her appearance is dramatic, her beautiful face with dark eyes and bright red lipstick and her fashionable dress making her a captivating figure. The old gentleman finds her and her fellow dancers very appealing and orders champagne. The girls enjoy teasing him and sitting on his knee. They entertain him with an excerpt from their cancan show, and he responds enthusiastically by providing more champagne.

Valentin finds La Goulue overwhelmingly attractive, and waits on her eagerly. She rewards him with a marvellous solo dance. Despite entreaties from the barmaid, Valentin eventually leaves arm in arm with La Goulue. The other customers also leave one by one, and the barmaid is left to clear up and contemplate her sad circumstances.

Although *The Bar at the Folies Bergère* seems to have confused the Moulin Rouge with the Folies Bergère, and to have a rather romantic image of the beauty of La Goulue, Grille d'Egout and their associates, it remains one of the few theatrical works to have focused on the cancan dancers of 1890s Paris. It was an interesting idea to develop a ballet from a painting, and the device of having the dancers enter through the audience reminded one of an evening at a *café-concert* in Montmartre. The music for the ballet is from Chabrier's *Dix pièces pittoresques*.

These ballets were by no means the first to feature the cancan. In the late nineteenth century, ballet had mixed fortunes, condemned by some as immoral because of its displays of female legs. This was especially true in Britain, and music halls, which had included some form of dancing in their programmes from the 1840s, soon became the only outlet for ballet. Some

FIG. 63. 'La Goulue' and 'Valentin' the waiter (Maud Lloyd and Walter Gore) in *The Bar at the Folies Bergère* at the Duchess Theatre in London in 1937. This ballet is a rare example of the stars of the 1890s being portrayed on stage. *Theatre Museum, V&A Picture Library.*

inevitable cross-fertilisation occurred: ballets often had to contain some form of sensation to keep a less-cultured audience interested, while at the same time the general quality of dance in the music halls was lifted to a higher standard through the influence of trained dancers. Inevitably, the cancan or 'Parisian quadrille' was often included in new ballets devised at this time.[20]

It would perhaps be easy to dismiss much of the music-hall ballet, on the assumption that a predominantly working-class audience would have rejected anything too artistically demanding. Certainly, a little extra excitement, through special lighting and other effects and dramatic 'transformation' scenes, was provided to ensure that the customers did not become bored, but this does not mean that they did not appreciate the dancing. On the whole, ballets were well received in music halls, and the dancers were respected performers. Ultimately, music halls became recognised for their patronage of ballet, and prominent dancers often appeared at the Empire, Coliseum, Alhambra and other London halls, a number of which had their own resident companies.[21] Even after these had been disbanded, the music halls continued to present ballet. *La Boutique Fantasque* was premiered at the Alhambra in 1919.

The Bal Mabille provided the inspiration for *Mabille in London*, which was staged at the Alhambra in 1868 and starred the Parisian *cancaneuse* Finette. She had come to London originally to appear in a pantomime at the Lyceum theatre by W. S. Gilbert, entitled *Cock Robin and Jenny Wren*, and neither performance caused any offence. This could not be said about the ballet *Les Nations*, which was staged at the Alhambra in 1870 and which provided an opportunity for Mademoiselle Colonna's troupe to excite and shock the public. Mlle Colonna (real name Newman) and her dancers, including the famous Sarah Wright, known as 'Wiry Sal', caused the theatre to lose its licence that year. The Alhambra's proprietor was not easily dissuaded from granting London audiences a sight of the famous Parisian dance, and only waited a few months after regaining his licence in April 1871 before presenting Esther Austin in the 'Quadrille du Grand Opéra de Paris'.[22] The cancan appeared regularly after that in various productions, including *The Black Crook*, which *The Times* condemned, causing the French dancers to be omitted in subsequent performances.[23] The next production, Offenbach's *La Belle Hélène*, included the triumphant return of Sarah Wright and her troupe.[24]

Wright had not been without work in the meantime. Emily Soldene, an accomplished singer who had made her name in comic opera (and who was the sister of Esther Austin), was now directing condensed versions of operettas at the Philharmonic Music Hall in Islington. She had witnessed the Colonna Troupe at the Alhambra, and when the theatre was closed she immediately engaged the dancers for a production of *La Grande Duchesse de Gérolstein*, also by Offenbach. In recognition of the talents of the extraordinarily supple Sarah Wright, Soldene renamed her 'Mademoiselle Sara' (after Sara Bernhardt) and made her the leader of the troupe.[25] Soldene presented her English Opéra Comique company in America in 1876, and she took with her a group of "human, healthy, handsome girls and a female who kicks in a style unparalleled in the annals of gymnastic experience". The *Boston Globe*'s critic disapproved, and wrote: "How any man who respects a woman can take her to witness one of these performances surpasses understanding; how any woman can sit through without a feeling of shame and mortification for herself and resentment against the man who subjects her to such a humiliation is still a more perplexing reflection". When he then described the "vicious gymnastics of the cancan", Emily Soldene and her company were assured of success.[26]

Soldene was by no means the only operetta director to use Offenbach's music as an excuse to give audiences a sight of the notorious French dance. Her example was followed in countless productions at the end of the nineteenth century, and continues to be so, with many of the composer's operettas being staged with a cancan troupe appearing in the final act regardless of whether this has any relevance in the context of the story. Offenbach's galops lend themselves so readily to the cancan, and it has always been tempting to apply them in this way, especially as the dancers' performance often brings the house down. He intended his music to be used in the dance halls for the cancan, but he would no doubt be surprised today to find the dance-hall tradition imported so often into the theatre and incorporated in his works.

In response to the feverish excitement generated by La Goulue and Jane Avril across the Channel, London music halls presented a number of new ballets containing a form of cancan in the 1890s, including *Round the Town* (1892) and *La Frolique* (1894).[27] The latter was based on a German original and concerned a dancer who causes a *jardin public* to be closed through her high-kicking *chahut*. Florence Levy, who played La Frolique, wore an unusual costume made from grey silk, with wide-legged, accordion-pleated culottes.[28] Clearly, this was not as revealing as the dresses of the *chahuteuses* of contemporary Paris—it was the dance itself which was supposedly so offensive. Energetic cavorting by women was still frowned on. The ballet ends with La Frolique managing to persuade the court to acquit her of offending public decency, and she is eventually joined in a wild galop by the judge, barristers and court officials.[29]

The score for *La Frolique* was described in a review at the time as "clever and pleasing", though its composer had "no special gift for dance rhythms".[30] Much of the music written for such works has been forgotten, being of little value except in its function of accompaniment to ballets which were quickly dated. The idea of 'Gay Paree' was a popular theme of ballet and operetta, and numerous ephemeral works produced in European cities concerned the adventures of a foreigner in the French capital, including his exposure to the naughty *danseuses* that seemed to inhabit every part of the city. The ballet *A Day in Paris* was one of these, and it typically reached its climax in a final scene set in the Moulin Rouge. If none of these products of a limited imagination has stood the test of time, it is partly because one operetta was soon to appear which swept triumphantly through the Western world, and which contained a matchless impression of the delights that Paris held for the foreigner. And naturally, it featured the cancan. This was Franz Lehár's *The Merry Widow*.

The secret of *The Merry Widow*'s phenomenal success lay in its unusually frank portrayal of sexual licence during the *belle époque*. Illicit affairs are a constant theme of the work, which is set in contemporary Paris, where apparently anything was permitted, or so Lehár's Viennese audiences believed. The libretto was inspired by a three-act comedy written by Henri Meilhac, one of Offenbach's librettists, which had first been performed in Vienna in 1863.[31] Victor Léon and Leo Stein adapted the story, keeping the action in Paris, but updating it from the Second Empire to the turn of the century. By this time the era of the *grande horizontale* courtesan was almost over, but ordinary women were beginning to assert themselves more sexually. They were now less likely to tolerate a dull, sterile marriage for long, and wives' infidelities were becoming more common. In *The Merry Widow* almost everyone seems to be indulging in some form of extramarital romance, and spending little time doing anything else. Count Danilo, the male lead, has a number of mistresses and also enjoys visiting Maxim's restaurant, where he passes the time pleasurably in the company of the *grisettes*, the cancan-dancing *demi-mondaines*. This is all explained to us in conversations between the Pontevedrian ambassador, Baron Zeta, and his secretary, Njegus, and is confirmed

JUNE 9, 1894   *BLACK AND WHITE*   705

"LA FROLIQUE" AT THE EMPIRE

THE new ballet at the Empire, although, perhaps, it suffers by comparison with some of its predecessors, is bright and gay, like all Madame Katti Lanner's inventions. It opens with a series of dances of Pierrots, Pierrettes, Harlequins, Columbines, Débardeurs, Sapphos, &c. During this an elderly man—Monsieur Severe—cleverly played by Signorina Cavallazzi, pays unequivocal attentions to most of the pretty girls. Then "variations" were done by the agile Signor de Vincenti and Signorina Brambilla—a pretty woman, and clever, brilliant dancer. Mdlle. Cora and eight ladies then dance a Spanish measure. This is a prelude to the appearance of Senorita Candida, the wonderful artist who delighted us in the *The Magic Opal*, and who now performs a dance full of strange, wild beauty. Next enters Miss Florence Levey as La Frolique, in a curious costume that has separate accordion-pleated skirts for each leg. The young lady defies the police prohibition of the *chahut*, and is arrested in the middle of a vigorous dance. She and her companions are dragged off to the police-court. She asks leave to convince the Court that the dance is pardonable, and the judge allows her to plead her cause with her dance. No sooner does she begin to dance than the others join in, till at length every person in the court is taking part in a wild quadrille, and then galop till the curtain falls. The music is lively and strong in rhythm, and shows considerable sense of humour.

FIG. 64. A story of how the cancan was banned. The *chahuteuses* are at the bottom, apparently dressed in carnival costumes that could hardly be described as improper—it was the dance itself that was so offensive to the authorities. BLACK AND WHITE, *9 June 1894, by permission of the British Library.*

when Danilo makes his entrance and enthusiastically regales us with the delights of Dodo, Lolo, Joujou, Margot, Cloclo and Froufrou, from whom he has just taken his leave.

The main story of *The Merry Widow* centres around the fortune of the widow herself, Hanna Glawari, which Zeta is desperate to keep in his country. Danilo is the prime candidate to marry her, the ambassador believes, but he refuses for two reasons. In the first place, he was once in love with Hanna at home in Pontevedro, but his family had objected to him marrying her because she was not from an aristocratic family. Danilo now resents the fact that she chose to marry a multimillionaire instead. Secondly, he enjoys his freedom and above all the attentions of the *grisettes*. However, it is clear throughout that Danilo is still in love with Hanna, and she with him, and they spend much of the first two acts skirting around each other, finally resolving their differences and proposing marriage in Act Three. A sub-plot of the operetta concerns the affair, or potential affair, between the ambassador's young wife, Valencienne, and Camille de Rossillon, a handsome French officer. She is initially reluctant to deceive her husband, but Camille's persistence pays off and he overcomes her misgivings, only for their tryst in the garden of Hanna's Paris residence to be discovered by her husband. Fortunately, Hanna manages to convince Zeta that he was mistaken and that he really saw, not Valencienne, but Hanna herself in the arms of Camille. This solves one problem, and also succeeds in making Danilo visibly jealous, proving once and for all that, despite his denials, he is in love with the merry widow.

The entrance of the *grisettes* near the beginning of Act Three is a wonderful moment in the operetta, and is also important to the story. Hanna has decked out her gardens to resemble Maxim's and invited the girls from the famous restaurant to help complete the illusion. It is a treat for Danilo, to prove her love for him, and to show him that marrying her does not mean eschewing entirely the pleasures of Paris nightlife. The *grisettes* also provide Valencienne with the opportunity to assert her independence, and she shocks her husband by joining them in their cancan. With this demonstration of her freedom, she hopes to make it clear to Zeta that she will no longer put up with his complacency about her feelings for him. He is obviously chastened and embarrassed by the effective masquerade, although perhaps a little proud as well.

The *grisettes*' song and cancan have a sensuality and seductiveness far removed in style from the Offenbach galops. Lehár's music may not be ideal for the dance, but in the context of the operetta it is superb. *The Merry Widow* is full of songs which reflect the erotic nature of the plot, being either suggestive (as in Valencienne's Act One 'Respectable wife'), passionate (Camille and Valencienne's love duet in Act Two) or simply unrestrained statements of the joys of a permissive lifestyle ('I'm off to Chez Maxim'). The *grisettes* sing of their life as streetwalkers, and how they also entertain at Maxim's with their high kicks, cartwheels and splits. The music is cheeky and provocative, giving ample opportunity for the girls to tease and entice, strutting around the stage showing a few flashes of black stockings and frilly petticoats. Then a fanfare sounds and they launch into their dance: again the music has a more decadent, saucy quality, and less of the relentless, helter-skelter energy of Offenbach's tunes. This is appropriate, as the flamboyant gaiety of the Second Empire had been replaced by the unashamedly naughty 1890s and the extravagant *belle époque*. Conventional morality was being seriously challenged, and the *grisettes* are proud to be at the forefront of the revolution.

The first night of *The Merry Widow* was a success with the audience and some of the critics, although box-office takings were poor and remained so until the show's twenty-fifth performance. Complimentary tickets handed out in the first weeks made sure that all Vienna was talking about Lehár's new work, and it became fashionable to see it.[32] Soon it was being staged all over Austria. The director of the Theater an der Wien, Wilhelm Karczag, at last realised that he had a hit on his hands, and he spent more money on the sets, ball gowns and dress uniforms, and new frills and finery for the girls from Maxim's. This extra investment paid off, and on 24 April 1907, *The Merry Widow* celebrated its four hundredth appearance in Vienna.[33]

FIG. 65. Lily Elsie, the original Merry Widow in London in 1907. The operetta was changed considerably to suit British tastes, with many names altered and a finale set in Maxim's itself. *Theatre Museum, V&A Picture Library.*

Lehár's masterpiece quickly spread throughout Europe and the Americas, under different guises and names. George Edwardes, the impresario who owned London's Gaiety Theatre, demanded numerous changes because he lacked confidence in this new Viennese product. Many of the names of the major characters were altered, and several irrelevant comedy routines were interpolated. Apparently London audiences needed humour to keep them interested. They also needed spectacular sets, and Edwardes shifted the action of Act Three to Maxim's itself. As a result, *The Merry Widow* was lauded by theatregoers and critics alike.[34]

In the United States, the operetta inspired an impressive array of products, including hats, shoes, cigars, chocolates, perfumes, escalopes, liqueurs, even restaurants and express trains, all named 'Merry Widow'. Unsurprisingly, 'Merry Widow' dance competitions were organised—waltzes not cancans, one assumes—and, perhaps inevitably, 'Merry Widow' corsets were the ultimate in underwear style, giving the wearer the feeling that she was being a little daring, even though she was probably outwardly demure.[35]

The Merry Widow had numerous imitators, some with titles as lacking in subtlety as *The Merry Widower*, some showing slightly more wit, like *The Troublesome Widow* (in German *Die lästige Witwe*, rather than *Die lüstige Witwe*).[36] If it had not been before, Paris was now a firm favourite as the setting for operettas. Lehár himself tried to repeat his success with *The Count of Luxembourg*, which remains popular today. Set in the artists' milieu of Montmartre, it has a farcical plot, dealing with two people who marry for convenience, and who later fall in love without realising that they are married to each other. The score contains no cancan as such, although one piece, 'The Champagne Call', is marked *à la cancan*, and in some productions is danced accordingly. Really the music is inserted more for atmosphere, in much the same way as Offenbach used the sounds of cancan music in *Ba-ta-clan*. *The Count of Luxembourg* also contains a flavour of Parisian cabaret *chansons*, as well as romantic waltzes, lively polkas and marches.

The quality of Lehár's music has rarely been equalled by other composers who tried to emulate his particular style of Viennese operetta. His closest rival was Emmerich Kálmán, who included a stronger Hungarian flavour in his work, the most highly regarded of which is *The Csárdás Princess*. This is not a formula work: the action takes place in Budapest and Vienna, and does not feature foreigners tasting the delights of a naughty city. Well, not quite. When it first appeared, in 1915, Hungary was still ruled from Vienna, which had something of a reputation as a pleasure capital. The central character is a Hungarian cabaret star who performs her famous *csárdás* for the delight of the Viennese cosmopolitan crowd. There is no real political message, however, and the general air of frivolity is underlined when the dancers of the cabaret put on a performance of a certain well-known French import.

There were various other minor operettas written in the early twentieth century which featured the cancan but which have not stood the test of time. Slightly more durable has been Jean Gilbert's *Die keusche Suzanne* (literally 'chaste Suzanne'), which was set in Paris, partly at the Moulin Rouge. Gilbert was in fact a German, born in Hamburg, and the operetta is quite Germanic, although the original story is from a French farce *Fils à Papa*. The operetta, originally produced in Magdeburg in 1910, was particularly popular in France, Spain and Latin America.[37] Light operas with a Parisian setting and the cancan much in evidence were still being written as late as the 1950s. Hans May and Sonny Miller's *Wedding in Paris*, produced in London in 1954, was one example, with the opening scene of the second act being devoted to the dance. Unfortunately, despite the presence of the popular stars Evelyn Laye and Anton Walbrook, this work was almost instantly forgettable.[38] In any case, it appeared at the wrong time in Britain, where the American musical was taking the West End by storm. The story lines of the Broadway successes had more bite than those of the operettas still being churned out in Europe, and they had exciting dance sequences that were integral to the plot.

Oklahoma! by Richard Rodgers and Oscar Hammerstein appeared on Broadway in 1943 and set the scene for a whole series of shows with strong scores, multifaceted plots and imaginative, colourful staging. A daring innovation of this particular musical was the inclusion of a lengthy 'dream ballet' at the end of the first act. Choreographed by Agnes de Mille, the dream focused on the heroine Laurey's confusion and fears about her lover's conflict with Jud, the hired hand on her aunt's farm. Jud is portrayed in the musical as a lecherous and violent man, but at the same time his loneliness is treated sympathetically. Inevitably, he is a frequenter of low-life saloons and during the girl's dream, or rather nightmare, he appears with a group of dance-hall floosies. These entertainers have a sinister quality, their skirt play is aggressive and threatening, and all in all they are as far away as possible from the conventional image of cancan dancers. It is an ingenious image for a nightmare, in which attractive, harmless people and objects can assume a distorted aspect, and be all the more frightening by undermining one's cosy view of the world. Saloon girls in the 'Wild West' were in many ways as tough as the cowboys they entertained, and Jud's companions are also seen as a threat to Laurey's innocence and her position as a representative of the farmers who are trying to cultivate the area, in more ways than one. There may also be a hint of a moralistic stance towards cancan dancers in Rodgers and Hammerstein's writing. Laurey is the epitome of 'good', but she feels drawn towards the 'evil' represented by Jud and his girls.

Rodgers and Hammerstein's musicals were often on American themes (although *The King and I* and *The Sound of Music* clearly were not), but they were influenced by European styles. Many of their American contemporaries had concrete links with Europe, being first or second generation immigrants, or having studied music in Europe, or both. Important among these are Frederick Loewe and Cole Porter, who both wrote music for the cancan. Frederick Loewe and Alan Jay Lerner, the writer and lyricist, had a somewhat difficult relationship, but nevertheless succeeded in producing some of the most durable musical shows of the 1950s. Loewe was the son of opera singer Edmund Loewe, who created the role of Count Danilo when *The Merry*

Widow was first staged in Berlin (the original Danilo, Louis Treumann, was still playing the part in Vienna at the time). The young Frederick was heavily influenced by the Viennese tradition in light opera, particularly the style of Franz Lehár, which was to be expected in view of his father's close involvement with the composer's most successful work. Fortunately, Lerner frequently chose European themes with which to exploit Loewe's obvious talents.[39]

Gigi had deliberate echoes of Vienna, despite being set in Paris. Loewe correctly pointed out that the French capital, in common with most cities of Europe in the first decade of the twentieth century, had completely surrendered to the charms of *The Merry Widow*. The popular tunes heard at restaurants and dance halls were Viennese waltzes, and so Loewe made a conscious effort to imitate Lehár's style in *Gigi*.[40] It was originally written as a screen musical, which, while it swept away nine Academy Awards in 1959, is almost completely lacking in dance numbers and suffers as a result. Only in the early 1970s, when it was rewritten for the stage, was this problem put right.

Gigi is a charming piece, and on stage has an intimate quality not achieved in the film. The story concerns a girl who is being groomed to be a courtesan, but who is 'saved' from this by Gaston, a family friend and *bon vivant*, well acquainted with courtesans. In common with Danilo, Gaston spends much of his time at Maxim's, but their characters are totally different, Gaston being highly dissatisfied with his life. The last straw for him comes when he observes that the innocent, but adolescent Gigi, is about to be sullied by being introduced into the world of high-class prostitution. The climax of the show occurs at Maxim's, with Gaston accompanying Gigi on her début in fashionable society, and realising that he is in love with her. The sparkle of the occasion is supplemented by a spirited cancan from the resident dance troupe.

There are many parallels with *The Merry Widow* in *Gigi*, although Loewe's music often has a harder, more ironic edge to it. Gaston's song 'She is Not Thinking of Me' is a Viennese waltz, but it has a distinctly bitter-sweet mood. If the protagonists in *Gigi* seem more blasé than those in *The Merry Widow*, it is possibly because they are native Parisians. The entry of the cancan dancers is an enjoyable diversion for the customers at Maxim's, but it is never likely to have much bearing on the plot because they have seen the dance performed many times before. Without question, Loewe is admirably successful in conveying a Parisian atmosphere in his music, especially in the songs originally written specifically for Maurice Chevalier in the film. There is also something of the spirit of *fin-de-siècle* decadence which continued into the *belle époque*, and which is evident in the novel by Colette on which the musical is based.

Lerner and Loewe's other musical containing a cancan was *Paint Your Wagon*, and this time it is much more important in the story. The musical has a Californian Gold Rush setting, making the date of the action around 1850. It is most unlikely that the cancan was being performed anywhere in America at this time, certainly not in this form, but musicals are of course fantasy. Essentially, the plot involves a group of itinerant gold prospectors who discover a gold nugget accidentally while they are burying one of their fellows who has recently died. A town is set up on the spot, and they all work hard looking for the gold that they believe must be there somewhere. One of the men, Jake Whippanay, dreams of making his strike and building a music hall where his girl, Cherry, can star. The other men also dream of the music hall, and of the girls who will perform there, because the town is at present populated almost solely by men. Jake eventually makes his strike and builds his saloon, and Cherry arrives on the stagecoach with dancers for the show. The arrival of the women is the cue for some spectacular dance routines, which were choreographed by Agnes de Mille in the original production. The highlight of Act Two is a colourful cancan sequence, led by the French dancer, Suzanne, and which eventually involves all the girls and the men. It is a poignant moment, however, because the gold has run out, and the music-hall dancers are making their final appearance. Eventually, nearly everyone leaves the town for a new strike, forty miles away. Among those who stay are Ben Rumson and his daughter, Jennifer, who found the first nugget, and after whom the town is named.

The musical was a hit with audiences, although some critics pointed out that the script rather lacked balance. There were long periods of intense moodiness while the men contemplated their lot, and things only improved with the appearance of the women at the end of Act One and the beginning of Act Two. All the dance routines were therefore concentrated at one point in the story, which may have had a certain logic, but was thought to be unsatisfactory as entertainment.[41] It should be pointed out that the film version of *Paint Your Wagon* bore little resemblance to the stage show, and, like *Gigi*, had little or no dancing. Some of Loewe's music was dropped, and new songs written by André Previn were added. It also starred three non-singers: Lee Marvin, Clint Eastwood and Jean Seberg. The stage show definitely has flaws, and Loewe's music is less inspired than in his other collaborations with Lerner, possibly because he was not writing for a European setting, but it still has some memorable songs, and the cancan sequence is particularly fine.

The musical Western *Calamity Jane* also includes the dance, presented for the cowboy regulars at the Golden Garter saloon. This is another musical that started out as a film, starring Doris Day, and it was only later when it was adapted for the stage that the cancan number was inserted. The music is by Sammy Fain. A transvestite presentation of the cancan occurs in Jerry Herman's *La Cage aux Folles*, based on the French stage farce by Jean Poiret. That the cancan should provide part of the entertainment at this nightclub in the south of France is not entirely surprising. In its latter evocations the dance has become an expression of ultra-femininity, with its stress on the frilly underwear of the late nineteenth century. Female impersonators may therefore view the cancan as fair game for exploitation, and in *La Cage* the performance has a distinctly satirical edge. The quality of protest against Victorian morality is undeniably undermined by the men dressed as women, but the musical as a whole has some important things to say about late-twentieth-century hypocrisy instead. There is considerable historical precedent for a transvestite cancan at the Carnival balls of the Second Empire, where the guests frequently cross-dressed and where the Quadrille des Clodoches was so popular. There is no record of the sexual orientation of the 'female' members of Clodoche's troupe, but we can always speculate.

Cole Porter's inspiration for *Can-Can* came from direct experience of Parisian nightlife during many years spent in the city. He first visited Paris in 1908, at a time when the cancan was still at the height of its popularity. The composer's Francophilia was reinforced by his studying music in the city (under Vincent D'Indy in 1919) and by meeting his wife, Linda Lee Thomas,

FIG. 66. Gwen Verdon as Claudine in the original production of Cole Porter's *Can-Can*, another story of how the cancan came to be banned in Paris. It was Gwen Verdon's cancan and *apache* dancing that largely ensured the show's success on Broadway. *Bob Willoughby.*

there—and indeed marrying her there. He wrote other musical items with a French theme before *Can-Can*, for example a revue *Mayfair and Montmartre* (1922), produced only in London; *Paris* (1928); *Fifty Million Frenchmen* (1929), which was also filmed; and the British musical *Nymph Errant* (1933), which featured a scene at a Paris cabaret and was choreographed by the then largely unknown Agnes de Mille. The latter never transferred to Broadway, despite Porter being very proud of his score, possibly because it was too English.[42]

By the time he wrote *Can-Can*, Porter was a well-respected songwriter in his native country, and he had high hopes for his new musical. He studied French music-hall songs from the 1890s, and tried to write similar material, only in a more modern idiom. He also made great efforts to integrate his songs with the story written by Abe Burrows.[43] Unfortunately, he was not entirely successful, producing what really amounts to an American idea of Parisian *chansons*, and probably failing to please either French or American ears. A few of the songs are excellent, particularly the dramatic and emotive 'I Love Paris'.

Can-Can was choreographed on Broadway by Michael Kidd, and starred the French actress Lilo as La Môme Pistache, proprietor of the Bal du Paradis. Gwen Verdon had a supporting role as Claudine, and she largely stole the show, much to Lilo's apparent disgust.[44] Despite the fact that Porter's musical is set in the 1890s, the dance routines seem more influenced by the French Cancan of the 1920s onwards, than the *quadrille réaliste* of La Goulue and Valentin-le-Désossé. The story concerns the battle between Pistache and the authorities who try to shut down her cabaret because she insists on presenting the scandalous cancan. When the curtain opens, we find a group of girls in court accused of performing this very dance the previous night. They insist they are actually merely laundresses and protest their innocence with the song 'Maidens Typical of France'. They are released anyway, because none of the arresting police officers is prepared to give evidence. The young judge, Aristide Forestier, a man of high moral standards, decides to visit the Bal du Paradis himself and investigate. Inside the cabaret, Pistache tells Aristide that she has evidence in her room of the bribery and corruption of police and court officials, and she invites him up, hoping to seduce him. Unfortunately, he proves to be incorruptible, and when the cancan is danced later, a photograph is taken, and she realises she has been tricked and that he now has evidence that will convict her. However, the judge is soon in trouble himself, when he is photographed at the *Bal des Quat'z Arts*, held at Pistache's nightclub, and the picture appears in the newspapers. He is summarily suspended from the bar, and expresses his indignation by joining Pistache in her new *café-concert* venture. Aristide and Pistache both end up appearing in court on charges of opening an unlicensed café. They admit their guilt, but Pistache also makes a plea for a more enlightened interpretation of the obscenity laws and points out that there is nothing really wrong with the cancan, which closes the show.

This is certainly a musical for lovers of the cancan, because the dance is featured in both acts. The music is more successful in the 'Quadrille' version in Act One, than in the finale, accompanied by the song 'Can-Can', which has a somewhat jerky rhythm. The show also has an *apache* dance and comedy and love interest, and would have been a great success, if had not been for some of the songs, with which even Cole Porter himself admitted he was unhappy.[45] The critics did not like the score, and audiences were apparently intolerant of the story—many Americans found it difficult to believe that a puritanical attitude had ever existed in Paris. Nevertheless, box-office takings were considerable, and the show was booked up for weeks ahead during its initial run.[46]

Burrows's book is a little puzzling, because he must have researched the subject, and the idea that the cancan was banned anywhere in Paris in the 1890s beggars belief, when so many cabarets and music halls had their versions of the dance, and the first striptease revues were being presented in some theatres. The London revival of *Can-Can* in 1988, for which Julian More adapted the story, presented a more plausible scenario, with the *cancaneuses* at Pistache's nightclub impudently removing their knickers to provide an even more shocking display (although discreet use of body stockings kept things decent for a family audience at the Strand Theatre).

Porter's flawed homage to Paris has been revived several times, but has largely failed to attract either critical or audience approval. This is a pity, as the show has some potential, and the right stars, good costumes and sets, and perhaps some rearrangement of the music could bring it success. Presumably there was very little right with the Broadway revival of *Can-Can* in 1981, starring Zizi Jeanmaire, which has the dubious honour of being in the *Guinness Book of Theatre Facts and Feats* as the most expensive flop in theatre history. It closed after only five performances, losing over two million dollars.[47]

After one person has tried, and only half-succeeded, it seems unlikely that a musical or operetta which accurately portrays the naughty nineties in Paris will ever be written. This is regrettable, because a theatrical representation of the excitement generated by the cancan and its stars in Montmartre could be an exhilarating experience. Of the works that have been devised on this subject, Porter's will continue to be revived periodically, and probably with some rewriting could prove to be more satisfactory. *The Bar at the Folies Bergère* of Dame Ninette de Valois could see the light of day again, but as already mentioned it has considerable defects as a historical record. Mikhail Baryshnikov's restaging of *Gaîté Parisienne* for his American Ballet Theatre in 1988 purported to have changed the period from Second Empire to the 1890s, but the costumes of Christian Lacroix rather swamped the production with excessive colour, and certainly bore little resemblance to the outfits worn by La Goulue and her contemporaries. The only satisfactory images we have of the dancers of the Moulin Rouge and the other cabarets at the turn of the century are in contemporary paintings and lithographs, and to some extent in films produced in various countries. In the next two chapters, we shall see how well artists and film directors have dealt with this great era in popular entertainment.

CHAPTER 5 / LA GOULUE "TOUS LES SOIRS"
The Cancan in Art

THE NAME OF THE PAINTER HENRI DE TOULOUSE-LAUTREC WILL BE FOREVER associated with the image of La Goulue, kicking her leg defiantly in the air, petticoats flying around her form. The Moulin Rouge poster and other lithographs and paintings that he produced in the 1890s have established him as the artist most frequently linked with the cancan dancers of Montmartre. But he was by no means the only noted painter to be inspired by the dance at the turn of the century, and he and his contemporaries were influenced directly or indirectly by a number of less well-known artists of the Second Empire. Nevertheless, his contribution is unique insofar as he was the only artist to stress the importance of individuals, in particular La Goulue and Jane Avril. With a few exceptions, others who painted the dance halls and the cancan gave their pictures anonymous titles, even when on occasions they undoubtedly were portraying real people.

Lautrec not only painted singers and dancers in the dance halls and *café-concerts*, but also circus scenes, theatrical performers and, most controversially, prostitutes and brothels. He is certainly one of the most famous of all late-nineteenth-century artists, and reproductions of his posters and paintings of La Goulue, Jane Avril, Yvette Guilbert and Aristide Bruant can be seen everywhere. Much mythology has grown up around him, partly because of his physical appearance and partly because his aristocratic background seemed at odds with his very public fascination with the 'low life'. The film *Moulin Rouge* and the novel by Pierre La Mure on which it was based are largely responsible for a very distorted picture of the life of this extraordinary man.

Toulouse-Lautrec's stunted growth seems likely to have been due to a congenital disease known as pyknodysostosis, which was partly fostered by the intermarrying that was prevalent in his family. His grandmothers were sisters, and there was at least one other case of dwarfism amongst his cousins. Having said that, he was not that diminutive—he was nearly five feet tall—but he was often seen in the company of rather tall friends, such as his cousin Gabriel Tapié de Céleyran. The explanation that accidents in his childhood were responsible for his condition was probably spread by his parents in order to cover up the existence of the disease. Other symptoms were, however, obvious to anyone who knew anything about it: his large nostrils, thick lips and short-sightedness were all signs. His father, Comte Alphonse, admitted to the nature of the disease in a letter to a former teacher after his son's death in 1901. He wrote of hoping to meet Henri in another life where "the attraction of two who really love each other will not be forbidden and punished in the fruit of the same blood which should never have been allowed to marry".[1]

His parents traced their ancestry back to the medieval counts of Toulouse and were proud of the family name, at first forbidding their son to use his real name when signing paintings in case he brought the family into disrepute.[2] As he gradually gained recognition, their attitude definitely soft-ened, and the fact that his father insisted on driving the hearse at Henri's funeral showed that they were finally very proud of him.[3] There was cer-tainly never any break between him and his family, as has sometimes been suggested. Several letters exist from him to various members of the family which show that he maintained a good relationship with them throughout his life.[4] He was particularly close to his mother, whom he painted on a num-ber of occasions. The count certainly did not disapprove of his son's lifestyle: he also enjoyed attending the music halls and brothels of Paris and appar-ently had an insatiable sexual appetite.[5] On the other hand, he perhaps may have wished that Henri would be more discreet, instead of recording his experiences in paint and pastels.

Lautrec inherited his father's love for the theatrical and enjoyed dressing up. Photographs exist of him as an altar boy at a *Courrier français* ball, in Japanese samurai costume, as a female Spanish dancer, and even dressed in Jane Avril's hat, coat and feather boa. His father had a whole collection of cos-tumes and was often seen in a variety of bizarre outfits both in his home town

FIG. 67. Henri de Toulouse-Lautrec Monfa, the artist who made the dancers La Goulue and Jane Avril famous, first in Paris and now throughout the world. He was the only major artist to recog-nise cancan dancers as individuals. *Musée Toulouse-Lautrec, Albi.*

LE COURRIER FRANÇAIS

11

Le Bal du Moulin-de-la-Galette.

Dessin de LAUTREC.

FIG. 68. *Le Bal du Moulin de la Galette*, a drawing which appeared in the magazine *Le Courrier français* and which was the basis for a painting by Toulouse-Lautrec of the popular *guinguette*, situated close to his studio. LE COURRIER FRANÇAIS, *19 May 1889, by permission of the British Library, M.F.85.*

of Albi and in Paris. He once came down to lunch at the family home wearing a ballet dancer's tutu. The painter's love of caricature and artifice probably owed much to his childhood experiences.[6]

Within the bounds of his physical abnormality, Lautrec was quite active, but nevertheless he was aware of his limitations. He once praised his friend Louis Anquetin "whom I cramp with my slow, small person by keeping him from walking at his own pace, but he pretends that it doesn't bother him".[7] On the other hand, he had no doubts about his sexual abilities, and he likened himself to a coffee pot with a large spout.[8] His love of portraying the dancers of the Moulin Rouge may in part be due to vicarious pleasure that he gained from their athletic prowess, in addition to the more direct enjoyment gained from watching them perform. In many of his works there is an emphasis on the legs of his subjects, which it could be argued is inevitable when painting dancers, but the fascination with the *cancaneuses* and other performers at the Moulin Rouge seems also to be linked to his own slight deformity. He certainly paid great attention to the physical appearance of his subjects, to their faces and bodies, and he sometimes exaggerated features for effect. The figure of Valentin-le-Désossé in the Moulin Rouge poster, for example, is more angular and elongated than the dancer was in real life. However his antics on the dance floor gave the impression that he truly was boneless and made of rubber, and Lautrec's image of him conveys some of the sense of this eccentric movement through the unavoidably static form of a poster. His caricatures were not always flattering. Yvette Guilbert had occasion to object strongly to the way Lautrec portrayed her and she pleaded in a letter to him "for the love of Heaven, don't make me so ugly!"[9]

Lautrec began his studies in Paris in 1883 under Fernand Corman at a studio in rue Constance, halfway up the Butte Montmartre—ideally placed for visits to the Moulin de la Galette and the Elysée-Montmartre. Among his many fellow-students was Louis Anquetin, whose work Lautrec grew to admire. Anquetin was also greatly interested in the world of cabaret and music hall, and was partly responsible for bringing Lautrec into contact with Aristide Bruant, who was to commission posters from Lautrec and also exhibit his works in his cabaret theatre, the Mirliton. Lautrec showed his admiration for Anquetin by acknowledging his influence, and Anquetin returned the compliment in 1893 with a large canvas entitled *La Salle de danse au Moulin Rouge*, which actually contained in it the image of Jane Avril from Lautrec's *Jardin de Paris* poster and some features of his *Le Bal au Moulin Rouge*. Anquetin and Emile Bernard, another fellow-student, both also produced works featuring La Goulue in the 1880s.[10] Apart from Anquetin and Bernard, Lautrec was influenced by the artists who contributed to the satirical magazines. Lautrec contributed to the magazines himself, and some of his well-known paintings appeared as line drawings in the *Le Courrier français*.

Lautrec was observing modern life and through his art made subtle comments on the people who inhabited his world. Sometimes the images seem unnecessarily cruel (particularly in self-portraits), but often affection for his subjects is the overriding impression. He is not afraid of depicting other people's sadness, of showing that behind the artifice of popular entertainment the performers are real people with real emotions, sometimes skilfully hidden from the public. Although he is best known for his posters of La Goulue and Aristide Bruant, there is little doubt that Jane Avril was his favourite model, and she appears in a variety of guises, experiencing a variety of moods. She is seen dancing at the Moulin Rouge and the Jardin de Paris, she appears in the audience in his poster for the Divan Japonais, and she is on his design for the cover of *L'Estampe originale*, published in 1893. There are also paintings of her arriving at and leaving the Moulin Rouge, discreetly dressed in a long coat and hat. She was one of the four members of the Troupe de Mademoiselle Eglantine whose poster he produced in 1896, and in 1899 one of his last lithographs shows her attired in a clinging black dress with a snake coiled somewhat bizarrely around her. His paintings of her are almost devoid of the caricature elements found when he portrayed La Goulue or Yvette Guilbert, and if he exaggerated anything it was to make Avril's slender outline even more willowy.

FIG. 69. Toulouse-Lautrec's first commissioned poster, and a departure from previous posters advertising the Moulin Rouge in its focus on one of its stars, La Goulue. Valentin-le-Désossé, is shown in grotesque silhouette. *Musée Toulouse-Lautrec, Albi.*

The famous La Goulue poster was commissioned by the Moulin Rouge in 1891, by which time the dancer was already well known through her appearances at the Moulin de la Galette and the Elysée-Montmartre. Lautrec's poster certainly helped to turn her into a star, the first real star of the cancan in the 1890s. Although her partner, the enigmatic Valentin-le-Désossé was also clearly shown in the picture, albeit almost in silhouette, it was only her name which appeared next to that of the dance hall, with the promise: *Tous les soirs.*

Lautrec admired the work of Jules Chéret, who had designed the earlier posters for the dance hall. Chéret specialised in simple semi-erotic pictures of attractive women (sometimes known as Chérettes), and also designed posters for other Parisian dance halls, including the Jardin de Paris. His Moulin Rouge poster had featured a number of anonymous Chérettes riding donkeys in the parade, but Lautrec decided on a simpler but much more provocative image for the new work. Earlier studies for the La Goulue lithograph reveal that he had begun with more detail and gradually pared down the image to its essentials. When the posters appeared on the streets of Paris they captured the imagination of the public as much as Chéret's ground-breaking three-colour posters for *Orpheus in the Underworld* had in the 1850s. Collectors recognised their value almost immediately, and they often disappeared from the walls before they had had time to fulfil their functions as advertising.[11]

It is interesting to consider the extent to which La Goulue actually deserved such promotion when compared with other dancers. Grille d'Egout, for example, was reputedly as accomplished and in some ways more attractive, and yet Lautrec virtually ignored her as a subject. She is probably to be seen partnering La Goulue on the cover of the 29 December 1886 issue of *Le Mirliton* in a drawing entitled *Le Quadrille de la chaise Louis XIII à l'Elysée-Montmartre*, but she is not seen in any of his major works. Neither, for that matter, is Nini-Patte-en-l'Air. La Môme Fromage possibly appears in the painting *Au Moulin Rouge*, but is only included because she is La Goulue's companion. La Goulue has certainly remained the most famous cancan dancer of all time, but just how much this is due to her talent and appeal compared to her contemporaries and how much is due to Lautrec's undoubted devotion to her as a subject is unclear.

Another poster—for the trip to London of the Troupe de Mademoiselle Eglantine—has the same simplicity and directness, and the same sense of movement. The photograph used by Lautrec as the basis for the lithograph shows the four dancers awkwardly holding a pose with legs raised and skirts held up. 'Fast' film was yet to be invented and subjects were required to stay in the same position for some minutes, which explains why no photographs exist of the 1890s *cancaneuses* in the midst of their acts. Lautrec was able to use his vast experience of seeing the dancers at work to transform the rather lifeless image in the photograph into one of vitality and excitement. The white of the dancers' petticoats has been likened to the clouds in the Japanese paintings which were so popular in Paris at the time, and which Lautrec and his contemporaries were keen to imitate.[12]

FIG. 70. Jane Avril was Lautrec's favourite model and it seems he also counted her as one of his friends. Note that her name is featured on this poster for the Jardin de Paris, rather the name of the establishment. *Musée Toulouse-Lautrec, Albi.*

It was Jane Avril who asked Toulouse-Lautrec to design this poster (see fig. 71), and her slim figure appears on the left of the group, with Eglantine on the right and the two lesser dancers in the middle. The poster for Avril's appearances at the Jardin de Paris was also commissioned at her request.[13] Lautrec depicted her in an uncharacteristically bright orange skirt, her leg raised with one arm cradling it and her underwear largely hidden from the spectator. It is surprisingly reminiscent of the cancan dancers of the Second Empire, as seen in the *Journal pour rire*, with the emphasis on the raised leg rather than display of petticoats. As skirt manipulation was a major aspect of Avril's performance, one wonders how much the image in the poster was governed by the need to hold her leg steady while posing for the photograph which Lautrec used. It is worth noting, incidentally, that the photograph shows her with a cheeky smile, whereas in the poster she appears rather haughty and superior.

Jane Avril was not only an artist's model for Lautrec, she was also a friend whom he valued. He introduced her to a number of his circle and took her to dinner at expensive restaurants. She also persuaded him to visit the Bal Bullier with her, where she gave the Latin Quarter regulars a free demonstration of what the bourgeoisie paid to see at the Moulin Rouge and the Jardin de Paris.[14] It is sometimes said that Lautrec gave Avril an untypically melancholy aspect in his work. Certainly the photographs of her and posters by other artists, including her husband Maurice Biais, show a much happier girl. But perhaps Lautrec was looking deeper into her soul, reflecting something of the traumas of her past.

Lautrec certainly captured Jane Avril's elegance and refinement, and her bourgeois appearance when out of the limelight. The two paintings of her entering and leaving the Moulin Rouge show a quiet, contemplative woman seemingly at odds with her reputation as La Mélinite. Even in *Jane Avril dansant* (1892) she appears as a figure of incredible contrast, her face showing none of the excitement that the almost unrealistic gyrations of her lower limbs signify (see colour illustration no. 7). In the poster for the Divan Japonais she is a picture of sophistication, adopting the pose of a confident fashionable lady whom Lautrec felt it important to focus on, rather than the unfortunate Yvette Guilbert on stage whose head cannot be seen.

Lautrec was as accurate in portraying La Goulue's confident sexuality, not only while she was dancing but also strolling around the Moulin Rouge dance floor accompanied by her fierce-looking sister, adjusting her hair in front of a mirror or being escorted by two women (her sister again and possibly her lover, La Môme Fromage) wearing a dramatically low-cut dress. The artist must also have had a soft spot for La Goulue, because he agreed to paint the panels for her fairground booth when he knew that she was past her prime and needed the recollections of her former triumphs to support her in her new venture. It was not just flattery that motivated him in depicting her dancing for an audience composed of famous people, including Oscar Wilde: only a few years previously she had been cheered on each night by such luminaries at the Moulin Rouge and the Jardin de Paris. She is seen in her new guise as a

FIG. 71. Jane Avril was responsible for asking Toulouse-Lautrec to design this poster for the Troupe de Mlle. Eglantine's trip to London, and she is the dancer on the far left. It is doubtful that the poster was ever used. *Musée Toulouse-Lautrec, Albi.*

belly dancer, for which she has added a cancan speciality—the high kick. The panels were affixed to the outside of the booth either side of the entrance, and were thus exposed to the elements. Fortunately for their survival, La Goulue was forced to remove them and sell them because she needed the money. They were still not safe, however, and an unscrupulous art dealer into whose hands they later passed decided to cut them up and sell the pieces separately. The Louvre eventually managed to acquire all the pieces and reassembled them—ironically in the year of La Goulue's death, 1929.[15]

Apart from the panels for La Goulue's booth and the poster for the Eglantine troupe, Lautrec rarely portrayed the cancan after the early 1890s. As Montmartre changed in the latter part of the decade, so he drifted away from the area and transferred his attentions to the higher class *café-concerts* of the Champs-Elysées. One of his last paintings of the cancan (from 1893) is one of a solo performer on a *café-concert* stage, entitled *La Roue* (*The Cartwheel*).

Unusually, this is of an unnamed dancer, the important thing in the painting apparently being the illustration of one of the cancan 'steps'. The work belongs to a series that Lautrec produced for *Le Figaro illustré* showing the pleasures of Paris. He had painted anonymous dancers in some of his other works, for example in the 1892 painting of the commencement of the *quadrille naturaliste* at the Moulin Rouge and the earlier painting of Valentin-le-Désossé training a new dancer. It is interesting to speculate as to who they might have been, whether they were soon to be famous or whether they would fail to make the grade and fade into obscurity.

In the latter years of his life Toulouse-Lautrec turned his attentions to the theatre; he always preferred popular theatre but was also to be found at the Opéra, the Comédie Française and some of the more avant-garde venues. One of his subjects was the actress Réjane, who learnt the cancan for a stage role from Grille d'Egout.[16] He also became well known for his sympathetic intimate studies of life in the rue des Moulins brothel, where he is said to have lived for some time.[17]

Lautrec died in 1901 at the early age of thirty-six, partly as a result of the hereditary disease which had caused his stunted growth, but more significantly through a combination of syphilis and chronic alcoholism. At one point during 1899 he had begun suffering from hallucinations caused by delirium tremens and he had been admitted to a nursing home.[18] His alcoholism may have been a form of escape from what many would have assumed was a miserable life, but the evidence of his art and his letters suggest otherwise. His physical appearance and limited mobility may have upset him, but he rarely allowed himself to be too introspective, enjoying socialising and meeting new people. He loved visiting the cabarets and watching the dancers, and he also appreciated them as people whose friendship he valued. Drinking to excess was a problem he shared with many in his circle—this was, after all, the golden age of the notorious absinthe—and in Lautrec's case probably had little to do with his personal 'tragedy'.

Before Lautrec's Moulin Rouge poster portrayed the cancan on the streets of Paris, drawings of famous dancers had frequently appeared in popular magazines. Lautrec himself contributed some material to such journals in the 1880s, and La Goulue had already appeared in designs in *Le Courrier français* by Louis Legrand and Ferdinand Lunel before Lautrec received his Moulin Rouge commission. But the tradition of showing the cancan in realistic, cartoon form had been established by other artists during the Second Empire, particularly in the *Journal pour rire* (retitled *Journal amusant* in 1857). Lautrec and his contemporaries owed something of a debt to these earlier artists for their inspiration and style.

Gustave Doré, who was later to make his name with grotesque and fanciful drawings for illustrated editions of Rabelais, La Fontaine, Dante and the Bible, was among the first artists to portray the cancan. He was also responsible for designing sets and some of the costumes for Offenbach's *Orpheus in the*

Underworld, and later painted the operetta's final climactic *galop infernal* (see fig. 57), showing the gods and mortals consumed by a Bacchanalian frenzy. Doré began his working life in the late 1840s as an artist on the *Journal pour rire*, which had just been launched by the publisher Charles Philipon. Doré was only sixteen when Philipon persuaded his father that he should be allowed to pursue a career as an artist. The young Doré had taken some of his drawings to Philipon's shop in the place de la Bourse in Paris, and the publisher had found them very impressive. He was engaged to provide caricatures for Philipon's new venture, and thus became self-supporting, although his father insisted that he continue with his general education.[19]

Doré lived life to the full as a young man in Paris. He was seen at gatherings organised by the rich and famous in the city, and associated with prominent figures in the arts and entertainment. He attended the *samedi soirs* of Rossini, which also attracted the writer Alexandre Dumas, the painter Délacroix, and the composers Saint-Saëns, Gounod, Liszt, Meyerbeer and Verdi. At Offenbach's dances he used to dress up in different costumes and entertain the guests in eccentric fashion.[20]

The artist was very close to his mother and lived with her until the end of her life, sleeping in a room adjoining her bedroom, but his devotion to her did not stop him having love affairs with some of the famous *grandes cocottes* of the Second Empire. He had a two-year relationship with the celebrated Cora Pearl, although it was never serious and he probably only sought her company because she was fashionable (and expensive). His liaison with Alice Ozy, another high-class courtesan, was more intense. She was twelve years older than him, and it has been suggested that he was possibly looking for a mother figure.[21]

Doré's caricatures in the *Journal pour rire* were witty observations on society and were usually less than flattering to their subjects. His designs for books were full of romantic imagery—weird and wonderful scenes prompted by the text of the works which he had chosen to illustrate. It seems unsurprising that Doré was inspired to paint the final scene of *Orpheus in the Underworld*. The pseudo-mythological subject was bizarre enough to appeal to his taste, and it must have reminded him of the scene at a Carnival ball when the entire dance floor was crowded with people in costume indulging in a wild cancan. He had drawn such a scene for the *Journal pour rire* as early as 1850 and had entitled his picture 'Le Galop Infernal' (see fig. 45). Offenbach borrowed this title for his famous piece of music that has ever since been firmly associated with the cancan. So the originator of the title *galop infernal* was not Offenbach, despite its appropriateness to his operetta, but whether Doré had invented the term or whether the name had already been used by others to describe the Carnival ball cancan is impossible to ascertain.

Doré's colleagues on the *Journal pour rire* also drew cartoons of the cancan, often with witty captions. Through them we can discover how the *"danse nationale de France"*(as it was frequently referred to in the magazine) was developing in the 1850s and 1860s. Men and women were shown in a variety of costumes at the Carnival balls, the men often dressed as women and vice versa, high kicking the night away. There were special features on the Chaumière, the Closerie des Lilas and most often the Bal Mabille where the *grisettes* and *cocodettes* were to be seen entertaining the crowds with their *ports d'armes* and *grands écarts*.

If the *Journal pour rire* reflected the witty and satirical side of life under the Second Empire, the illustrator Constantin Guys was responsible for giving a clearer image of the moral and social aspects. The vast majority of his works show people in the pursuit of pleasure, and he was particularly fond of portraying women, both from the *haut-monde* and the *demi-monde*. He was a superb visual historian of the period, although he has sometimes been criticised for ignoring the lives of ordinary working people.[22]

Guys's life is surrounded by mystery, because he deliberately avoided publicity. There are sometimes periods of several years when the only information we have about him is his drawings. He might have been largely forgotten today if it had not been for a series of essays written by his friend, the poet Baudelaire, in the newspaper *Le Figaro*. Guys objected strongly to the

FIG. 72. The 'painter of modern life', Constantin Guys represented the Second Empire *demi-monde* in a distinctive manner which brought out the courtesans' splendour but also a sense of the decadence of the era. *Musée du Louvre/Réunion des Musées Nationaux.*

idea of his work being described in a popular daily, and he agreed to Baude-laire writing about him only on condition that his name was never mentioned. Baudelaire therefore referred to him throughout as 'M.G.'.[23]

Guys had no formal academic training, but had a remarkable gift for recording exactly what he saw, and his work certainly influenced Toulouse-Lautrec and also Manet and Degas. He was well travelled in Europe, and was familiar with all the major capital cities. He told Baudelaire that he wanted to be remembered as a "man of the world" rather than as an artist, although it is clear from his output that his "world" most frequently meant the good life in Paris.[24]

In his hundreds of drawings, some of which were enhanced with water-colour, he showed people in search of pleasure—riding, dancing, at the the-atre or at court receptions. He delighted in military parades and sometimes drew the emperor himself on horseback. Above all he loved painting beauti-ful, fashionable women. They are to be seen filling carriages in the Bois de Boulogne with their vast crinolined dresses, some carrying parasols, or talk-ing to dandies under the trees in the park. There are numerous pictures of courtesans, perhaps arriving at the Bal Mabille, resplendent in their jewels with daring *décolletages*, carelessly lifting the edges of their skirts to reveal their calves and the lacy edges of their drawers. Then there are the cancan-dancing *cocodettes*, confidently kicking their legs high into the air at the *bals publics.*

Baudelaire said that Guys painted the modern woman, and so had no need to study the old masters for lessons in style. They had no experience of illustrating the latest fabrics and how they looked over a crinoline or starched muslin petticoats. They also would not have understood the gestures and car-riage of the woman of the Second Empire, nor how she invested her clothes with a life and physiognomy which were different from women of the past. According to Baudelaire, Guys loved to show women in all their sophisticated finery, but regardless of their luxurious attire he managed to reveal differences in status. The *demi-mondaines* were thus distinguishable from the high-society women and the *grandes dames*.[25]

When the empire fell in 1870, Guys found that his old haunts mostly dis-appeared with it. He became much poorer, and resorted to brothels and pub-lic dance halls for his subjects. He continued to observe the pursuit of pleasure, but at a lower level of society. He now painted ordinary prostitutes rather than *cocottes*. In 1885, he was knocked down by a carriage while cross-ing the rue du Havre, and he was unable to walk for the last eight years of his life. It is thought that he was distracted by the sight of a pretty woman.[26]

The first major work of art to feature the cancan in the 1890s was not by Toulouse-Lautrec, as might be believed, but by Georges Seurat. *Le Chahut* is generally considered to be one of his finest paintings, executed in the pointil-list or divisionist style. It shows four dancers—two men and two women—all high kicking in chorus-line style on a stage. It seems that Seurat was anticipating the evolution of the cancan in later years in portraying the dance in such a manner. In 1890, when the painting was completed, the cancan was still performed in Paris in the *quadrille naturaliste*, mostly on dance floors rather than on cabaret stages, and it still relied a great deal on individual flair from its exponents. So the artist's treatment of the subject may appear somewhat puzzling, but his general approach to his work was governed by a natural tendency to rebel against convention, and this painting was no exception.

Despite his unremarkable middle-class Parisian family background, Seurat soon showed considerable talent as an artist. He studied at the Ecole des Beaux-Arts, and was influenced by the work of Ingres and Puvis de Chavannes, but it was not long before he began to develop his own style. He usually made several studies from nature before executing a painting, but had an overall concept in mind which was not to be governed by his observations.[27] *Le Chahut* is a perfect example of this: an examination of his Conté crayon drawing of a performance at the Divan Japonais in around 1888 reveals that it is clearly the basis for *Le Chahut*, but only one dancer is shown on the stage, with perhaps a second in the background. In the final painting, Seurat was embellishing his presentation to enhance the effect, using artistic licence. Seurat believed that emotions could be conveyed through line in painting, and for him the uplifted leg along the diagonal signified 'happiness'.[28] To have this reiterated by each dancer in turn without doubt emphasises this statement. The development of the idea can be seen in further studies that the painter executed before beginning work on the final version. The first painted study shows three dancers, and a fourth is added, along with other members of the orchestra, in the second painted study (see colour illustration no. 9). The Divan Japonais was a very small cabaret, too small in reality to allow more than one or two dancers to appear on stage at any one time.

Le Chahut is something of departure from Seurat's earlier works, which mainly showed men and women living in harmony with nature. The nightclub as a setting for human activity is far removed from his famous *Sunday Afternoon on the Island of La Grande Jatte*, but in a sense follows a similar theme: Parisians enjoying themselves.[29] In this way, he was following the same path as Guys, although his depiction of the pursuit of pleasure was very different. It has been said that *Le Chahut* has elements of satire, and it certainly is not a realistic portrayal of the dance. Georges Lecomte describes the dancers as "performing their libidinous acrobatics" with "their upper bodies impeccably rigid, heads held high, and from beneath the eyelids that speak of their conquests they cast an eye over the temptations they have unleashed". He implies that Seurat was trying to emphasise the performers' awareness that they were giving an erotic display for money.[30] This suggests that Seurat was taking a very moralistic view of the cancan, which seems unlikely. Like Lautrec he admired the work of Chéret, and to some extent *Le Chahut* is a homage to this master of poster art.[31] Chéret was not criticising when he depicted Parisian entertainments, and there is no reason why Seurat should have been either. The faces of the dancers in *Le Chahut* in any case bear close relationship to those of the circus performers in *Le Cirque*, which Seurat painted at around the same time. In this work, the central figure is a female bareback rider, and the audience is composed mostly of women, some with children. There can surely be no suggestion here of moral disapproval.

Seurat was reflecting one aspect of nightlife in the French capital, bringing together the excitement of the small-scale *café-concerts* and the larger dance halls within one picture. If anything, his dancers have proud expressions on their faces, being aware that they are challenging conventional morality through their performance. The picture gives an impressive sense of the thrill of the spectacle, of the movement and the sounds, but it somehow lacks the immediacy of a Toulouse-Lautrec. Whereas Lautrec was clearly closely involved with his subjects, Seurat's cancan is seen from a more detached viewpoint, content being less important than style.

The artists Jean-François Raffaëlli and Adolphe Willette, both of whom influenced Toulouse-Lautrec, also painted the dancers of the *quadrille naturaliste* in the 1880s and 1890s. Raffaëlli painted La Goulue on more than one occasion, and a painting of four dancers, two male and two female, in a quadrille, almost certainly shows her with her partner Valentin-le-Désossé. Willette was perhaps more inclined to exaggerate his female subjects' sexuality. He idealised their bodies and facial features, giving them a irresistibly coquettish appearance, and emphasised the erotic aspects of their dress, particularly the corseted waist and petticoats. This style is evident in his illustrations for the book *Paris Dansant* (published in 1898) by Georges Montorgueil, including one of the *quadrille naturaliste* and a scene at the Jardin de Paris (see colour illustrations nos. 5 and 10). Willette, who designed the Moulin Rouge for Joseph Oller and some of the interiors of the Bal Tabarin for Auguste Bosc,[32] portrayed many aspects of life in Montmartre in his work, notably in his painting *Parce Domine* 1884 for the ceiling of the Chat Noir cabaret. This ambitious work showed entertainers, revellers at a masked ball, prostitutes and their customers, artists, and a variety of fantasy figures apparently being swept along in what Willette called "a whirlwind of pleasures and vices".[33] Further examples of these pleasures and vices can be found in his *Paris Dansant* paintings. In the foreground of the one showing the *quadrille naturaliste* two lesbians can be seen, and in another a violent encounter at a *bal musette* is graphically depicted. Like Lautrec, Willette contributed to satirical magazines.

Many artists from abroad came to Paris in the 1880s and 1890s, some of whom encountered Toulouse-Lautrec and were influenced by him or inspired by the same subjects. Charles Conder, whom Lautrec painted on more than one occasion, produced a painting of the *quadrille naturaliste* at the Moulin Rouge in 1890, as did William Warrener, the model for Lautrec's *L'Anglais au Moulin Rouge*. Perhaps the most famous artist to have painted the cancan at this time, apart from Seurat and Lautrec, was the Norwegian Edvard Munch, then resident in Paris. In the early twentieth century, two prominent artists followed Toulouse-Lautrec's lead in portraying the *café-concerts* and dance halls of Paris. Their style was obviously influenced by him, but they each took a highly individual approach which represented a distinct phase in their artistic development, and perhaps reflected their very different backgrounds.

Georges Rouault was born in dramatic circumstances in a working-class district north of Paris while the Commune was at its height. His family were sheltering in a cellar from a government bombardment when his mother went into labour. His very first experience of life was thus traumatic, and he grew up in the tense aftermath of the tragic events of 1871. When he came to paint clowns, dancers and prostitutes, his approach was one of compassion. He showed more of an understanding of their lives than did Toulouse-Lautrec, who was from a different class and a different town.[34]

Rouault began his working life as an apprentice to stained-glass painters, but then decided to be an artist and went to study at the Ecole des Beaux-Arts under Gustave Moreau. Moreau, who also taught Matisse, advised Rouault not to follow the official route to success as a painter.[35] This ultimately allowed his talent to be fully exploited and not be constrained by the need to paint in the official, conservative style guaranteed to win acceptance by the Salon. On the other hand, because Moreau was barely tolerated by the artistic establishment, Rouault suffered isolation when his mentor died in 1898.[36]

Moreau had taught Rouault to be an individual and to obey his instincts. Most of the major artists in France from the Impressionists onwards had suffered ostracism by the establishment because of their independence of thought. Toulouse-Lautrec, for example, was not really accepted until about twenty years after he died.[37] So perhaps the situation worked to Rouault's advantage. He was able to choose controversial subjects and paint them in a truly unique style, with strong dark colours and heavy black outlines reminiscent of the stained-glass work of his youth.

FIG. 73. *Bal Tabarin (Le Chahut)* by Georges Rouault is hardly the most attractive image of the cancan but it conveys a sense of the energy of the dance, perhaps more so than in the works of Toulouse-Lautrec. *Musée d'Art Moderne/ Photothèque des Musées de la Ville de Paris.*

His paintings of the cancan date from the early 1900s when the Tabarin had recently opened and the Moulin Rouge had decided to dispense with the *quadrille naturaliste*. *Bal Tabarin (Le Chahut)* (1905) and *Danseuse (au Tabarin)* (1906) show individual dancers in the midst of their routines. These are hardly pretty images—the faces of the dancers are grim and hard featured—but they exhibit a vibrancy and energy that even Toulouse-Lautrec had been unable to convey. The dark, gloomy appearance of the paintings contrasts effectively with the dramatic, thrusting high kicks of the dance. These dancers were no longer stars in the way that La Goulue and Jane Avril had been in the 1890s, and Rouault preserves their anonymity. This is stressed in *Danseuse et Monsieur Loyal*, also from 1905, in which an unnamed *cancaneuse* executes her routine apparently without conviction on the stage behind 'M. Loyal'.

One other painting by Rouault which might at first appear to have links to the cancan, in fact turns out to have a misleading title. *Jeu de massacre—la Noce de Nini-patte-en-l'air* (1905) actually depicts a fairground game in which large puppets were knocked down with sponge-filled balls. The central figure was always a bride, and when she was knocked down her feet would rise into the air as she fell backwards—hence Nini-patte-en-l'air. Obviously named after the famous dancer, it nevertheless would not have mattered if contestants had never heard of her.

Perhaps a surprising inclusion in a list of artists who painted the cancan is Pablo Picasso. He remains the twentieth century's most well-known painter, but mostly because of his innovative abstract style and his development of Cubism. In his early working life, he painted more naturalistic images, influenced by some of the great French artists of the late nineteenth century.

Picasso first visited Paris in 1900 at the age of nineteen. He had already seen the work of Toulouse-Lautrec in satirical magazines such as *Le Rire*, which was available in his home city of Barcelona, but he said later that he had not realised how great an artist Lautrec was until he had seen his works in the environment in which they had been created.[38] One of Picasso's first works executed in Paris was *Le Cancan* (1900) which appears to be almost a mirror image of the poster of the Troupe de Mademoiselle Eglantine. It is more detailed than Lautrec's work, being a pastel study rather than a lithograph, and shows such ornamentation as the ribbons on the dancers' bloomers. It is imbued with a gaiety absent from Lautrec's poster, simply by virtue of the laughter in the faces of the girls. Another of Picasso's paintings from this period is of the Moulin de la Galette, inviting comparison with Renoir's treatment of the same subject in the 1880s. Again the faces of the women make a difference, the brightness of their lipstick being caught by the electric light which had been installed since Renoir's time.[39]

Picasso produced a number of other drawings and paintings of the cancan during his two initial trips to Paris in 1900 and 1901, revealing the excitement that the young man must have felt in encountering Paris nightlife for the first time. It is quite possible that he had never witnessed the cancan in Barcelona. He also produced a watercolour 'poster' of the Jardin de Paris and

FIG. 74. *Danseuse de French Cancan*—one of many drawings and paintings of the dance executed by Picasso in his first two years in Paris, 1900–01. It is clear that the cancan made quite an impression on the young man. *Musée National Picasso/Réunion des Musées Nationaux.*

portrayed scenes at the Folies Bergère and the Moulin Rouge. His most dramatic approach to the dance was in *French Cancan* (1901), his only oil painting of the subject, and contrasting with his earlier works with its dramatic use of colour, anticipating the Fauvist movement.

Picasso's paintings of cancan dancers display an affection for and appreciation of the Parisian cabarets in the *belle époque*. He may have first become aware of the dance through the works of Toulouse-Lautrec but his approach was very different, more vibrant and colourful, and he made little attempt to explore behind the gaiety of the spectacle to show the reality of the dancers' lives, as did Rouault. Picasso was just reacting to the dance as entertainment, and was highly successful in demonstrating its escapist charms.

The well-known and respected artists who painted the cancan at the turn of the century have been followed, and imitated, by lesser artists so numerous that it would be impossible to mention them all. It is worth recording, however, that the dance even provided inspiration for those who painted in distinctly unusual, non-naturalistic styles—for example, the Cubism of the Italian, Gino Severini. Perhaps the most widely known and durable of works portraying the cancan in the twentieth century have again been posters—for the Moulin Rouge and other cabarets, and for films such as *French Cancan* and *Moulin Rouge*. Although including some original features, these have often borrowed from the style of Toulouse-Lautrec. Some of the Moulin Rouge posters have incorporated Lautrec's images of La Goulue and her partner Valentin-le-Désossé in acknowledgement of his contribution to the development of the poster and his promotion of the dance hall. Other poster designers have apparently been influenced by the frothier, more erotic style of Chéret. In the 1920s the cancan settled down into a format which continues to be repeated today, but nevertheless prevailing fashions have tended to influence certain aspects of what is essentially a Victorian dance costume. Similarly, posters have also responded to changing tastes, and it is possible to identify, for example, 1930s- or 1950s-style cancan posters, despite there being supposedly no difference in subject matter. Particularly striking are some produced in the 1950s, a time when long, full skirts with voluminous petticoats were once again in fashion.

CHAPTER 6 / A FEAST FOR THE EYES
The Cinema and the Cancan

FILMS HAVE PROBABLY BEEN RESPONSIBLE FOR PERPETUATING MORE MYTHS AND misconceptions about the cancan than any other art form. The dance has often been used as light relief in dramas set in the late nineteenth century, and what has generally been shown is the French Cancan of Paris nightclubs at the time the films were made, rather than anything approaching the *quadrille naturaliste* style that would have been more appropriate. Having said that, film-makers have provided us with some really beautifully staged, costumed and choreographed versions of the dance and it is perhaps a little pointless and ungrateful to demand historical accuracy in every case. It does seem unfortunate, however, that there is not even one major film that manages to re-create the atmosphere and the appearance of the dance in either the Second Empire or the 1890s.

A brave attempt at conveying the images of the dance halls of Montmartre, and more specifically the performers as seen through the eyes of the painter Toulouse-Lautrec, was made by John Huston with his 1952 film *Moulin Rouge*. The first twenty minutes are devoted to presenting the entertainment at the famous dance hall in about 1890. According to Huston, the filming actually took place at the Bal Tabarin, which presumably had a more suitable interior than the actual Moulin Rouge did in the 1950s.[1] In the opening scene, La Goulue is portrayed dancing in a quadrille with another girl and two men, a combination that rarely occurred at the Moulin Rouge. The quadrille itself is unconvincing, and makes one wonder what the excitement engendered by the famous dancer could have been all about. There is much flashing of lingerie by the two women, but little sign of the classic cancan steps. In fact their dance is performed at a sedate pace, the music being too slow for a galop. Some success is achieved in conveying La Goulue's vulgarity, both in the performance and afterwards, and she and her female rival later have a fight in front of Toulouse-Lautrec, much to his amusement.

More disappointing is the film's portrayal of Jane Avril, played by a badly cast Zsa Zsa Gabor. Surprisingly, she makes her entrance, at the top of a staircase, singing the film's theme song, the *Moulin Rouge Waltz*. In reality, Jane Avril rarely sang, and in *Moulin Rouge* that is all she does, which amounts to a sad misrepresentation of someone who by all accounts was a much-admired dancer. To add insult to injury, Zsa Zsa Gabor's part makes Avril appear to be an empty-headed flirt, whom Toulouse-Lautrec finds exasperating. As we know, he had a deep affection for her, and she was probably his favourite model.

La Goulue and Jane Avril both appear periodically throughout the film. Whereas Avril is portrayed as having pursued a successful career as a singer, La Goulue is shown more accurately letting success at the Moulin Rouge go to her head, and finally being forgotten by the Paris public. In one scene, late in the film, she is found by Toulouse-Lautrec drunk and desperately trying to

FIG. 75. Toulouse-Lautrec and Jane Avril, José Ferrer and Zsa Zsa Gabor, in the 1952 film *Moulin Rouge*. An impressive film in many ways, it unfortunately failed to show the famous dancer actually dancing. *Romulus Films*.

convince fellow down-and-outs that she was once a famous dance-hall star. Although this encounter, supposedly set in 1900, is pure fiction and highly implausible, it is true that La Goulue had degenerated quickly from her starring role as a *cancaneuse* in the early 1890s. It is possible, as the film suggests, that Toulouse-Lautrec's poster of her had contributed markedly to her pride, and ultimate fall.

The evening at the Moulin Rouge is rounded off with a fine, if rather short, French Cancan, expertly choreographed, and performed by six dancers to the music of Offenbach. This is certainly one of the best versions of the cancan to be seen in any film. The costumes are very attractive and realistically Victorian—lace blouses and long, full skirts, and particularly frothy underwear, with long diaphanous bloomers through which can be seen black stockings and suspenders. The excitement of the dance is enhanced by the film techniques, with its mixture of close-ups and long shots and occasional views of audience reaction. The faces of the dancers themselves are often shown in close-up, clearly enjoying every minute of their performance. Some amusement is gained at the expense of apparently English members of the audience, one of whom lets his monocle fall from his eye in amazement (or possibly shock) when presented with an array of lace-covered bottoms as the girls emulate La Goulue's party trick. The dancers perform again in a later part of the film, this time more sumptuously attired in gold dresses to signify the success of the Moulin Rouge.

The only trouble with this cancan is that it is anachronistic and is more reminiscent of a stage performance than something belonging to the dance hall. Carefully choreographed ensemble routines were not part of the Moulin Rouge fare in the 1890s, and the cancan did not really emerge strongly in this form until the early decades of the twentieth century. Of course, *Moulin Rouge* is Hollywood-style fantasy, and its version of the life of Toulouse-Lautrec is only barely accurate. In fact, this was recognised by John Huston himself at an early stage.[2] It is perhaps in keeping with this that he was determined to treat the opening sequence as a feast for the eyes and pulled out all the stops to present an apotheosis of the cancan rather than a strictly factual record. Something

FIG. 76. The *Moulin Rouge* dancers beginning their performance, which is certainly one of the best cancan sequences ever filmed, even if it is anachronistic. The beautiful costumes are more true to the period. *Romulus Films.*

of Huston's intentions are revealed in a conversation with José Ferrer, who played Lautrec, when he was trying to persuade the actor that the book *Moulin Rouge*, by Pierre La Mure, was ideal material for a film. Ferrer in fact owned the rights to the book, and had intended to turn it into a stage play, but Huston thought otherwise: "Forget the stage. This thing has got to be done for the screen—in colour, on the streets of Paris, with interiors at Maxim's and the Deux Magots. . . . We'll fill it with cancan girls in black stockings and music and brothels and champagne. With you as a bearded dwarf in a top hat. Well, kid, what do you say?" Ferrer was convinced, and said yes! [3]

La Mure's book was a highly romanticised view of the painter's life, which ignored some of the more sordid details, and Huston realised that it would present few problems with regard to censorship. Prostitution was a taboo subject in Hollywood, and could only be hinted at, certainly not presented as a major aspect of Toulouse-Lautrec's daily life, even though it was. So Huston's promise to Ferrer about the brothels was largely unfulfilled. He more than made up for this with the dancers, however, although even these presented some problems in small-town America. As the director recalled: "When I contemplate the censorship of the time and the absurdities of it, it is hard to believe. I remember there was one scene where the girls raise their dresses and show their pantaloons, and in some places this was deleted."[4]

Dramatically *Moulin Rouge* is extremely thin, but Huston's aim was really more to convey in cinematic terms the art of Lautrec. He used Technicolor in a revolutionary manner to reproduce the effects of the paintings. Previously this process had concentrated on showing everything in shot as clearly as possible, and the Technicolor laboratory initially objected to his ideas. In the end Huston managed to produce attractive impressionistic images on the screen that Technicolor were highly pleased with: sometimes the picture was hazy or quite dark, depending on what was required by the paintings; the foreground may have been in sharp focus, but the backgrounds were often blurred, with subtle blending of colour.[5]

Ferrer, as Lautrec, is shown frequently in the opening sequence, at his table by the dance floor, sketching the performers. When his drawing is seen in close-up, the hand is actually not Ferrer's but that of the artist Marcel Vertès, who had once made a living from producing impressive forgeries of Toulouse-Lautrec's work. Several times throughout the film Lautrec is to be seen adding little touches to his paintings, and each time it is Vertès's hand that we see, ensuring apparent authenticity in the use of the brush.[6] This attention to detail on Huston's part is admirable, although many other facets of the artist's appearance in the film are not so accurate. Ferrer had to walk around with his calves strapped back and with his shoes on his knees to appear as short as Lautrec, and with beard, bowler hat and pince-nez he certainly looked the part.[7] It is a shame, therefore, that the story of his life should have been distorted in the film. The section dealing with his early life contains the erroneous suggestion that an accident led to his stunted growth, rather than the congenital condition that really was the case, and the body of the plot concentrates on a romanticised and highly fictionalised view of his love life. There is little,

FIG. 77. An ensemble presentation of La Goulue's famous party trick by the cancan dancers in *Moulin Rouge*. It was the promise of dancers in black stockings which was at least partly responsible for José Ferrer agreeing to participate in the film. *Romulus Films.*

therefore, to commend *Moulin Rouge* as a serious biographical account. However, even Huston admitted that he had not attempted to make a film that would be strong on historical detail. He had been motivated from the beginning by an idea he had had for the final scene in the film, in which Toulouse-Lautrec would be seen on his death-bed visited by ghostly figures of the dancers at the Moulin Rouge, and as the music of the cancan started he would breathe his last. This was the first thing that had come into his mind after reading the novel. He described it as a "truly happy ending", and it is probably the most successful, if over-sentimental, scene—apart from the opening twenty minutes set at the dance hall itself.[8]

Moulin Rouge proved to be a box-office success, even though it was poorly received by the critics. It is a very beautifully photographed film, and apart from its ingenious use of colour to present its images in the style of oil paintings, it also contains two more direct examinations of Toulouse-Lautrec's art.

One is a narrative explanation of the process of lithography, by which his posters were produced. The other occurs when whole sequences are devoted to a montage of his works, accompanied by music from the dance hall. These details, together with the film's visual evocation of turn-of-the-century Paris and the magnificent cancan, make the film well worth seeing, even if the acting and dialogue are rather disappointing.[9]

Jean Renoir's *French Cancan* followed so closely (in 1954) after *Moulin Rouge* that it is possible that the one inspired the other. Renoir was not the first choice for director, but he was pleased to be offered it because it "corresponded to a great desire I had to make a film in a very French spirit, which would allow an easy and convenient contact . . . between myself and the French public".[10] Renoir had just returned to France after spending a number of years in Hollywood, and now wanted to re-establish his credentials as a French director. The subject was chosen by the producer, but Renoir was given a free hand in deciding how to construct the film.[11] The story he chose deals in a highly fictionalised way with the development of the French Cancan and its presentation on the opening night of the Moulin Rouge. The film is also a homage to the small *café-concerts* and their performers, including Yvette Guilbert. The director remembered being taken to *café-concerts* himself aged five by his Uncle Henri, who clearly thought it was necessary for his education.[12] But *French Cancan*'s main strengths lie in its gentle evocation of life in Montmartre in the 1880s, idealised through non-naturalistic studio sets designed by Max Douy, some reminiscent of paintings by the director's father, Auguste. There is little attempt at historical accuracy in the film, but somehow this matters less than in *Moulin Rouge*, which after all gave the impression of being a serious treatment of the life of a famous painter. In *French Cancan* the central story is lightweight and romantic, and not meant to be taken seriously at all.

French Cancan is a more balanced film than *Moulin Rouge*, the latter seeming distinctly anticlimactic and turgid after the thrill of the opening twenty minutes. In Renoir's film, the main dance sequence is saved until the end, and the whole film is geared towards this, gradually gathering pace as excitement is enhanced by the sense of anticipation. The story focuses on the impresario, Danglard, played by Jean Gabin, and his vision of opening a new cabaret venue with the cancan as the centrepiece of the evening's entertainment. His inspiration for this comes when he visits the Reine Blanche, an insignificant working-class dance hall in Montmartre, where he is captivated by a young laundress, Nini, played by Françoise Arnoul, who surprises and delights him by spontaneously dancing the *chahut*. He is convinced that the cancan danced by twenty or more pretty girls like Nini would transform Parisian night-life, and he resolves to take over the site of the Reine Blanche and build a new, more opulent dance hall in which to present his new show. This is not such a simple proposition, because money is needed for the project and Danglard is also faced with the task of finding enough talented dancers and other performers to make his new venture a success.

Money proves not to be a major obstacle, as Danglard's mistress, La Belle

FIG. 78. Nini's audition in *French Cancan* looks a little painful! Madame Guibole's dancing school was fictional, but she had a real-life counterpart in Nini-Patte-en-l'Air. The character of Danglard was based on Zidler, the manager of the Moulin Rouge. *The Kobal Collection.*

Abbesse (Maria Félix) persuades another of her lovers, Baron Walter, to finance Danglard's cabaret, which is to be called the Moulin Rouge. Danglard then begins the search for dancers with the help of dance teacher and former *cancaneuse*, Madame Guibole. Auditions are held at Madame Guibole's school, and it soon becomes clear that there is no shortage of young women who are keen to dance the cancan. Once the best have been selected, rehearsals begin and the French Cancan gradually begins to take shape.

The progress towards the opening night is hardly without difficulties, caused not least by Danglard's increasing affection for Nini, who is to be his star dancer. This enrages La Belle Abbesse and during the ceremony to lay the foundation stone for the Moulin Rouge, due to be carried out by a cabinet minister, she is overcome by jealousy and attacks Nini, kicking her on the leg. In the ensuing mêlée, which seems to involve everyone present, Danglard is knocked down and injured by Nini's boyfriend.

The impresario's hectic love life causes more serious trouble on the opening night of the new dance hall, when Nini refuses to lead the cancan because she realises she has lost him to the 'street singer' Ester Georges. However, Danglard convinces her that her art is more important than her private life, and that she is threatening to harm not him but the public who have come to see her. In the end, Nini realises that he is right, and joins in the dance with the rest of the girls. Her boyfriend, Paolo, who had objected to her becoming a cancan dancer is seen angrily watching her but then gradually growing closer to a friend of Nini, who had been rejected by Madame Guibole. Danglard emerges from backstage to join the audience when he is sure that his French Cancan is a success, and he finds himself drawn to yet another woman, one of the spectators. The film is rounded off with close-ups of the main characters' faces, each of them looking contented despite their earlier troubles, these having been effaced (perhaps briefly) by the infectious joy of the cancan.

Renoir's film is a wonderfully nostalgic view of life in Paris in the late nineteenth century. Despite not being a historical account, it nevertheless manages to convey in a light-hearted fashion some of the important features of social change in this era. The growing sexual freedom for women is reflected in the love lives of La Belle Abbesse and Nini, and in the French Cancan itself, which allows them to express their sexuality openly and triumphantly. The underwear in the cancan is a magnificent display of lace and ribbons, an example of the general extravagance of women's dress at this time, despite increasing emancipation. Earlier in the film, Danglard is seen lacing up La Belle Abbesse's corset, and she orders him to pull the laces tighter, so that she can achieve a more perfect figure. He responds that men are mere slaves of women—a wry comment on the controversy over the corset itself. The entertainment of a typical *café-concert* is portrayed at Danglard's original theatre, the fictional Paravent Chinois, where La Belle Abbesse performs her belly dance and where another star of the opening night at the Moulin Rouge, a whistling clown, makes his début.

The atmosphere of several of the real music halls of the 1880s is evoked when Nini leads an admirer, the Balkan prince Alexandre, on a tour of Parisian nightlife. In one scene, the 'little sparrow' Edith Piaf appears briefly to impersonate a *chanteuse* of yesteryear, Eugénie Buffet. Madame Guibole's dancing school could have been modelled on that of Nini-Patte-en-l'Air, although Guibole herself is an older woman and supposedly a cancan star from the Second Empire. She does not invite men to observe her dancers rehearsing, as Nini-Patte-en-l'Air did, but two government officials who arrive during the auditions to discuss with Danglard his plans for the site of the Reine Blanche seem eager to stay and offer their opinions. When an attractive, sophisticated and proud *demi-mondaine* enters, hoists up her skirts, but then proves to be hopeless as a dancer, the two men ask what is going to be done with the rejects.

An important acknowledgement of the origins of many *cancaneuses* is found in the character of Nini, who is working as a laundress when she is 'discovered' by Danglard. The majority of the hopefuls who come for auditions are working-class girls looking for a chance to better themselves. They are taking a risk opting for the world of entertainment; whereas Madame Guibole achieved moderate success with her studio after her career as a dancer came to an end, at the other end of the scale is Prunelle, once the toast of Paris as a cancan dancer (as Danglard informs Nini) but now reduced to being a rag-picker, virtually a beggar.

So *French Cancan* is not afraid of social comment. More is to be found in Renoir's own poignant lyrics for the film's theme song, which is about a girl dying of consumption, and is delivered at the Moulin Rouge by Ester Georges. The music is hauntingly beautiful, and appears throughout the film in different contexts, sometimes played on a barrel organ in the street while Nini and her friends deliver their baskets of laundry. It adds to the delicate atmosphere of the nostalgic scenes in Montmartre. Jean Renoir may have recognised the difficulties of life in nineteenth-century Paris, but he never lets the mood descend to gloom. The film always appears bright and colourful, in contrast to the often dark, and depressing *Moulin Rouge*.

French Cancan succeeds best in its dance scenes, the finale being one of the greatest choreographic spectacles ever filmed. The momentum builds gradually towards the presentation of the first French Cancan. Nini's *chahut* in the Reine Blanche is brief, as is a spirited re-creation of her own cancan days by Madame Guibole, when she inspires her pupils with a few high kicks and a brave demonstration of the splits. Rehearsals for the girls are shown at various stages of competence, from their early exercises to improve high kicks and *grand écarts* (often looking rather painful), through rather untidy attempts at synchronous movement, to, eventually, a triumphant ensemble routine rounded off with a *grand écart* by each dancer in turn. Danglard stands watching this scene with his back to the camera, his dark figure silhouetted against the white of the dancers' underwear.

On the opening night of the Moulin Rouge, the cancan is what everyone has come to see, but Danglard (like Renoir) is determined to make the audience wait. A succession of acts is introduced by the master of ceremonies, including La Belle Abbesse, performing a belly dance in the guise of Catherine the Great of Russia, and Ester Georges's plaintive, dramatic singing. After the backstage drama in which Nini nearly abandons her career as a dancer before it has started, and during which the crowd begins to chant her name impatiently, the French Cancan is finally announced.

The *cancaneuses* appear from all around the hall, over tables, down from ropes, through false walls. Nini drops down from the orchestra gallery into arms of eager admirers, from whom she quickly extricates herself. She and the other girls push the spectators out of the way on the floor, and begin the dance. It is balletic and graceful, thrilling and sexy. The dresses are colourful, the petticoats a frothy profusion of lace frills and coloured ribbons. The music constantly changes, with several well-known tunes appearing, including Lottie Collins's 'Tara-ra-ra-boom-de-ay' and the *galop infernal* of Offenbach. The whole sequence is breathtaking, and lasts almost ten minutes.

Renoir uses several different approaches in filming the dance; there are some close-ups, but often long shots which give us a chance to witness the spectacle as if we are part of the audience. It is difficult to count them all, but it seems that as many as twenty-four dancers are involved in this magnificent French Cancan, which *Variety* described as "the finest film-painting ever seen on any screen".[13] During the dance there are also brief cuts to Danglard sitting backstage, listening to the audience reaction, and hoping that his show is a success. At one point he is caught by a wardrobe assistant gently lifting his own leg up and down in time with the music. Eventually convinced that his gamble has paid off, he ventures out to watch the final minutes.

French Cancan is a film about dedication to ideals in show business, and the duty of those involved in the profession to their audience. It is also a labour

FIG. 79. The superb finale of *French Cancan* with twenty-four dancers performing supposedly on the opening night of the Moulin Rouge. Historical inaccuracy can be forgiven in this wonderfully costumed and choreographed dance sequence. *The Kobal Collection.*

of love on the part of Renoir in his determination to honour a fine French product, the cancan itself. It is interesting to compare the British-produced version of the cancan in Huston's film, with the genuine French article. It is difficult to identify quite why, but the French do seem slightly to have the edge. The acting performances in *French Cancan* are far superior. Jean Gabin, who had often worked with Renoir in the past, was an excellent choice to play Danglard. Françoise Arnoul and Maria Félix in the two lead female roles are superb, with Arnoul pretty and petite, but strong, and Félix proud and beautiful. Incidentally, not only were the characters of Nini and La Belle Abbesse rivals, but there were also moments of hostility between the two actresses during the making of the film. According to Renoir, during the 'fight' at the laying of the foundation stone, Arnoul accidentally scratched Félix with her bracelet, and a real fight began. The cameras were ready to roll as the two attacked each other, but Renoir intervened before medical assistance was necessary.[14]

The character of Nini was originally to have been played by Leslie Caron, an accomplished dancer who had already established her credentials as a performer in a musical. She had starred with Gene Kelly in *An American in Paris* and in the dream ballet had appeared as a cancan dancer from a Toulouse-Lautrec painting. Renoir told her that he had written the part in *French Cancan* especially for her, but ultimately her Hollywood commitments ruled her out and Françoise Arnoul stepped in. As Renoir said, Arnoul was a good actress—but she was not really a dancer.[15] If you look carefully you can see that another dancer takes her place in long shots for the particularly difficult manoeuvres of the cancan, with Arnoul being shown in close-up immediately afterwards as if *she* had carried them out.

Following the British *Moulin Rouge* and the French *French Cancan*, America responded by attempting to film Cole Porter's *Can-Can*. This film was subject to a large amount of pre-release publicity because of the Soviet leader Khrushchev's outburst about Western immorality. It was prompted, apparently, by the sight of Shirley Maclaine's backside as she rehearsed for the main dance routine during his visit to Hollywood. One might suspect that the studio had paid Khrushchev to make his remarks to boost audiences for what turned out to be a mediocre film. It has nothing of the sparkle of *French Cancan*, and the dance routines and costumes are unimpressive. The main problem is that it has no sense of period, and, as one critic said, owes more to Las Vegas of 1960 than Paris of the 1890s.[16]

The story and score were adjusted to suit the stars who were invited to take part. Thus, Frank Sinatra appears as François, a character who did not feature in the original stage musical, and there are two judges, rather than one—in addition to the young, 'moral' Philippe Forestier, played by Louis Jourdan, there is the corrupt Paul Barrière, played by Maurice Chevalier. This pairing is obviously an attempt to repeat the success of *Gigi*, in which they starred with Leslie Caron, but in *Can-Can* their casting opposite Sinatra and Maclaine creates a confusion of cultures. The American and French accents clash with each other, and the film seems to fall between two stools, failing to establish whether it is trying to portray an American night-club version of Parisian entertainment or the real thing.

One of the most impressive songs from the stage musical, 'I Love Paris', only appears over the opening credits, and the song 'Can-Can' itself is just employed instrumentally, which is unfortunate to say the least. 'I Love Paris' deserves to be given more prominence and the cancan finale loses much of its appeal when the girls do not sing the witty lyrics of the title song. The dancing in the cancan sequences is competent, but lacks the energy and vitality of those in *French Cancan* or *Moulin Rouge*. The dresses and underwear are also not as attractive, the transparent black knickers worn over briefs seeming a particularly strange choice. The whole adds up to a rather tame presentation of something which is supposed to be exciting and sexy. The other dance sequences are poor, and the 'Adam and Eve Ballet' is neither original nor sinful. Juliet Prowse, as a non-singing Claudine, does emerge with some credit in the dancing, and so does Shirley Maclaine. It is not really their fault that the choreography, designs and music let them down.

The most unsatisfactory aspect of the film is the essential drawback of the stage musical: the suggestion that the cancan was a banned dance in late-nineteenth-century Paris. In Walter Lang's screen version this is compounded in the opening shot, captioned "Montmartre 1896", when the camera shows first of all the Moulin Rouge in the distance and then follows Sinatra and Chevalier to the entrance of the fictional night-club of Simone Pistache (Maclaine), the Bal du Paradis. Most people with any knowledge of turn-of-the-century Parisian nightlife would surely be aware that the cancan was performed nightly at the Moulin Rouge from the day it was opened without transgressing the penal code, and it therefore seems totally absurd that the nearby Bal du Paradis should be invaded by the police whenever it is performed there.

The cancan has appeared in many other films based on musicals or operettas, rarely satisfactorily. In *Oklahoma!* (1955) the dancers actually come across as being even more sinister and threatening than had been the case on stage. When *Paint your Wagon* was filmed, the cancan and other dances which formed the highlight of the stage show were dispensed with, and the story was considerably rewritten. Jean Gilbert's operetta *Die Keusche Suzanne* has been filmed a number of times, and the three French versions—*La Chaste Suzanne* (1938 and 1951) and *La P'tite Femme du Moulin-Rouge* (1950)—all contain the French Cancan.

Lehár's *The Merry Widow*, which would seem to offer great opportunities to film-makers, has been unfortunately treated rather disrespectfully by the cinema. The best version is that of Ernst Lubitsch, made in 1934 in Hollywood and starring Maurice Chevalier as Danilo and Jeanette MacDonald as the widow. Both are well cast, with Chevalier playing his role as the dissolute count with great panache, and MacDonald clearly relishing her part as the seductive Sonia. The story is, however, considerably altered, and, lamentably, there are no *grisettes*. There is a brief but attractive cancan performance at Maxim's, which is some consolation. It is certainly far superior to the execrable dancing in the 1952 version, starring Lana Turner. The latter film is best summed up in *Halliwell's Film Guide* as a "Chill, empty remake".[17]

FIG. 80. Ernst Lubitsch preparing to direct the cancan in *The Merry Widow*. He dispensed with the *grisettes'* song in favour of a large-scale choreographed routine performed to the music from the operetta. *The Kobal Collection*.

The ballet *Gaîté Parisienne* was filmed in Hollywood in 1941 as *The Gay Parisian*. This and another film of the Ballet Russe de Monte Carlo, *Capriccio Espagnol*, represent the first real attempts to bring ballet into the cinema. Alexandra Danilova, who was dancing the role of the glove seller at the time, took a screen test for the film with the rest of the company, but it was decided that she was not photogenic enough. Danilova was told that "the film public must have pretty and innocent heroines", despite her protests that French-women were usually witty and charming rather than simply pretty, and that the glove seller could hardly be described as "innocent". Hence, Mlada Mladova, one of the corps de ballet, was offered the role and Danilova had to coach her for it.[18]

The ballet was specifically adapted and condensed for the cinema, and close-ups, camera angles and cutting were used, which infuriated ballet purists when the film was released. They evidently felt that they should be able to watch the ballet as if seeing it on stage in a theatre.[19] At one point the dancers are reflected in a wall mirror. It is a colourful rendition of the ballet, although

Mladova's interpretation of the central role is dull in comparison to that of Danilova.[20]

The Gay Parisian or *Gaîté Parisienne* was, like the operetta it was based on, set in the Second Empire. The style of cancan dancing in the ballet belonged very much to a later time, but this could be forgiven easily as artistic licence, especially as the story was so light and insignificant. It might be expected that films based on serious novels set in the same period would be more accurate. This has rarely been the case, in fact. Jean Renoir's *Nana* (1926), based on Zola's ultimately tragic novel, was a good example. The director admitted to some licence in his choice of costumes for the protagonists in the film, choosing to dress them in fashions from a later period rather than the extravagant crino-lined dresses that would have been more in keeping. He said that he hoped he would be "pardoned a small historical error which I deliberately perpetrated by costuming my artists in the more curious fashion of 1871".[21] If we can for-give him for this deliberate error, perhaps we can also make allowances for the fact that the cancan dancers in the film appear in dresses which seem to owe more to the styles of the 1920s than the 1860s. It is true that the dancers at the Moulin Rouge in the 1920s wore costumes that above the waist would have seemed highly fashionable, but had the necessary (for the dance) long full skirts and petticoats that had disappeared from women's dress two decades earlier. Renoir may have borrowed these very dresses for the film—even the hair styles belong more the Charleston era than that of the *quadrille naturaliste*.

The cancan itself is the choreographed form that took shape in the 1920s rather than the highly improvised dancing of the likes of Finette la Bordelaise or Alice la Provençale at the Bal Mabille. Having said that, other details are more accurate: when Nana and her friends arrive at the famous dancing gar-dens, a gentle quadrille is in progress, performed by humble artisans and working women. The orchestra leader lets fire with pistols, like Musard did when he was conductor at the Opéra balls. Nana's participation in the cancan ends with her kicking top hats out of the hands of gentlemen admirers—although this was perhaps not as daring as contemporaries who managed to knock hats from the *heads* of spectators. Finally, when she quarrels with her jealous lover, she is comforted by the lavatory attendant, an older woman who reveals that she is none other than the former Reine Pomaré. This is a nice touch by Renoir, showing that not all of the cancan stars of the 1840s ended their days in luxury. Unfortunately, Pomaré was a bad choice, because she died of tuberculosis in her early twenties.

The dance sequence is cleverly filmed, and long shots through a smoky atmosphere with the spectators' heads dominating the foreground alternate with close-ups portraying the excitement in the faces of the dancers. This seems to have been a trial run for *French Cancan*, in which some of the same techniques were used. Renoir said that he had really needed colour and sound for *Nana*, and he may have ultimately gained some satisfaction through the later film.[22] It is easy to find parallels between the two, allowing for the fact that technological advances helped the director achieve so much more with *French Cancan*. The contrast in moods between the films could not, however, be more marked, and while Nini is the star of the show on a joyful occasion at the Moulin Rouge, Nana is attempting to forget her own miseries by losing herself in the dance.

Nana had a budget of a million francs, and was ultimately a failure essentially because Catherine Hessling in the central role came across, in Renoir's words, as "a marionette". He said that he meant this to be a compliment, but unfortunately 1930s audiences wanted realism. Despite a lavish première in the big hall of the Moulin Rouge, which was then a cinema, with the orchestra playing tunes by Offenbach, and extensive publicity with posters of Hessling all over Paris, Renoir lost his million.[23]

The general appearance of the Mabille in Renoir's *Nana* seems accurate if compared with contemporary drawings of the establishment. In a more recent film, based on Eugène Sué's novel *Les Mystères de Paris*, and directed by André Hunebelle, the dancing gardens are also featured, and look very similar, if more opulent. The film is somewhat tedious on the whole, but does have the merit of showing something close to a genuine cancan of the time, with one man executing some impressive high kicks in the centre of the floor to the admiration of fellow-dancers. It is all too brief, but does give an idea of what it may have been like at the Mabille in its heyday.

The end of the Second Empire and the Paris Commune provide the setting for the Soviet film *New Babylon*, made in 1929. This was a silent film for which the composer Dmitri Shostakovich wrote an orchestral score. The revolutionaries on the barricades are shown at one point triumphantly dancing the cancan, and Shostakovich cleverly used excerpts from Offenbach's *galop infernal* intertwined within his own music.

The Elysée-Montmartre dance hall is the setting for a somewhat stylised cancan in Max Ophuls's film *Le Plaisir* (1952), which consists of three stories originally written by Guy de Maupassant. In the first of these, a ball is in progress at the famous dance hall when a mysterious figure wearing a mask suddenly appears and joins the revellers in their wild gyrations. Before long, he collapses onto the floor, and a doctor is called. When his mask is removed, he is found to be an old man. When he is taken home his wife reveals that he has never been reconciled to his lost youth, and cannot resist returning to his former haunts to try to recapture the pleasures of his past. Maupassant's novel *Bel Ami* has also been filmed, on a number of occasions. In *The Private Affairs of Bel Ami* (1947), George Sanders and Angela Lansbury can be seen dancing a rather restrained *chahut* at the Reine Blanche. The dance hall that replaced the Reine Blanche, the Moulin Rouge, crops up again in *So Long at the Fair* (1950). The cancan is incorporated in a rather fanciful (not to say inaccurate) portrayal of some of the famous features of the dance hall. The dancers appear sliding down a chute out of the side of the cardboard elephant, and then take part in a parade riding donkeys in the middle of their performance. However, the dance itself has the right mixture of fun and sexiness, even though its presentation is a world away from the real *quadrille naturaliste* of 1889.

In the 1950s, the same decade that produced *Moulin Rouge*, *French Cancan* and *Can-Can*, a number of French films were released that contained images of the contemporary cabarets at Paris nightclubs. Among them were *La Tournée des Grands Ducs* (1952), which featured several scenes of dancing at the various cabarets, and *Tabarin* (1957), which was a drama set in the famous dance hall, with the Bluebell girls performing several tableaux. The Tabarin had by now closed for business, and was reopened briefly for the making of the film. Both films included an exhilarating French Cancan.

The Tabarin was most probably the setting for a scene in the 1990 film *Mr and Mrs Bridge*, starring Paul Newman and Joanne Woodward. Mr Bridge is somewhat taken aback, and not a little delighted, when one of the cancan dancers in the night-club deposits herself briefly on his lap in the middle of the show.[24] The film is primarily about the middle-class hypocrisy of an elderly couple living in a small town in 1930s America. The incident with the dancer during their holiday in Paris gives Mrs Bridge the chance for some gentle teasing of her husband, whose response is to say that he is planning to send the girl some flowers. He is, however, clearly embarrassed by the episode, much to Mrs Bridge's satisfaction! The cancan in *Mr and Mrs Bridge* is a fine traditional performance of the dance, evoking the period of the Tabarin's pre-eminence before the Second World War.

British and American Victorian music-hall settings have also been employed attractively by film-makers, with the cancan often presented in visually stunning fashion. The nineteenth century is a popular period for Gothic horror, and the dancing seems often to have been used to contrast with the more serious sides of the films, which usually have slightly absurd, melodramatic plots. In *House of Wax* (1953), the heroine is invited to a music-hall performance to take her mind off a frightening experience she had had the previous night. When she sees the cancan dancers, she asks her companion if "nice" people normally go to such establishments, where women reveal their "talents". Unsurprisingly, he seems more interested in watching the show than in conversation. Incidentally, the film was made in 3-D, and consequently members of the cinema audiences probably felt the dancers' high kicks were too close for comfort!

A grimmer tale, in that it is based on real incidents, is told in *Jack the Ripper* (1958), although it bears little relation to the facts of the case. In this film, one of the cancan dancers eventually becomes a victim of the murderer. The original (British) version of *Gaslight*, made in 1939, also features a music-hall performance of the cancan. An evil husband, played by Anton Walbrook, who is trying to drive his wife insane, takes the housemaid to a show at which the manager proudly announces that the next act will be a troupe of French dancers. He then apologises for turning his back on the audience, because he wants to see their performance for himself. *Fanny by Gaslight* (1944), not to be confused with the aforementioned film, is partly set in what is more like a brothel than a music hall, where cancan dancers supply an aphrodisiac function. All three of these films contain impressive, though rather short versions of the dance.

The American Western film, with its cowboys and saloon girls, has always been fertile ground for the cancan, even as far back as the silent era. Comedy

Westerns are particularly likely to contain sequences featuring high kicking dance-hall girls. Laurel and Hardy's *Way out West* (1937) and the Marx Brothers' *Go West* (1940)were both early examples, although the dancers appear for less than a minute in each case, and despite flashing their underwear and stockings they cannot really be said to be dancing the cancan in either. *Destry* (1954), George Marshall's own remake of his earlier success *Destry Rides Again*, is more of a true musical with songs and dances. Mari Blanchard plays the saloon queen Brandy, and Audie Murphy is the pint-sized innocent who drinks milk and does not carry a gun, but whose father, Tom Destry, was a famous gunfighter. Young Destry may not seem a match for the villains, but he succeeds in saving the town. Among the musical numbers is the song 'If You Can Can-Can', which may not be a very original title, but does allow for spirited dancing by Brandy and her girls.

A strange feature of *Destry* and many other American films of the 1940s and 1950s, including *House of Wax*, is that it seems to have been impermissible to show what James Laver has described as "thigh eroticism", i.e. the few inches of bare flesh between stocking tops and knickers.[25] Presumably the censors felt that this was too suggestive, especially in 'family' films—although it had not bothered them in the 1930s, for example in the musicals of Busby Berkeley. Dancers in post-war American films therefore nearly always wore tights rather than stockings, which sometimes led to absurd situations. In the musical *Silk Stockings* (1957), Cyd Charisse disappears behind a screen to put on the stockings of the title only to emerge, miraculously, wearing tights! In *House of Wax*, the poster outside the music hall shows a dancer clearly wearing stockings and suspenders, but the dancers on stage do not. The cancan loses something of its essential appeal as a result, not to mention its authenticity. This strange unwritten rule seems to have been relaxed at the end of the 1950s in time for *Can-Can*. Other countries were not affected, and John Huston was not thus constrained when making *Moulin Rouge* because he worked with a British production company, although, as mentioned earlier, he did experience some difficulties with local censorship when the film was shown in America. It could not have been censorship problems which restricted the makers of *Darling Lili* as late as in 1970. This American film, set in the First World War, has a very fine cancan sequence, with beautiful costumes. The image is only spoilt because under their skirts the dancers are, inexplicably, wearing totally inappropriate black tights.

Two films of the 1960s not subject to the above limitations, and belonging, loosely speaking, to the 'Western' genre were the British film *Carry on Cowboy* and the French *Viva Maria* (both 1965). The latter stars Jeanne Moreau and Brigitte Bardot as two entertainers, both called Maria, who get heavily involved in a Central American revolution. It somewhat lacks substance, and the cancan actually ends up as a striptease when Bardot's costume proves to be a little on the small side for her. So as far as the cancan is concerned it promises much more than it delivers, and it remains a matter for conjecture what the result would have been had two of France's most glamorous actresses been given full-rein to perform their country's most famous dance. *Carry on Cowboy*

FIG. 81. The Stodge City saloon girls on the set of *Carry on Cowboy*. Westerns and particularly comedy Westerns have often featured the cancan—usually a much more accomplished and attractive version of the dance than any real cowboys would have seen. *Canal+Image UK Ltd.*

very much follows the *Destry* theme, with Stodge City having been taken over by the Rumpo Kid (Sid James), and all hopes resting on a 'wet behind the ears' marshal, who is really a sanitary engineer. Unlike *Destry*, this is a film that constantly undermines any worries that it might be taking a serious turn. When the mayor, played by Kenneth Williams, comes into the saloon to complain about the "disgraceful exhibition" on stage (a cancan provided by the Ballet Montparnasse) the Rumpo Kid responds: "It's educational", and so it is.

It would be impossible to try to list all the films in which the cancan appears. There are too many, and some are disappointing and consequently not worth mentioning. However, there is one film remaining that must be recorded. Pierre Benoit's book *L'Atlantide* about the lost city of Atlantis may not seem promising material for a film featuring a cancan, but G. W. Pabst's 1932 version of the story, *The Queen of Atlantis*, is full of surprises. The central theme of the story is that Atlantis is buried, not beneath the sea as is usually assumed, but under the Sahara desert. When Saint-Avit, an officer in the French Foreign Legion, is captured by Tuaregs and taken there, he has some bizarre experiences, including having to play chess for his freedom against the beautiful, classically featured Queen Antinéa. One of the few other Europeans in this gloomy underworld is Count Bielowsky, an aging *bon vivant*, who drinks to escape his misery. When Saint-Avit asks him who the queen really is, he replies: *"Antinéa, c'est Paris!"*.

At this point the scene abruptly switches to a music-hall stage a few decades before where a magnificent French Cancan is in progress. On the very word *"Paris"*, spoken by the count, we see a close-up of a cancan dancer's petticoats and lacy knickers, the camera pulling back to reveal a chorus line of dancers, with a beautiful soloist leading the troupe. This is Clémentine, Antinéa's mother, who is full of the joy and the excitement of the dance—quite the opposite of her rather moody and frustrated offspring. This cancan is certainly one of the most effective ever filmed, and the whole sequence in the theatre and in the dressing room afterwards evokes the effervescent thrills of the *fin de siècle*. It is in sharp contrast to the rest of the film which is unremittingly claustrophobic.

It is revealed that Clémentine was the count's mistress, but he wanted to improve her status and succeeded in marrying her off to a Tuareg prince. Clémentine was very aware of the prince watching her in the theatre, and made sure she danced part of her solo routine right next to his box. He was captivated by her and their engagement was soon announced in *Le Figaro*. This is an imaginative variation on the theme of dancers marrying into the aristocracy. There is no record of a *cancaneuse* actually becoming a queen, let alone the queen of a mythical realm—but it may have happened.

Apart from the three major feature films which have the cancan as a central element, the others cited above are included to provide just a few illustrations of the many different contexts in which it has appeared. In fact, the cancan must qualify as the most filmed dance ever, considering the vast number of films showing anything from a tantalising glimpse of the dance to a full performance. It has been continually popular with directors because of its versatility in evoking moods, a sense of period or location in a way that almost nothing else does. It has been used to symbolise gaiety, immorality, freedom, rakish abandon or sheer joy and excitement. It can immediately transport the viewer to the end of the nineteenth century, the *fin de siècle*, the 'naughty nineties', the time of music hall and variety, with no further elucidation necessary. Above all it is a symbol of Paris, particularly in the nineteenth century, but also in the twentieth century, especially in films portraying a foreigner's eye-view of the French capital.

Whilst the superficial reason for the inclusion of the cancan may be clear, there are often sub-texts reflecting an attitude to the morality of the age in which the films were set which is influenced then by the morality of the times in which the films were made. The lack of 'thigh eroticism' in American films of the 1940s and 1950s is one example, but a more general change in approach to sexuality in America can be detected over the decades. The early 1930s were relatively liberal with regard to what was permissible in films, and hence the cancan tended to be portrayed in traditional costume, with no attempt to disguise or comment on its erotic nature. Towards the end of the 1930s censorship increased, and the post-war years brought a real reaction to all forms of liberalism. Cancan dancers when they appeared were unequivocally labelled as 'bad girls'—rather hypocritically, as they were usually included for their entertainment value. In *Destry* they have to leave when the town is 'cleaned up' by the hero; in *Oklahoma!* they are associates of the villain, Jud, who threaten the heroine's innocence. In other films which might logically have featured the cancan it was omitted because it would not have been acceptable to a family audience. One such film is *Tonight and Every Night* (1945), a Hollywood musical supposedly about the Windmill Theatre in London, which not unexpectedly also declines to portray the other Windmill speciality, the nude tableau.

In the late 1950s and 1960s, when sexual permissiveness returned and indeed became fashionable, the cancan was sometimes used as a vehicle for expressing this new mood, evoking an earlier time when the bounds of freedom were being extended. But when the final taboo on nudity in the cinema was removed, there seemed to be little place for a dance which relied so heavily on costume. The cancan may also have seemed innocent in comparison with the perceived advances in expressing sexuality. Moreover, the age of film musicals seemed to be largely over, the pop musicals that were produced reflecting confidence in the modern age but offering no scope for inclusion of a cancan.

This confidence has not lasted, and nostalgia has returned to popularity together with an understanding and appreciation that the experiences of the past can have relevance today. In *Mr and Mrs Bridge*, Mr Bridge's hypocritical attitude to sex in the 1930s has considerable meaning for the 1990s. His surreptitious enjoyment of the cancan at the nightclub is exposed when the dancer chooses to single him out for a little bit of 'audience participation'. Paul Newman's quickly changing expression from surprise, through embarrassment, to pride at being so selected by the uninhibited *cancaneuse* is a marvellous piece of acting, readily appreciated by anyone watching the film.

It is to be hoped that a film-maker experienced in dealing with historical subjects will one day successfully approach the story of the cancan and its performers, in the 1840s, the 1860s or the 1890s. It would be important to achieve a degree of realism which was absent from *Moulin Rouge* but not to forget that the cancan has only ever existed because it is entertaining. The kind of gritty realism that reduces everything to a political level would be misplaced, but total escapism would fail to demonstrate the human stories behind stars like Céleste Mogador, Rigolboche or La Goulue.

CHAPTER 7 / THE CANCAN TODAY

THERE IS SOMETHING ABOUT THE LIBERATED FRENCH ATTITUDE TO SEX THAT HAS appealed to foreigners, especially those in northern Europe, and latterly in America, for generations. The cancan has become symbolic of this attitude, even though, by many people's standards of what constitutes sexy entertainment, it is somewhat tame. But the image of 'Gay Paree' pre-dates the cancan and goes back at least as far as the peace of Amiens in 1802 between Britain and France. At this time British men visiting the French capital were surprised and delighted to encounter young women in extremely scanty versions of the Empire-line dresses then in fashion. Stories of topless and see-through versions of these outfits may have been exaggerated, as may the extent of the 'services' offered by these women, but as always people were prepared to believe the most shocking stories.[1] The idea of Paris as a pleasure city was reinforced by the vast array of unofficial 'guides' to the French capital published in the nineteenth and early twentieth centuries and has been sustained by the major cabaret venues which provide shows with a degree of nudity and eroticism which would not be tolerated in the mainstream in other countries.

The French seem to be relaxed about sex or sexiness in a way that other nationalities are not, although appearances may be deceptive. Certainly there is widespread use in English-speaking countries of 'French' to denote 'sexy': French knickers; the 'French maid'; French kissing; 'French letter' (it is of course ironic that the French equivalent of the latter is *la capote anglaise*); and the international popularity of French actresses like Brigitte Bardot in the 1950s and Béatrice Dalle more recently is more to do with their sex appeal than classical notions of beauty. Introducing the cancan to London in the 1860s, music-hall proprietor Charles Morton was aware that to prefix the name of the dance with the word 'French' would leave his audience in no doubt that what they were about to witness was in some way spicy or titillating. The continuing usage of the two-word combination 'French Cancan' in Paris is a recognition of this foreign view of what used to be termed in the satirical magazines of the 1850s and 1860s the *danse nationale de France*. Today it is obviously more important to the French that other nationalities have acknowledged their liberated morality, and the cancan has a significant historical role in this respect.

The cancan came to be regarded as the epitome of French naughtiness and was frequently criticised by moralists. When it first appeared it was condemned for its 'indecorous' movements and 'indecent' bodily contact between the sexes, and because it was liable to reveal women's underwear, legs and sometimes even their 'private parts'. Later, its associations with prostitution brought fresh criticism, and even when it became professionalised it was attacked for lewd exhibitionism, for its exploitation of impressionable young women or for the unacceptably open demonstration of sexuality by the dancers. More recently it has come under fire for being degrading and sexist, although such a view has little currency in France where 'political correctness' is hardly known as a concept.

How much political correctness has validity and how much it is really old-fashioned morality in a new guise is difficult to say, especially with regard to the cancan. The French may be admired in some quarters for their liberal attitudes, but they are also castigated by feminists abroad for their attitudes to women and sex. But does this seem a great deal different from the position of moralists in London more than one hundred years ago? Wiry Sal's performances were much criticised, but in the main the cancan in London was viewed as in better taste than the Parisian version because it was performed in more modest dress. John Hollingshead was not alone in admiring Finette's performance in *Mabille in London* and defending it as superior to the cancan at the real Bal Mabille. A correspondent of the London magazine *The Mask*, "A Humorous and Fantastic Review of the Month", saw Finette at the Lyceum and remarked that "we cannot say we saw anything to hurt sensitive people beyond what applies to general ballets". Referring to the cancan as seen in Paris, the writer observed that "there is a difference in a dance performed in male costume, and the same, much exaggerated, danced by a woman in ordinary petticoats, which from their length suggest, when raised for the free elevation of the leg, what even short ballet-skirts do not hint at". Apparently oblivious of the fact that Finette had made her name at the Mabille, he referred to the "gross" exhibitions at the famous dancing gardens "exercised by savages, whose only idea of wit lies in indecency".[2]

Something of this intolerance of the style of Parisian nightlife remains today in English-speaking countries. Prudery dictates that nothing like the semi-erotic spectaculars of Paris exists in Britain, North America, Australia or New Zealand. This also partly explains why so many British dancers have ambitions to work in Paris. As one of the Moulin Rouge's Doriss Girls told the magazine *Marie Claire*, in Britain "it's out-and-out sex shows or nothing". The Moulin Rouge show "could never work back home", she added.[3] Of course, there are "out-and-out sex shows" in Paris too, but they are not mainstream entertainment. The exception may be the Crazy Horse revue, which is considerably more risqué than any of the other *spectacles*. Significantly, Jean Trocher, writing at the end of the 1950s, saw the advent of the Crazy Horse as a threat to traditional Parisian culture, and particularly the cancan. He described striptease as "Anti-Cancan" and said that many intelligent Frenchmen would regard it as a sign of "serious decline" if striptease became popular. For Trocher, this American import was "the opposite of what until recently one understood as the more refined eroticism, an eroticism in which French taste was universally known to be competent". By way of clarification, he added that "French eroticism has always gone hand-in-hand with a great deal of humour and wit".

To be fair, it must be said that the Crazy Horse revue is not devoid of humour, but this may support Trocher's argument insofar as it shows that even striptease is susceptible to being transformed by the peculiarly French form of eroticism which he described. He was of course putting the case for the cancan, which he regarded as epitomising French eroticism and it is true that the cancan is nothing if not a fun dance—at least for spectators and, for the most part, the performers. He maintained that striptease was the product of a puritanical culture, "a decked-out speculation upon the desires of men who either cannot, or can only with a bad conscience, be erotic". He said that there was no link between the cancan and puritanism and that the cancan was essentially French, "particularly so, as the French rarely suffer a bad conscience over eroticism".[4] British ballet dancer Alison Smith has confessed that dancing the cancan made her feel "tarty", but she admitted that this was probably because of the "middle-class attitudes" that prevail in Britain, so there is something in what Trocher said.

It seems likely that a puritanical culture was at the root of the campaign in Whitehorse, Canada, in 1992 against the cancan dancers of the 'Sourdough Rendezvous' by the local newspaper editor. Peter Lesniak, writing in his *Yukon News*, said that it was time to "can the can-can dancers". "When women lift their skirts and flaunt their fannies for leering men, no matter how good-naturedly it's done, they do their sex a grave disservice. They undermine years of hard work by the feminist movement," he continued.[5] Lesniak was completely ignoring the cancan's feminist credentials and this was reflected in

FIG. 82. The Frantic Follies revue in the former Gold Rush town of Whitehorse, northwest Canada. These dancers were the centre of a series of acrimonious incidents in 1992 when a local newspaper editor tried to get their performances banned. *Yukon Government Photo.*

some of the letters of protest his editorial provoked. Many of the correspondents were clearly enraged by his comments, but one which took a calmer, more reasoned approach wrote:

Women (and men, as the case may be) do other women a great disservice by not acknowledging the myriad of ways that women become or feel empowered. The hard work done by feminism often goes by the wayside because feminism is, itself, often so judgmental and ill-equipped, theoretically and practically, to accept women's differences and diversity of women's empowerment strategies.[6]

Certainly the cancan has great power and its significance as a feminist assertion of sexuality should not be underestimated, not simply from a historical viewpoint. Clare Parker's troupe, based in Norfolk, England, were criticised after they appeared on television in a series about modern feminism: "One write-up said you can't profess to be a feminist and wave your frilly bottom in the air. Well, can't you? I can. I mean, surely being a feminist means that you have the same rights as everybody else. If I intend to exploit my sexuality I should be free to do it." The television programme showed the boyfriend of a dancer in the troupe complaining about her performing for other men, while the girl herself defended her right to do whatever she liked.

The historical roots of the cancan provide other excuses for disparaging it. In the 1890s, the bourgeoisie were attracted by the easy-going culture of the working class but on the other hand were repelled by it. The thought of being unencumbered by the neurotic obsession of having to keep up appearances was very appealing, but at the same time it was a sign of a lack of education and refinement to behave like their 'inferiors'. The cancan was not subtle, especially when performed by La Goulue, and the middle classes were in a dilemma over whether it was acceptable to enjoy it. It was fun and it was exciting, but was it not a sign of loose morality or even an open attack on middle-class values? Something of this class prejudice survives today: the cancan is viewed as belonging to more sordid surroundings than other forms of dance, despite its incorporation in a number of successful ballets. It may feature in well-known operettas and musicals, but these are also regarded as 'popular' entertainment, far removed in terms of refinement from grand opera or even the lighter works of Mozart. If you find the cancan enjoyable, it may still be unwise to admit it in polite circles.

The cancan is a dance of freedom, as Rigolboche recognised, and not just from a working-class or a feminist viewpoint. It retains its anarchic image, even if the element of improvisation has largely disappeared, and it is imbued with an eroticism which few dances can lay claim to, certainly in the West. Dance purists may find it offensive for these reasons, but the cancans found in the ballets of Massine have brought the dance into the bounds of respectability and there is certainly less opposition within the dance world to this particular form of dancing than might be thought. This is partly because professional dancers are aware that the history of ballet is littered with as much opprobrium as that heaped on the cancan, all female stage dancers in the early part of the nineteenth century being regarded as little better than prostitutes, and that it was only towards the end of the century that this stigma began to be lifted.

The cancan is appealing to most men, but there is something about it that also makes it as enjoyable (in a different way) for women in the audience. They can admire the cancan dancers for what they do, even if they object to other dance acts. According to Sue Wilson, a former cancan dancer and choreographer, when her girls performed in bikinis some women in the audience actually turned their backs in protest, but when it came to the cancan they lightened up considerably. It is the humour in the dance which makes the difference, and separates it from so-called erotic spectacles. Star of the Moulin Rouge Jacqueline Alcock said: "It is perhaps the only dance in which the onlooker becomes part of the show, part of the theatre and part of its world of magic." The dancers seem clearly to be enjoying themselves in their exuberant display; laughs, smiles and shrieks of excitement are as much a part of the cancan as anything else. Then there is the suggestive contrast of the demure—the long, Victorian-style skirts and blouses or dresses, with the provocative and abandoned—the way those skirts are lifted up to show what should be hidden, and the way the dancers leap about in a totally unrestrained manner. The overall effect for those watching is a feeling that the women know that what they are doing is naughty, but nice, sexy, but harmless.

So there is definitely something about the cancan that attracts both men and women, but it would be less than frank to deny that some male spectators find the dance erotically stimulating. In the 1950s, Jean Trocher commented that the costumes "are consciously aimed at the arousing of fantasies, wishes and desires. . . . [I]t is made unmistakably clear to the male onlookers where to look, what to think, and what to wish".[7] Today in Paris there are usually male performers (wearing trousers of course) doing acrobatics with the girls, but it is still the girls who are the centrepiece of the show, and few people when asked would regard the cancan as anything but a women's dance. So how much truth is there in the charge that women dancing the cancan are being exploited for the purposes of male entertainment? This was an accusation levelled against the Moulin Rouge one hundred years ago, when feminism was in its infancy. As always, it depends on your point of view, but perhaps it might be worth taking note of the opinions of some of those involved in the dance in more recent years.

Bridget Crowley danced at the Folies Bergère in the late 1950s and views the cancan as something of a feminist statement. She regards it as having been more "bawdy" than "sexy". "I think those women [in the 1890s] knew exactly what they were doing." One sign that there is little coercion needed today to encourage women to dance the cancan is the large number of amateur groups performing the dance around the world. A member of Clare Parker's troupe said: "Women sometimes say what we do is degrading, but we don't agree. We enjoy performing. . . . We're not trying to provoke reactions from blokes."[8] A dancer in another Norfolk-based cancan troupe also suggested that dancing the cancan was as much about pleasing yourself as entertaining: "When I dress up in my cancan gear, I feel like a completely different person. When I do the

FIG. 83. La Goulue 'clones' representing the Moulin Rouge in a veteran vehicle rally through the streets of Paris in the 1950s. The famous night-club had finally recognised the importance of the cancan in attracting customers, and it has been the climax to its nightly *spectacle* ever since. *Popperfoto.*

dance, I feel uplifted—there is a real feeling of freedom, even when I am just practising on my own."[9] Anne Holmes, choreographer of the Golden Heart Dancers, a successful amateur group in Fairbanks, Alaska, also highlights the enjoyment of the cancan. "The comment we hear most is that it looks like we're having so much fun while we're performing". Even Alison Smith acknowledged that, despite her reservations, the cancan is "tremendous fun if you're in a good mood".

It is fun, but at the Moulin Rouge they take it very seriously in rehearsals. One dancer told *Marie Claire* that on her first day there "we had to kick our right legs for a solid two hours. My right thigh swelled to double its size."[10] Peter Wallace, who choreographs the show at the Nouvelle Eve, says that more acrobatics have crept into the cancan in the last twenty years, but all the effort involved is worth it when it comes to performing because it is so *"agréable à faire"*. The audience reaction is very positive and very important for the dancers, he adds. He acknowledges that the cancan brings more than its fair share of injuries. Alison Smith once strained her groin performing the *grand écart* on an unsuitably narrow strip in front of the orchestra pit during a performance of Offenbach's *Bluebeard* and feels she has never fully recovered.

The cancan may take its toll, but there are many dancers around the world whose ambition is to work at one of the famous Paris cabarets. Another dancer at the Moulin Rouge told *Marie Claire*: "The Paris shows are so different from anything we have in Britain. My mother runs a ballet school and since I was a child I'd heard all about the Moulin. I came to see the show in 1989 and loved the beautiful girls, the wonderful costumes, and I knew I wanted to work here." Of course many who go for auditions are disappointed. Star of the show at the Moulin Rouge, Jacqueline Alcock, was auditioned in the Pineapple Dance Studio in London. Madame Doris Haug, the *maîtresse de ballet* at the cabaret, put her through a ballet combination and then a series of cancan movements to test her suppleness before offering her a job—in the event, not as a cancan dancer, but as a *danseuse-nue* (topless). The two roles are usually kept completely separate at the Moulin Rouge, and both types of performer get paid the same rate. Despite the glamorous image of Parisian nightlife, auditions are not always held in the most salubrious of environments. Bridget Crowley was less than impressed with her audition for the Folies Bergère. She remembers going through her paces in a flat, which she describes as "really, really sleazy", somewhere not far from London's Oxford Street.

The five main *specialités* of the cancan are the *battement* (high kick), the *rond de jambe* (fast rotary movement of the lower leg, with the knee raised), the *port d'armes* (rapidly rotating on one leg, with other leg raised to a vertical position and held around the ankle with one hand, the other arm and hand being outstretched), the *roue* (cartwheel) and the finale *grand écart* (flying or jump splits).[11] Because these steps and variations on them have to be performed during an energetic routine while manipulating heavy skirts, the dancers themselves need to be skilful and very fit if they are also to give the impression of being carefree and fun-loving at the same time. Highly trained dancers, often those with ballet training, are employed by today's Paris nightclubs, and at the

Moulin Rouge and the Nouvelle Eve they are mostly British. Peter Wallace says that, although the Nouvelle Eve does recruit dancers from elsewhere, those in Britain can be relied on to be of high standard. It may seem ironic, but British dancing schools seem able to train dancers ideal for the Paris *spectacles* despite there being no equivalent style of show in Britain itself.

The tradition of recruiting ballet-trained British dancers for Paris shows stretches back a long time. Bridget Crowley remembers that in the 1950s some of the dancers at the Nouvelle Eve were from the Royal Ballet in London, and she was trained at Rambert. Many of the dancers in Paris in the 1950s were from Britain, including the Jackson Girls at the Folies Bergère and the Bluebells at the Lido, but there were also many from local schools. At the Drap d'Or and the other more intimate night-clubs, less popular with foreign tourists, most of the dancers were French. Another reason for British dancers' popularity is that they are thought to be taller on average than French girls, and it was this that provided the Bluebells with their initial impact in the 1930s. The Doriss girls are expected to be at least five feet seven inches tall, which is indicative of the change that has taken place to the cancan in the last one hundred years.[12] The Moulin Rouge cancan was made famous worldwide by the short, squat figure of La Goulue, whose main attraction was her anarchic, provocative, spontaneous performance. She would contrast startlingly with today's tall, slim dancers who are drilled for hours so that they can execute a precisely choreographed cancan routine, characterised by unison high kicks.

In a sense, the cancan can be over-choreographed, and really precision dancing has no place in it. It also does not pay to make it *too* acrobatic, and some of the amateur groups succeed in providing a saucier, more suggestive performance than their professional counterparts because they take it at a slightly slower pace. There must be something about the cancan which attracts the amateur performer, because there are so many of them around the world, performing at French theme nights, Wild West shows, Gold Rush revues, charity events, private parties and open air events and carnivals. The roots of the cancan are in public dance halls and dancing gardens and so it seems appropriate that the dance is still performed by women for the love of the dance, rather than it being solely a professional activity, even though the amateur dancers today perform something more like the professional stage dance than the original cancan of the 1830s. Amateurs often have some professional training and they still have to be fit, yet they apparently do not need to be young. The Golden Heart Dancers have a fifty-year-old in their ranks, who in some ways outperforms the younger dancers "flirting with an entire room at once, men and women", according to Anne Holmes. One movement that the amateur dancer can cheat with in the cancan is the splits: a variation, known as the American splits, in which the back leg remains bent, with the knee forward, is easily hidden by the voluminous skirt.

The professional shows in Paris which feature the cancan—at the Moulin Rouge, the Nouvelle Eve and Paradis Latin—take different approaches with their treatment of the dance. At the Moulin Rouge, it forms the climax of a tableau built around the characters portrayed by Toulouse-Lautrec, including a dancer as La Goulue, costumed as for his famous poster, except that she wears short frilly knickers rather than bloomers. Jane Avril is played by the star of the show (at the time of writing), Jacqueline Alcock, wearing the famous 'snake' dress from one of the artist's paintings. Unfortunately, she does not dance but simply sings a couple of songs from old Montmartre. Despite the traditions of the Moulin Rouge, the emphasis today is on large-scale spectacular, and there are often thirty or more dancers on stage at one time performing the cancan. The two other cabarets are on a more intimate scale. The Nouvelle Eve has endeavoured to create a more Parisian-style of music-hall entertainment over the past few years, and in doing so has attracted more French customers. Peter Wallace, who trained at the Moulin Rouge and was the male dance captain there, says he respects the technique of the dance of one hundred years ago in his choreography for the Nouvelle Eve, and as a result his cancan has a more traditional feel than that of its better-known neighbour. In a small venue like this, performers can get greater rapport with the audience, who clap along with the music during the cancan. Naturally they demand an encore, which is duly provided. The Paradis Latin's show is also regarded as Parisian in flavour, with its attractive cancan forming the climax.

Although the dance is seen as being typically French, its international popularity has been crucial in sustaining it. It is no coincidence that the Moulin Rouge opened its doors in the same year as the Paris Exhibition of 1889, when numerous foreign visitors were in the French capital. This helped to spread the fame of the dance far and wide. But it was the Bal Tabarin which established the tradition of the French Cancan in the 1920s and which the Moulin Rouge, the Nouvelle Eve and the Paradis Latin now imitate in their shows. Bridget Crowley remembers hearing people talk about the Tabarin when she was working at the Folies Bergère in the 1950s. It had relatively recently closed, and there were some who still longed for it to reopen. Pierre Mariel, in his book *Paris Revue*, recalls meeting an old man at the Lido who was unimpressed with the show there, comparing it unfavourably with the Tabarin. But he said: "perhaps it is not the loss of the Tabarin, the Tabarin of Bosc and Sandrini, which I mourn, but the loss of my youth". According to Mariel, he appeared to be "surrounded by enchanted phantoms, touching and caressing him. He hears, it seems, the *froufrou* of the petticoats of the cancan dancers."[13]

Soon after the demise of this once great cabaret, many of its competitors began to present their dinner shows featuring the French Cancan, and in the 1950s and 1960s you could see the cancan at the Lido, the Moulin Rouge, the Folies Bergère, the Nouvelle Eve, the Alcazar and many others. Bridget Crowley performed the cancan at the Drap d'Or, where the clientele were predominantly French. One interesting phenomenon of the 1950s was that male dancers once more came into their own and were recognised as individuals. Starring at both the Drap d'Or and the Folies Bergère was the charismatic Roger Stéfani: "He was incredible—his legs just went up round his ears," said Crowley. Roger used to be employed by several different cabarets at the same time: "He would come in literally 10 minutes before, go on, dance and be gone. There would be a cab waiting for him to go on to the next one." At the Moulin

The CONCENTRATION OF A PROLIFIC FUND MANAGER IS NOT EASILY BROKEN.

No one concentrates harder on investment management than Prolific – after all, that's all we do. Perhaps that's why we have such a strong, long-term investment record.

But why take our word for it? For an objective view of our track record, contact your independent financial adviser. However, if you don't have one, simply call the:

IFA Promotion Line on Freephone 0800 387 946

for a list of independent financial advisers in your area. Alternatively, complete the coupon.

Please send me details about the range of Prolific's unit trusts & PEPs
Please return this coupon to Prolific Unit Trust Managers Ltd. FREEPOST London EC4B 4JY

NAME

ADDRESS

POSTCODE

Prolific CONCENTRATING ON INVESTMENT

Please remember that past performance is not necessarily a guide to the future. The price of units and the income from them may go down as well as up. Exchange rates may also cause the value of underlying overseas investments to go down or up

FIG. 84. The cancan is often used in advertising, often to sell French products but not necessarily. This, for example, is an advertisement for an investment management company found in the business pages of a major newspaper. *Gered Mankowitz/The Harwood Company.*

Rouge in the 1950s, the equally supple Jean-Louis Bert was the principal male dancer. Both these dancers no doubt felt proud to be following in the footsteps of the legendary Valentin-le-Désossé. There were female soloists in the Paris of the 1950s, but it was the men who stood out and are remembered, because there were so few of them. Now, there are many more men taking part in the cancan at the three cabarets. This is sign of the times, as today male dancers are expected to be looser than their predecessors, and so it is not unusual to find them able to do the high kicks and splits required for the dance. As a consequence, they have slipped back into anonymity, along with the women.

Apart from the familiar cancan 'steps', what are the essential features of the dance today? Yes, it should be sexy—that is its *raison d'être*—although, according to Sue Wilson, today it is never shocking. "Not many people know the origins of the cancan, so most people enjoy it for what it is; it's lively, noisy and they enjoy the skirts and the stockings and suspenders. I don't think you'll offend anyone with the cancan." Clare Parker deplores cancan performances by girls who are too young: "Young girls from ballet school haven't got a clue about sexuality, and if you're going to dance this type of thing, you've got to get this across." It might also be said that the notion of pre-pubescent girls being expected to perform a provocative dance is decidedly suspect. The cancan's reputation was built on its sensualism and its cheeky gestures, and a certain maturity is needed to carry these off successfully. Perhaps the most risqué gesture in the cancan, and the one that audiences seem to enjoy the most, is the La Goulue party trick, when the dancers turn their backs, bend over and hoist their skirts over their heads revealing their frilly bottoms. The idea that the cancan was commonly danced without knickers is still around, and Clare Parker's troupe were once offered "a lot of money" to dance like this at a private party. They refused, less on moral grounds than because this is not what the cancan is about. It needs to be sexy, but not crude. Furthermore, without knickers a dancer would be less in control and the power of the dance would be undermined, leaving her feeling vulnerable.

Relentless movement and energy are still essential to the cancan and important to this overall effect is the music; unsurprisingly, Offenbach remains the predominant choice. Parker finds the famous galop from *Orpheus in the Underworld* inspiring: "It still excites me, even though I have heard it endlessly over the last 13 years." With many cancan routines lasting ten minutes or more, other Offenbach tunes are used, together with Strauss polkas and galops and other cancan music such as that of Cole Porter. Some routines build up slowly, perhaps using the famous 'I Love Paris' from *Can-Can*, with the girls performing delicate balletic movements before launching into the frenetic cancan itself.

Much of the essence of the dance comes from the costume. The cancan is about underwear at its most beautiful and erotic: the lace, the ribbons, the bloomers or frilly French knickers, the stockings, the garters or suspenders, are all as important to the dance as nudity is (ultimately) to striptease. For the best effect, white or pale-coloured underwear is contrasted with deeper-coloured dresses. Black stockings, or possibly fishnet black stockings, are also essential. If tights or stockings in any other colour are worn something of the fundamental sexiness of the cancan is lost. Cancan dresses today tend to be made of lighter-weight material than those of one hundred years ago, even if they superficially resemble them; many dancers today are amazed that their antecedents could perform such an energetic dance wearing such heavy clothing. Footwear varies from ballet shoes to knee-high boots, but the most attractive are the familiar ankle boots.

The cancan is often different when performed in cabaret from when it appears in operetta, musicals or ballet. The latter tend to keep to a more traditional style, fitting the period in which the works are set, whereas the cabarets feel able to experiment a little more. But essentially the dance remains very similar to that of the 1920s, and the basic movements would still be recognised by La Goulue if she were alive today. If a visitor to Paris feels short-changed after seeing the French Cancan at its 'home', the Moulin Rouge, it is most likely because the faster, flashier, bigger version does not appeal in the same way as the more subtle and sensual performances seen in the past, provided by a much smaller *corps de ballet*. But it has to be acknowledged that some visitors want drama and spectacle, and the Moulin Rouge provides it. The smaller cabarets in Paris are a better choice for anyone who wants to see a more 'typically French' cancan.

Dancers, choreographers and theatre managers all agree that the cancan is the one dance in the repertoire of variety shows that is guaranteed to enliven the most jaded of audiences. It has an infectious quality which engenders a feeling of *joie de vivre* like nothing else, and it is this quality which has ensured the dance's survival as an image of pleasure and fun, recognised throughout the world. It has now been established as part of the Parisian entertainment scene for more than seventy years, and it is also performed regularly in cabaret and revues in many countries. Operettas, musicals and ballets featuring the cancan still appear frequently in the repertoire of professional companies and many an amateur musical production is enlivened by a cancan in the final act. 'Old-time' music hall and variety shows would not be complete without it. Directors of period films continue to use troupes of dancers with frilly petticoats and black stockings as a convenient device with which to fix the action in Paris, the 'naughty nineties' or the Wild West. The famous works of John Huston, Jean Renoir and others are often broadcast on television, as are some of the hundreds of other films in which the cancan appears. It is a hugely popular image in advertising—for French holidays, food and wine, cognac and, less obviously, for products as diverse as washing powder and computers. It is essential to 'French' evenings celebrating Bastille Day or the arrival of Beaujolais Nouveau. In short, it seems to be everywhere.

But will it last forever? Sue Wilson says: "I've found as a dancer and choreographer that dance crazes come and go, but the cancan has remained." Peter Wallace of the Nouvelle Eve has no doubts: "As long as Paris exists, the French Cancan will be here!"

NOTES AND BIBLIOGRAPHY

NOTES

INTRODUCTION / THE 'NAUGHTY NINETIES'

1. David Thomson, *Europe since Napoleon* (London: Penguin Books, 1966), pp. 395–96.
2. Ivor Guest, 'The Heyday of the Cancan', in W. H. Holden, ed., *Second Empire Medley*, (London: British Technical and General Press, 1952), p. 11.
3. Pierre Mariel and Jean Trocher, *Paris Cancan* (London: Charles Skilton, 1961), p. 27.
4. Eugène Rodrigues (Erastène Ramiro), *Cours de Danse fin de siècle*, quoted in Raoul Charbonnel, *La Danse* (Paris: Garniers Frères, n.d.), p. 285.
5. Ivor Guest, 'Bal Mabille', *Ballet* (London), February 1947.
6. Ivor Guest, 'The Opera Balls', *Ballet* (London), March 1950.
7. Siegfried Kracauer, *Offenbach and the Paris of his Time* (London: Constable, 1937), p. 29.
8. Aileen Ribeiro, *Dress and Morality* (London: B. T. Batsford, 1986), pp. 129–130.
9. Michael Harrison, *A Fanfare of Strumpets* (London: W. H. Allen, 1971), p. 38.
10. James Laver, *Taste and Fashion* (London: George Harrap & Co., 1937), p. 64. According to Laver: "Without wishing in any way to accuse the entire mid-Victorian world of shoe fetishism, one can hardly resist the conclusion that the erotic significance of boots and shoes received partial encouragement from the invention of the crinoline".
11. Nancy Bradfield, *Costume in Detail: Women's Dress 1730–1930* (London: George G. Harrap & Co., 1981), p. 249.
12. Ribeiro, *Dress and Morality*, p. 120 and pp. 148–49. Ribeiro writes that drawers were introduced in the Empire period only "after prolonged opposition" because of the association with prostitutes "and—this was almost the same in the eyes of many—professional dancers". Ribeiro points out that when drawers were shown in fashion magazines towards the end of the nineteenth century, they were usually drawn folded up so that it was not possible to see that they had legs. She also refers to a book by Pierre Dufay, *Le Pantalon Feminin*, published in 1916, "an erotic excursion into the delights of female underwear", in which he devotes an entire chapter to discussion of the open or closed type of knickers, concluding that the open type could be seen as inviting a sexual encounter. She comments that part of the excitement of the cancan lay in its promise of a sight of this titillating underwear, as well as the frilled petticoats.
13. Ibid., p. 135.
14. Roy Busby, *British Music Hall* (London and New Hampshire: Paul Elek, 1976), p. 39.
15. Elizabeth Ewing, *Dress and Undress* (London: B. T. Batsford, 1978), pp. 105–06.
16. C. Willett and Phyllis Cunnington, *The History of Underclothes* (London: Faber & Faber, 1981), pp. 124–25.
17. Ewing, *Dress and Undress*, p. 83.
18. Willett and Cunnington, *The History of Underclothes*, pp. 128–29.
19. Laver, *Taste and Fashion*, p. 175.
20. Ribeiro, *Dress and Morality*, p. 149.
21. Emil Zola, *Nana*, tr. George Holden (London: Penguin, 1972), p. 155.
22. See Elinor Glyn, *Visits of Elizabeth* (London: Duckworth and Co., 1900), pp. 74–75. Elizabeth's French companions find too few rooms available at an inn in rural France and are shocked at the suggestion that married couples may have to share.
23. Deborah Gorham, *The Victorian Girl and the Feminine Ideal* (London: Croom Helm, 1982), p. 54.
24. Eugen Weber, *France Fin de Siècle* (Cambridge: Harvard University Press, 1986), pp. 59–60.
25. Ibid., pp. 88–9.

26. Theodore Zeldin, *France, 1848–1945: Anxiety and Hypocrisy* (Oxford: Oxford University Press, 1981), p. 181.
27. Anne de Margerie, Marianne Théry and Dominique Brisson, eds., *Le temps Toulouse-Lautrec* (Paris: Editions de la Réunion des Musées Nationaux/Textuel, 1991), pp. 66–68.
28. Ibid., pp. 86–87.
29. Anonymous, *Paris by Night* (London: Rozez & Co., 1871), p. 27.
30. Bernard Denvir, *Toulouse-Lautrec* (London: Thames & Hudson, 1991), pp. 66–67.
31. Marianne Ryan, ed., *Toulouse-Lautrec* (London: South Bank Centre, 1991), p. 407.
32. Charles Castle, *The Folies Bergère* (London: Methuen, 1982), pp. 37–38.
33. Anonymous, *Paris by Night*, p. 1.
34. Denvir, *Toulouse-Lautrec*, p. 142.
35. Ibid., p. 142.
36. Ronald Pearsall, *The Worm in the Bud* (London: Pelican, 1971), pp. 50–51.
37. Gertrude Aretz, *The Elegant Woman*, tr. James Laver (London: George Harrap & Co., 1932), pp. 215–16.
38. Weber, *France Fin de Siècle*, p. 92.
39. Kracauer, *Offenbach and the Paris of his Time*, p. 205. Kracauer writes that it was almost impossible to distinguish between high-society women and the *demi-mondaines* in public places because the former copied the styles of the latter. He points to the artificiality of crinoline and cosmetics, which both classes adopted.
40. Anonymous, *Paris by Night*, p. 4.
41. Joanna Richardson, *The Courtesans* (London: Weidenfeld and Nicholson, 1967), pp. 6–7.
42. *Le Figaro* (Paris), 2 April 1857.
43. Ivor Guest, 'Cora Pearl plays Cupid', *Ballet* (London), May 1948.
44. Weber, *France Fin de Siècle*, p. 81.
45. José Shercliff, *Jane Avril of the Moulin Rouge* (London: Jarrolds,1952), pp. 55–59.
46. Weber, *France Fin de Siècle*, p. 97.
47. Ribeiro, *Dress and Morality*, p. 134; Sir Sacheverell Sitwell, *La Vie Parisienne* (London: Faber and Faber, 1937), pp. 32–33. Ribeiro claims that the courtesans eagerly took up the new fashion "which outlined the bust and the shape of the thighs", but, if Sitwell is to be believed, this was not a universal feeling.
48. Harrison, *Fanfare of Strumpets*, pp. 9–11, pp. 21–22.
49. Weber, *France Fin de Siècle*, pp. 90 and 92.
50. Ribeiro *Dress and Morality*, pp. 142 and 147.
51. Bernard Grun, *Gold and Silver: The Life and Times of Franz Lehár* (London: W. H. Allen, 1970), p. 149.
52. Mariel and Trocher, *Paris Cancan*, pp. 34–37.
53. Weber, *France Fin de Siècle*, pp. 32–40.
54. See chapter 2.
55. De Margerie, Théry and Brisson, eds., *Le temps Toulouse-Lautrec*, p. 11.
56. Weber, *France Fin de Siècle*, pp. 164–65 and note on p. 171.
57. Castle, *The Folies Bergère*, p. 19.
58. A copy of *The London Cancan* can be seen in the British Library.
59. J. H. Billington, *Mikhailovsky and Russian Populism* (Oxford: Oxford University Press 1958), p. 76.

CHAPTER 1 / HOW IT ALL BEGAN

1. Guest, 'The Heyday of the Cancan', p. 10; 'Des Chercheurs et Curieux', *L'Intermédiaire* (Paris), 25 April 1891, column 280. Guest describes the early cancan as "a veneer of improvisation, in fact, accompanied by abundant gestures and a violent, unrestrained activity, that was superimposed upon the popular dances of the time". In 'Des Cher-

cheurs et Curieux', a correspondent writes that the cancan and the galop appear to have been amalgamated in the 1830s or 1840s. Indeed, the cancan was often referred to as a galop—for example, Offenbach's *galop infernal* in *Orpheus in the Underworld*.

2. 'Des Chercheurs et Curieux', column 278. A correspondent describes how in the eighteenth century *"les débardeurs et mariniers, porteurs et gens de la Halle"* used to dance something like the *chahut* or the cancan.

3. Ibid. The same correspondent writes that the students imported the dance into the Latin Quarter after 1830. See also Gaston Vuillier, *A History of Dancing* (London: William Heinemann, 1898), p. 319.

4. A. H. Franks, *Social Dance: A Short History* (London: Routledge and Kegan Paul, 1963), p. 134.

5. Derek and Julia Parker, *The Natural History of the Chorus Girl* (Newton Abbot and London: David and Charles, 1975), p. 29.

6. Vuillier, *A History of Dancing*, p. 337. Vuillier does not use the word 'cancan' to describe the dancing of La Goulue and her contemporaries.

7. Oscar Bloch and Walther von Wartburg, *Dictionnaire Étymologique de la Langue Française* (Paris: Presses Universitaires de France, 1994), pp. 103–04, entry on *cancan*.

8. Guest, 'The Heyday of the Cancan', p. 11.

9. *Collier's Encyclopedia*, vol. 7 (New York: Crowell-Collier & Macmillan), p. 691, says that the cancan imitates the fandango.

10. Curt Sachs, *World History of the Dance* (New York: Norton & Co., 1937), p. 441.

11. Ibid., p. 390. Sachs views this as "obviously a fertility dance".

12. Philippe de Vigneulles, *Chroniques de Metz*, quoted in 'Des Chercheurs et Curieux', columns 283–84.

13. Castil-Blaze (François Henri Joseph Blaze), *L'Académie Impériale de Musique: Histoire littéraire, musicale, choréographique de 1645 à 1855* (Paris 1855), p. 269.

14. F. de Ménil, *Histoire de la Danse* (Paris: Alcide, Picard & Kaan éditeurs, n.d.), pp. 207–08.

15. Ivor Guest, *Jules Perrot* (London: Dance Books, 1984), pp. 5–13.

16. Kracauer, *Offenbach and the Paris of his Time*, p. 28.

17. Vuillier, *A History of Dancing*, p. 319.

18. Jacques Boulenger, *Les Dandies*, quoted in Francis Gribble, 'The Origin of the Can-Can', *The Dancing Times* (London), April 1933, pp. 19–22.

19. Ludwig Rellstab, *Paris im Frühjahr (1843)*, quoted in Kracauer, *Offenbach and the Paris of his Time*, p. 29.

20. Guest, 'The Opera Balls'.

21. Guest, 'The Heyday of the Cancan', p. 17.

22. Vuillier, *A History of Dancing*, p. 310.

23. *Grande Larousse Encyclopédie*, vol. 2 (Paris 1960), p. 571.

24. Vuillier, *A History of Dancing*, pp. 309–10.

25. Gaston Robert, *Les Mystères du Bal Bullier*, quoted in André Warnod, *Les Bals de Paris* (Paris: Les Editions G. Crès & Cie, 1922), p. 13.

26. Vuillier, *A History of Dancing*, p. 311.

27. Guest, 'Bal Mabille'.

28. Mariel and Trocher, *Paris Cancan*, pp. 11–13.

29. Vuillier, *A History of Dancing*, p. 313.

30. Mariel and Trocher, *Paris Cancan*, p. 13.

31. Guest, 'Bal Mabille'.

32. Mariel and Trocher, *Paris Cancan*, p. 14.

33. Warnod, *Les Bals de Paris*, p. 14.

34. Mariel and Trocher, *Paris Cancan*, pp. 14–15.

35. Ibid., p. 16.

36. Françoise Moser, *Vie et Aventures de Céleste Mogador* (Paris: Éditions Albin Michel, 1935), p. 54.
37. Ibid., p. 76.
38. Ibid., p. 76.
39. Jacques Pessis and Jacques Crépineau, *The Moulin Rouge* (Stroud, Gloucestershire: Alan Sutton Publishing, 1990), p. 14.
40. Richardson, *The Courtesans*, pp. 206–08.
41. Pessis and Crépineau, *The Moulin Rouge*, p. 14.
42. Mariel and Trocher, *Paris Cancan*, p. 19.
43. Guest, 'The Heyday of the Cancan', p. 18.
44. Harrison, *A Fanfare of Strumpets*, pp. 68–69.
45. Ivor Guest, 'Queens of the Cancan: They Made Paris Gay', *Dance and Dancers* (London), December 1952.
46. Guest, 'The Heyday of the Cancan', p. 19.
47. Rigolboche (Marguerite Badel), *Mémoires* (Paris 1860), p. 85.
48. Anonymous, *A bas Rigolboche* (Paris 1860), p. 38.
49. Guest, 'Queens of the Cancan'.
50. Mariel and Trocher, *Paris Cancan*, p. 14.
51. Finette was probably the first to present a genuine Parisian cancan on the London stage. Charles Morton's introduction of the 'French Cancan' with Hungarian dancers at the Oxford music hall came a few years earlier.
52. John Hollingshead, *My Lifetime*, vol.1 (London: Sampson Low, Marston & Co., 1895), p. 224.
53. Townley Searle, *Sir William Schwenck Gilbert: A Topsy-Turvy Adventure* (London: Alexander-Ouseley, 1931), p. 12.
54. Hollingshead, *My Lifetime*, p. 225.
55. Ivor Guest, *Ballet in Leicester Square* (London: Dance Books, 1992), p. 19.
56. Hollingshead, *My Lifetime*, p. 225. Hollingshead said he had received this information from a friend who was a Foreign Office messenger. However, in *Paris Dansant* (Paris: Théophile Belin, 1898), p. 169, Georges Montorgueil suggests that Finette ended her days as the owner of a dyeing and cleaning shop.
57. *The Era* (London), 27 November 1842.
58. W. MacQueen-Pope, *The Melodies Linger On* (London: W. H. Allen, 1950), p. 118.
59. Guest, *Ballet in Leicester Square*, p. 21.
60. *The Days' Doings* (London), 22 October 1870.
61. John Hollingshead, *The Story of Leicester Square* (London: Simpkin, Marshall, Hamilton, Kent & Co., 1892), p. 68. Hollingshead also commented that the management of the Lyceum Theatre had "prudently arranged to get [the cancan] stamped with a legitimate theatrical stamp by inducing Mr E. T. Smith to stuff it into a pantomime written by Mr W. S. Gilbert".
62. *The Sketch* (London), 30 January 1895.
63. Guest, *Ballet in Leicester Square*, p. 25.
64. John Johnston, *The Lord Chamberlain's Blue Pencil* (London: Hodder and Stoughton, 1990), p. 128.
65. *The Era* (London), 2 March 1845.
66. Guest, 'The Heyday of the Cancan', pp. 19–21.
67. Ibid., pp. 15–16.
68. Franks, *Social Dance*, pp. 133–34. According to Franks, it was almost unacceptable to be regarded as a good dancer in French high society in the 1830s and 1840s. The contrasting energy of the public dance halls provided some impetus for change and the arrival of the polka harnessed this energy "into a less uncontrolled and unseemly direction".

69. Derek and Julia Parker, *The Natural History of the Chorus Girl*, p. 29.
70. Arthur Maria Rabenalt, *Voluptas Ludens* (München-Regensburg: Verlag Die Schaubühne, 1962), p. 244.
71. Guest, 'The Opera Balls'. Guest remarks that the stars of the *bals publics* were seen "capering and contorting themselves in as obscene a manner as they dared under the watchful eye of the ubiquitous *sergent de ville*".
72. Ibid.
73. Harold Scott, *The Early Doors* (London: Nicholson and Watson, 1946), p. 159.
74. Mariel and Trocher, *Paris Cancan*, p. 20.
75. Zola, *Nana*, p. 470.

CHAPTER 2 / FRILLS AND SPILLS IN THE MODERN AGE

1. Mariel and Trocher, *Paris Cancan*, p. 27.
2. Edmond and Jules de Goncourt, *Germinie Lacerteux* (London: Vizetelly & Co., 1887), pp. 95–96.
3. Michel Souvais, *Les Cancans de la Goulue* (Paris: Michel Souvais, 1991), p. 10.
4. Pessis and Crépineau, *The Moulin Rouge*, p. 22.
5. Ibid., p. 23; Mariel and Trocher, *Paris Cancan*, p. 28.
6. Pessis and Crépineau, *The Moulin Rouge*, p. 23.
7. De Margerie, Théry and Brisson, eds., *Le temps Toulouse-Lautrec*, p. 75.
8. Eugène Rodrigues (Erastène Ramiro), *Cours de Danse fin de siècle*, quoted in Charbonnel, *La Danse*, p. 285.
9. Pessis and Crépineau, *The Moulin Rouge*, p. 23.
10. Jacques-Charles, *Cent Ans de Music-Hall* (Geneva, Paris: Editions Jeheber, 1956) p. 230.
11. Valentin's surname was certainly Renaudin, but there appears to be some doubt about his first name. Pessis and Crépineau, in *The Moulin Rouge*, refer to him as Jacques (p. 34), he is Jules in Ryan, ed., *Toulouse-Lautrec* (p. 250) and Denvir refers to him as Etienne (*Toulouse-Lautrec*, p. 750). Montorgueil, in *Paris Dansant* (p. 190), who was writing within a few years of Valentin's stardom at the Moulin Rouge and might have been expected to know, takes no chances and simply calls him M. Renaudin.
12. Montorgueil, *Paris Dansant*, p. 189.
13. Denvir, *Toulouse-Lautrec*, p. 75; Ryan, ed., *Toulouse-Lautrec*, p. 250.
14. Pessis and Crépineau, *The Moulin Rouge*, p. 34.
15. Mariel and Trocher, *Paris Cancan*, p. 31.
16. Walter Sorell, *The Dance through the Ages* (London: Thames and Hudson, 1967), p. 153.
17. Shercliff, *Jane Avril of the Moulin Rouge*, p. 99.
18. Ibid., p. 99.
19. Vuillier, *A History of Dancing*, p. 337.
20. Shercliff, *Jane Avril of the Moulin Rouge*, p. 100.
21. Denvir, *Toulouse-Lautrec*, p. 126.
22. Pessis and Crépineau, *The Moulin Rouge*, p. 27.
23. Shercliff, *Jane Avril of the Moulin Rouge*, p. 31.
24. Ibid., pp. 31 and 41.
25. Ibid., pp. 44–47.
26. Ibid., pp. 50–51.
27. Ibid., pp. 58–59.
28. Ibid., pp. 76–81.
29. Ibid., p. 97.
30. Ibid., p. 92.
31. Ibid., pp. 96–97.
32. De Margerie, Théry and Brisson, eds., *Le temps Toulouse-Lautrec*, p. 71.

33. Shercliff, *Jane Avril of the Moulin Rouge*, p. 100.

34. Mariel and Trocher, *Paris Cancan*, p. 34.

35. Shercliff, *Jane Avril of the Moulin Rouge*, p. 101.

36. Mariel and Trocher, *Paris Cancan*, p. 37.

37. *St Paul's* (London), 15 February 1896, reviewing the visit of the Eglantine Troupe to London's Palace Theatre, reported that Eglantine was "no new comer to us for it will be recollected that the handsome, dark-eyed lady was one of the four nymphs who constituted the 'Nini Patte en l'Air' troupe, who appeared at the then Trafalgar Theatre, and later on at the Palace".

38. Mariel and Trocher, *Paris Cancan*, p.37; Pessis and Crépineau, *The Moulin Rouge*, p. 29.

39. Eugène Rodrigues (Erastène Ramiro), *Cours de Danse fin de siècle*, quoted in Charbonnel, *La Danse*, p. 287.

40. The programmes for their appearances show that the troupe were well down the bill—no.16 for the Saturday matinée on 21 April 1894, for example.

41. Pessis and Crépineau, *The Moulin Rouge*, p. 29.

42. Mariel and Trocher, *Paris Cancan*, p. 37.

43. Pessis and Crépineau, *The Moulin Rouge*, p. 29.

44. 'Des Chercheurs et Curieux', column 278.

45. Charbonnel, *La Danse*, p. 286.

46. Warnod, *Les Bals de Paris*, appendice, p. xxxi.

47. Charbonnel, *La Danse*, p. 286.

48. Ibid., p. 289.

49. Pessis and Crépineau, *The Moulin Rouge*, p. 29.

50. Ibid., p. 29; Mariel and Trocher, *Paris Cancan*, p. 35.

51. Guest lists several of the nicknamed dancers as an appendix to 'The Heyday of the Cancan'.

52. Postcards from the Moulin Rouge in the 1920s show cancan dancers with the nicknames 'Fleur de Lotus', 'La Panthère' and even 'Rayon d'Or'.

53. Shercliff, *Jane Avril of the Moulin Rouge*, pp. 97–98, states that among other things Père le Pudeur separated couples of the same sex dancing together.

54. Mariel and Trocher, *Paris Cancan*, p. 41.

55. An article in *Gil Blas*, included in Eugène Rodrigues (Erastène Ramiro), *Cours de Danse fin de siècle*, quoted in Warnod, *Les Bals de Paris*, appendice, pp. xxx–xxxi.

56. Montorgueil, *Paris Dansant*, p. 172.

57. Warnod, *Les Bals de Paris*, appendice, p. xxxi.

58. Montorgueil, *Paris Dansant*, p. 173.

59. De Ménil, *Histoire de la Danse*, p. 214.

60. Laver, *Taste and Fashion*, pp. 173–74.

61. Pessis and Crépineau, *The Moulin Rouge*, p. 30.

62. Warnod, *Les Bals de Paris*, appendice, pp. xxxiv–xxxv.

63. Shercliff, *Jane Avril of the Moulin Rouge*, p. 112; Vuillier, *A History of Dancing*, p. 337.

64. Jacques-Charles, *Cent Ans de Music-Hall*, p. 229.

65. Shercliff, *Jane Avril of the Moulin Rouge*, p. 106.

66. Busby, *British Music Hall*, p. 39.

67. George Bernard Shaw, *Music in London: 1890–1894*, vol 2 (New York: William H. Wise, 1931), p. 95.

68. Ernest Short, *Fifty Years of Vaudeville* (London: Eyre & Spottiswoode, 1946), p. 226.

69. *Black and White* (London), 28 May 1892.

70. Shaw, *Music in London*, p. 95.

71. J.E.Crawford-Flitch, *Modern Dancing and Dancers* (London: Grant Richards, 1913), p. 97.

72. Busby, *British Music Hall*, p. 39.

73. Short, *Fifty Years of Vaudeville*, pp. 226–27.

74. Shercliff, *Jane Avril of the Moulin Rouge*, pp. 148 and 150; Denvir, *Toulouse-Lautrec*, p. 123.
75. Ryan, ed., *Toulouse-Lautrec*, p. 302.
76. Shercliff, *Jane Avril of the Moulin Rouge*, p. 151.
77. Crawford-Flitch, *Modern Dancing and Dancers*, pp. 74–75 and 77–78.
78. *St. Paul's* (London), 15 February 1896 and 21 March 1896.
79. *The Times* (London), 3 February 1897.
80. Castle, *The Folies Bergère*, p. 35.
81. Robert C. Toll, *On with the Show* (New York: Oxford University Press, 1976), p. 218.
82. Edward B. Marks, *They All Had Glamour: From the Swedish Nightingale to the Naked Lady* (New York: Julian Messner, 1944), p. 45.
83. Toll, *On with the Show*, p. 222.
84. Billington, *Mikhailovsky and Russian Populism*, p. 76.
85. Khrushchev was apparently shocked by the sight of the cancan being performed when he visited the set of *Can-Can* in Hollywood in 1959. See later in this chapter and Chapter 6.
86. Warnod, *Les Bals de Paris*, appendice, p. xxxv.
87. Pessis and Crépineau, *The Moulin Rouge*, p. 23.
88. Shercliff, *Jane Avril of the Moulin Rouge*, p. 196.
89. Pessis and Crépineau, *The Moulin Rouge*, pp. 23–24; Denvir, *Toulouse-Lautrec*, p. 79.
90. *The Times* (London), 10 March 92.
91. Shercliff, *Jane Avril of the Moulin Rouge*, p. 167.
92. Ibid., pp. 134, 141–42, 149, 171, and 172.
93. Ibid., p. 183.
94. Ibid., p. 221.
95. Pessis and Crépineau, *The Moulin Rouge*, p. 29.
96. Ryan, ed., *Toulouse-Lautrec*, p. 291.
97. Warnod, *Les Bals de Paris*, p. 45.
98. Ibid., p. 51.
99. Jacques-Charles, *Cent Ans de Music-Hall*, p.150.
100. Ibid., p. 151.
101. Fred Majdalany, 'The Truth about the Cancan', *The Dancing Times* (London), June 1935.
102. *Dance Magazine* (New York), November 1959.
103. *Dance Magazine* (New York), October 1959.
104. Roger Wilmut, *Kindly Leave the Stage: The Story of Variety, 1919–1960* (London: Methuen, 1985), p. 138 and pp. 159–60.
105. *Yukon News* (Whitehorse, Canada), 18 March 1992.
106. *Whitehorse Star* (Whitehorse, Canada), 23 March 1992.

CHAPTER 3 / THEATRES, MUSIC HALLS AND DANCING GARDENS

1. Pessis and Crépineau, *The Moulin Rouge*, p. 11.
2. De Margerie, Théry and Brisson, eds., *Le temps Toulouse-Lautrec*, p. 57.
3. *Le Figaro illustré*, quoted in Ryan, ed., *Toulouse-Lautrec*, p. 244.
4. Shercliff, *Jane Avril of the Moulin Rouge*, p. 98; Philippe Jullian, *Montmartre* (Brussels: Phaidon, 1977), p. 97.
5. Jullian, *Montmartre*, p. 97.
6. Pessis and Crépineau, *The Moulin Rouge*, p.12.
7. Jullian, *Montmartre*, p. 100.
8. Pessis and Crépineau, *The Moulin Rouge*, pp. 52–53, has a list of the *redoutes* from 1894 to 1902.
9. Montorgueil, *Paris Dansant*, pp. 126 and 130.

10. Derval, *The Folies Bergère*, p. 10.
11. Lucien Muhlfeld, quoted in Warnod, *Les Bals de Paris*, p. 141.
12. Jacques-Charles, *Cent Ans de Music-Hall*, p. 229.
13. Warnod, *Les Bals de Paris*, pp. 139–42, compares the various pleasures on offer at the two gardens.
14. Ryan, ed., *Toulouse-Lautrec*, p. 250; Pessis and Crépineau, *The Moulin Rouge*, pp. 40 and 42.
15. Pessis and Crépineau, *The Moulin Rouge*, p. 43.
16. Ibid., pp. 77 and 58.
17. Jacques-Charles, *Cent Ans de Music-Hall*, p.150.
18. Pessis and Crépineau, *The Moulin Rouge*, pp. 59 and 112.
19. Ibid., p. 160.
20. Ibid., p. 159.
21. Albert D. Vandamm, *An Englishman in Paris*, vol.1 (London: Chapman and Hall, 1892), pp. 30–31.
22. Mariel and Trocher, *Paris Cancan*, p. 7; Vuillier, *A History of Dancing*, p. 318.
23. Mariel and Trocher, *Paris Cancan*, p. 7; Vandamm, *An Englishman in Paris*, p. 31.
24. *Journal pour rire* (Paris), 16 November 1852.
25. 'Des Chercheurs et Curieux', column 282. The correspondent claims that the cancan was not allowed to flourish like it should have done because of La Hire's strict regime at the Chaumière.
26. *Journal pour rire* (Paris), 16 November 1852.
27. Ibid.
28. Ibid.
29. Mariel and Trocher, *Paris Cancan*, pp. 10–11; Vuillier, *A History of Dancing*, pp. 337–38.
30. Gaston Robert, *Les Mystères du Bal Bullier*, quoted in Mariel and Trocher, *Paris Cancan*, p. 10.
31. Warnod, *Les Bals de Paris*, p. 10.
32. *Journal pour rire* (Paris), 1 July 1848.
33. Alfred Delvau, *Les Cythères parisiennes*, quoted in Warnod, *Les Bals de Paris*, p. 16.
34. Anonymous, *Guide des Plaisirs à Paris* (Paris 1907), p. 168.
35. 'Tales of Paris Dancing', *The Dancing Times* (London), December 1927, "culled from *Les Bals de Paris* by André Warnod".
36. Guest, 'Bal Mabille'; Mariel and Trocher, *Paris Cancan*, p. 15.
37. Guest, 'Bal Mabille'; Guest 'The Heyday of the Cancan', p. 14.
38. Guest, 'The Heyday of the Cancan', p. 14; Guest, 'Bal Mabille'.
39. Guest, 'Bal Mabille'.
40. Guest, 'The Heyday of the Cancan', pp. 16–17.
41. Guest, 'Bal Mabille'.
42. Guest, 'The Heyday of the Cancan', p. 18; Vuillier, *A History of Dancing*, pp. 332–34.
43. Guest, 'Bal Mabille'.
44. Ibid.
45. Guest, 'The Opera Balls'.
46. Ribeiro, *Dress and Morality*, pp. 104–05.
47. Guest, 'The Opera Balls'.
48. Ibid.
49. 'Des Chercheurs et Curieux', column 280; Guest 'The Opera Balls'.
50. *The Court Journal* (London), 1867, quoted in ibid.
51. Ibid.
52. 'Des Chercheurs et Curieux', column 282.
53. Guest, 'The Opera Balls'.
54. Jullian, *Montmartre*, p. 41.

55. Edmond and Jules de Goncourt, *Germinie Lacerteux*, p. 94.

56. Ibid., p. 96.

57. Warnod, *Les Bals de Paris*, p. 40.

58. Jullian, *Montmartre*, p. 46.

59. Ibid., p. 42.

60. Warnod, *Les Bals de Paris*, p. 41.

61. Ryan, ed., *Toulouse-Lautrec*, p. 238.

62. Charles Rearick, *Pleasures of the Belle Epoque* (New Haven: Yale University Press, 1985), p. 186.

63. Warnod, *Les Bals de Paris*, p. 26.

64. Q.v. an oil sketch by Toulouse-Lautrec from 1885–87 entitled *Au Moulin de la Galette, La Goulue et Valentin-le-Désossé*, located at the Musée Toulouse-Lautrec, Albi.

65. Warnod, *Les Bals de Paris*, pp. 26–27.

66. Jullian, *Montmartre*, p. 61.

67. Rearick, *Pleasures of the Belle Epoque*, p. 95. Rearick observes that within the urban population "social barriers and privilege remained strong and poverty widespread". Montorgueil, *Paris Dansant*, has a chapter devoted to the *bal musette*, illustrated with a design by Willette showing a violent encounter between two women.

68. Felix Barker, *The House That Stoll Built: The Story of the Coliseum Theatre* (London: Frederick Muller 1957), p. 35.

69. Scott, *The Early Doors*, p. 159. Scott reports that Clodoche and his "now professional" troupe appeared at the Princess's Theatre in 1866 and at Covent Garden in 1869, and that, when they appeared at the Philharmonic Hall, Wiry Sal was also on the bill, presumably shortly before her Alhambra performances led to that theatre's closure.

70. *The Observer* (London), 16 October 1870.

71. D. F. Cheshire, *Music Hall in Britain* (London: David and Charles, 1974), p. 86.

72. Ibid., pp. 38–39. Cheshire describes the Empire as "'a club' for colonial officials, soldiers, civil servants, 'advanced' clergymen as well as for the aristocracy, young bloods, Bohemians and ordinary music hall goers". He also reports that the relationship between prostitution and Wilton's music hall in the East End of London was even closer: the auditorium was actually situated within a brothel.

73. Ibid., p. 39.

74. Ibid., p. 42.

75. Archibald Haddon, *The Story of Music Hall* (London: Fleetway Press, 1935), p. 88.

76. Programme, Palace Theatre, 1896.

77. Richard Kislan, *The Musical: A Look at the American Musical Theatre* (Englewood Cliffs, N.J.: Prentice-Hall, 1980), pp. 39–41 and 48–49. Kislan points out that vaudeville gave women an equal chance for stardom and that opera singers and respected actresses often appeared in it. But eventually the wholesome concept became relaxed enough to allow the suggestive songs of Mae West and others.

78. Ibid., p. 12.

79. Toll, *On with the Show*, p. 143.

80. Ibid., p. 208. Toll observes that burlesque shows gradually became more risqué, eventually resorting to striptease in the 1920s and 1930s, and ultimately disappeared as a major branch of show business in America because other more respectable forms of entertainment, like vaudeville, successfully absorbed burlesque's "most sensual innovations".

81. Kislan, *The Musical*, p. 40.

82. Toll, *On with the Show*, p. 210.

83. Kislan, *The Musical*, pp. 65–66.

84. Poster for the Rentz-Santley troupe, 1902, Library of Congress, Washington, D.C.

85. Toll, *On with the Show*, p. 222.

86. Ibid., p. 227.
87. Ibid., p. 218.
88. Marks, *They All Had Glamour*, p. 45.
89. Ibid., p. 52.
90. *Everybody's* (London), 7 February 1953.
91. Ibid.
92. Ibid.
93. Cheshire, *Music Hall in Britain*, p. 94.
94. *The Bystander* (London), 12 June 1940; *Everybody's* (London), 7 February 1953.
95. Vivian Van Damm, *Tonight and Every Night* (London: Stanley Paul and Co.,1952), p. 136.
96. *Everybody's* (London), 7 February 1953.
97. Richard Traubner, *Operetta: A Theatrical History* (Oxford: Oxford University Press, 1989), p. 10, writes that the lower classes in Paris wanted "'pop' music, rather than pantomimes, or tumbling acts, or cheap farces".
98. Ibid., p. 10 .
99. Castle, *The Folies Bergère*, pp. 18–19.
100. Denvir, *Toulouse-Lautrec*, p. 71.
101. Castle, *The Folies Bergère*, pp.21–25.
102. See chapter 2 for more on this.
103. Anonymous, *Guide des Plaisirs à Paris*, p. 97.
104. James Macmillan, 'An Age Stripped Bare', *The Sunday Times Magazine* (London), 6 October 1991.
105. Jullian, *Montmartre*, p. 121; Denvir, *Toulouse-Lautrec*, p. 126; Shercliff, *Jane Avril of the Moulin Rouge*, p. 171.
106. Denvir, *Toulouse-Lautrec*, pp. 98–99.
107. Warnod, *Les Bals de Paris*, pp. 53–57; Shercliff, *Jane Avril of the Moulin Rouge*, p. 171. According to Shercliff, Jane Avril was one of the stars of the Moulin Rouge who appeared at the Tabarin, in 1909.
108. Jacques-Charles, *Cent Ans de Music-Hall*, pp. 150–51.
109. Ibid., p. 152.
110. Peter Leslie, *A Hard Act to Follow: A Music Hall Review* (New York and London: Paddington Press, 1978), p. 172.
111. Jacques-Charles, *Cent Ans de Music-Hall*, p. 153.
112. Mariel and Trocher, *Paris Cancan*, p. 92.
113. Castle, *The Folies Bergère*, pp. 296–97.
114. Paradis Latin publicity and programme for 'Viva Paradis' revue.

CHAPTER 4 / OFFENBACH IN THE UNDERWORLD

1. Ivor Guest, *The Romantic Ballet in Paris* (London: Dance Books, 1980), p. 125.
2. Traubner, *Operetta: A Theatrical History*, pp. 30–31.
3. Kracauer, *Offenbach and the Paris of his Time*, p. 145.
4. Ibid., p. 35.
5. Traubner, *Operetta: A Theatrical History*, p. 3.
6. Peter Gammond, *Offenbach: His Life and Times* (Tunbridge Wells: Midas Books, 1980), p. 49.
7. James Harding, *Jacques Offenbach: A Biography* (London: James Calder, 1980), p. 111 .
8. Traubner, *Operetta: A Theatrical History*, p. 10.
9. Alexander Faris, *Jacques Offenbach* (London: Faber and Faber, 1980), p. 71.
10. Traubner, *Operetta: A Theatrical History*, p. 35 .
11. Gammond, *Offenbach: His Life and Times*, p. 54.

12. Harding, *Jacques Offenbach: A Biography*, p. 117.

13. Faris, *Jacques Offenbach*, p. 77.

14. Ibid., p. 169.

15. Antony Tudor's ballet, *Offenbach in the Underworld*, uses the same music and setting, with a slightly different story. The protagonists are this time a famous operetta star, with her lover, the Grand Duke; a debutante and her friends; a young impoverished artist; and other celebrities who all visit a fashionable restaurant seeking unbridled pleasure. Again the story is slight; the high point of the ballet is the cancan, which leaves everyone exhausted but content.

16. Michael E. Williamson, 'La Boutique Fantasque', David Drew, ed., *The Decca Book of the Ballet* (London: Frederick Muller, 1958), p. 263.

17. Cyril W. Beaumont, *The Complete Book of Ballets* (New York: G. P. Putnam's Sons, 1938), pp. 721–22.

18. Alexandra Danilova, *Choura: The Memoirs of Alexandra Danilova* (London: Dance Books, 1987), p. 122.

19. *The Independent* (London), 29 July 1997.

20. Ivor Guest, *The Empire Ballet* (London: London Society for Theatre Research, 1962), p. 13.

21. Mary Clarke and Clement Crisp, *The History of Dance* (London: Orbis Publishing, 1981), p. 235.

22. Guest, *Ballet in Leicester Square*, p. 25.

23. *The Times* (London), 27 December 1872.

24. Guest, *Ballet in Leicester Square*, p. 33.

25. Emily Soldene, 'How the Alhambra Was Shut', *The Sketch* (London), 30 January 1895.

26. Marks, *They All Had Glamour*, pp. 52–53.

27. Guest, *The Empire Ballet*, p. 43.

28. *The Sketch* (London), 30 May 1894.

29. Kurt Gänzl, *The Encyclopaedia of the Musical Theatre* (Oxford: Blackwell, 1994), p. 218. According to Gänzl, the story of the cancan being banned and its performers being brought before a court of law originated with the Hungarian operetta *Cancan a törvényszék előtt* by István Friebeisz Rajkai and Jakab Jakóbi in 1864, and a century later Abe Burrows's story for Cole Porter's *Can-Can* had the same theme.

30. *The Sketch* (London), 30 May 1894.

31. Grun, *Gold and Silver: The Life and Times of Franz Lehár*, p. 111.

32. Ibid., p. 122.

33. Ibid., p. 122.

34. Ibid., pp. 124–26; Gänzl, *The Encyclopedia of the Musical Theatre*, p. 904.

35. Grun, *The Life and Times of Franz Lehár*, pp. 127–28.

36. Gänzl, *The Encyclopedia of the Musical Theatre*, p. 905.

37. Traubner, *Operetta: A Theatrical History*, p. 240.

38. Sheridan Morley, *Spread a Little Happiness* (London: Thames and Hudson, 1987), p. 136.

39. Gene Lees, *The Musical Worlds of Lerner and Loewe* (London: Robson Books, 1990), pp. 4 and 12.

40. Ibid., p 156.

41. Ibid., p. 255.

42. Morley, *Spread a Little Happiness*, p. 77.

43. George Eells, *Cole Porter: The Life that Once He Led* (London: W. H. Allen, 1967), p. 279.

44. Gänzl, *The Encyclopaedia of the Musical Theatre*, p. 217; Abe Laufe, *Broadway's Greatest Musicals* (Newton Abbot and London: David & Charles, 1978), p. 174. According to Gänzl, "Miss Verdon's threatening to steal the show resulted in her role being severely cut before opening, but she went ahead and stole it anyway". Laufe writes that following Verdon's success rumours soon spread that her part had been cut at Lilo's insistence.

45. Eells, *Cole Porter*, p. 283.
46. Ibid., p. 280.
47. Michael Billington, *The Guinness Book of Theatre Facts and Feats* (Enfield, Middlesex: Guinness Superlatives, 1982), p. 199.

CHAPTER 5 / LA GOULUE "TOUS LES SOIRS"

1. Denvir, *Toulouse-Lautrec*, pp. 9 and 204.
2. Ibid., p. 47.
3. Ibid., p. 18.
4. Richard Shone, 'A Giant Fills the Frame at Last', *The Times* (London), 5 October 1991. In *Toulouse-Lautrec*, Denvir quotes from a number of these letters, and also from a letter written by Lautrec's mother to her mother proudly describing an invitation by his teacher, Fernand Cormon, to collaborate with him on illustrations for a projected edition of Victor Hugo's works. She wrote: "They are now predicting for Henri a future of great fame, which seems unbelievable" (p. 48).
5. Denvir, *Toulouse-Lautrec*, p. 18.
6. Ibid., p. 17.
7. Ibid., p. 13.
8. Ibid., p. 145; Mariel and Trocher, *Paris Cancan*, p. 31.
9. Ryan, ed., *Toulouse-Lautrec*, p. 328.
10. Denvir, *Toulouse-Lautrec*, pp. 52–54.
11. Ibid., pp. 103–04.
12. Ryan, ed., *Toulouse-Lautrec*, p. 302.
13. Ibid., p. 298.
14. Shercliff, *Jane Avril of the Moulin Rouge*, p. 111.
15. Ryan, ed., *Toulouse-Lautrec*, p. 270.
16. Mariel and Trocher, *Paris Cancan*, p. 34.
17. Denvir, *Toulouse-Lautrec*, pp. 144–45.
18. Ibid., p. 189.
19. Millicent Rose, *Gustave Doré* (London: Pleiades Books, 1946), p. 19.
20. Joanna Richardson, *Gustave Doré* (London: Cassell, 1980), pp. 46–47.
21. Ibid., pp. 66–68.
22. Clifford Hall, introduction to Lillian Browse, ed., *Constantin Guys* (London: Faber and Faber, 1946), p. 10.
23. Ibid., p. 6.
24. Ibid., p. 6.
25. P. G. Konody, in C. Geoffrey Holme, ed., *The Painter of Victorian Life: A Study of Constantin Guys with Introduction and Translation of Baudelaire's 'Peintre de la Vie Moderne'* (London: The Studio, 1930), pp. 72–75 and 153.
26. Hall, introduction to *Constantin Guys*, p. 14.
27. John Rewald, *Seurat* (London: Thames and Hudson, 1990), pp. 17–18, 38 and 51.
28. Ian Chilvers, ed., *The Concise Oxford Dictionary of Art and Artists* (Oxford: Oxford University Press, 1990), p. 432.
29. Anthony Blunt and Roger Fry, *Georges Seurat* (London: Phaidon Press, 1965), p. 84.
30. Richard Thomson, *Seurat* (London: Phaidon, 1985), p. 208.
31. Ibid., p. 204.
32. Pessis and Crépineau, *The Moulin Rouge*, p. 12; Jacques-Charles, *Cent Ans de Music-Hall*, p. 150.
33. Ryan, ed., *Toulouse-Lautrec*, p. 227.
34. Pierre Courthion, *Georges Rouault* (London: Thames and Hudson, 1978), p. 102.
35. Ibid., p. 49.

36. Ibid., p. 73.

37. The opening of the museum dedicated to his works in Albi in 1922 gave Lautrec the recognition he deserved, but as Richard Shone ('A Giant Fills the Frame at Last') points out, the subject matter of his work had alienated many critics. Shone cites Herbert Read, writing in the 1930s, who blames a "'formidable tradition' of moral judgement in matters of art" for Lautrec's unpopularity in Britain, for example.

38. Pierre Daix and Georges Boudaille, trans. Phoebe Pool, *Picasso: The Blue and Rose Periods* (London: Evelyn, Adams and Mackay, 1967), p. 118.

39. Ibid., p. 33.

CHAPTER 6 / A FEAST FOR THE EYES

1. Gerald Pratley, *The Cinema of John Huston* (Cranbury, N. J.: A. S. Barnes & Co., 1977), p. 96.

2. Scott Hammen, *John Huston* (Boston: Twayne Publishers, 1985), p. 68.

3. William F. Nolan, *John Huston: King Rebel* (Los Angeles: Sherbourne Press,1965), pp. 111–12.

4. Pratley, *The Cinema of John Huston*, p. 94.

5. Stuart Kaminsky, *John Huston: Maker of Magic* (London: Angus & Robertson, 1978), p. 94; Nolan, *John Huston: King Rebel*, p 117.

6. John Huston, *An Open Book* (New York: Alfred A. Knopf, 1980), p. 211.

7. Kaminsky, *John Huston: Maker of Magic*, p. 92. Kaminsky adds that Ferrer also played Lautrec's father in the film, and for scenes in which both characters appeared Huston used a real dwarf instead of Ferrer in long-distance shots.

8. Huston, *An Open Book*, p. 205.

9. Hammen, *John Huston*, pp. 70–71.

10. Raymond Durgnat, *Jean Renoir* (London: Studio Vista, 1975), p. 301.

11. Ibid., p. 301.

12. Célia Bertin, trans. Mireille and Leonard Muellner, *Jean Renoir: A Life in Pictures* (Baltimore and London: Johns Hopkins University Press, 1991), p. 285.

13. *Variety* (New York), 1 June 1955.

14. Jean Renoir, trans. Norman Denny, *My Life and My Films* (London: William Collins, Sons & Co., 1974), p. 270.

15. David Thompson and Lorraine LoBianco, eds., Jean Renoir, *Letters* (London: Faber and Faber, 1994), p. 326.

16. *Variety* (New York), 16 March 1960.

17. John Walker, ed., *Halliwell's Film Guide*, 11th edn. (London: Harper Collins, 1995), p. 754.

18. A. E. Twysden, *Alexandra Danilova* (London: C. W. Beaumont, 1945), p. 127.

19. A. H. Franks, *Ballet for Film and Television* (London: Sir Isaac Pitman & Sons, 1950), p. 4. Franks says that many ballet lovers in England "were appalled at what they considered to be a wicked mutilation of their Art".

20. Twysden, *Alexandra Danilova*, p. 128.

21. Durgnat, *Jean Renoir*, p. 40.

22. Renoir, *My Life and My Films*, p. 83.

23. Ibid., p. 84; Bertin, *Jean Renoir: A Life in Pictures*, pp. 64–65.

24. The Tabarin would have been *the* place to see the cancan in the 1930s, but in the film Moulin Rouge-style windmills can be seen around the dance floor.

25. Laver, *Taste and Fashion*, pp. 173–74.

CHAPTER 7 / THE CANCAN TODAY

1. Ribeiro, *Dress and Morality*, p. 121.

2. 'The Antiquity of the Can-can', *The Mask* (London), March 1868.

3. Sarah Wise, 'Secrets of the Showgirls', *Marie Claire* (London), February 1994 .

4. Mariel and Trocher, *Paris Cancan*, pp. 85–87.
5. 'It's time to can the can-can dancers', *Yukon News* (Whitehorse, Canada), 18 March 1992.
6. Letter, *The Whitehorse Star* (Whitehorse, Canada), 24 March 1992.
7. Mariel and Trocher, *Paris Cancan*, p. 76.
8. *The Independent* (London), 15 October 1990.
9. Sarah Wise, 'Women with Alter Egos', *Marie Claire* (London), March 1995.
10. Sarah Wise, 'Secrets of the Showgirls'.
11. Majdalany, 'The Truth about the Cancan'; Michel Souvais, *Les Cancans de la Goulue* (Paris: Michel Souvais, 1991), p. 39, n. 7.
12. Wise, 'Secrets of the Showgirls'.
13. Pierre Mariel, *Paris Revue* (London: Neville Spearman, 1961), p. 97.

BIBLIOGRAPHY

BOOKS

A bas Rigolboche. Paris: Librairie Théatrale, 1860.

Aretz, Gertrude. Translated by James Laver. *The Elegant Woman*. London: George Harrap & Co., 1932.

Atwell, Lee. *G. W. Pabst*. Boston: Twayne Publishers, 1977.

Barker, Felix. *The House that Stoll Built*. London: Frederick Muller, 1957.

Beaumont, C. W. *The Complete Book of Ballets*. New York: G. P. Putnam's Sons, 1938.

Bertin, Célia. Translated by Mireille and Leonard Muellner. *Jean Renoir: A Life in Pictures*. Baltimore and London: Johns Hopkins University Press, 1991.

Billington, J. H. *Mikhailovsky and Russian Populism*. Oxford: Oxford University Press, 1958.

Billington, Michael. *The Guinness Book of Theatre Facts and Feats*. Enfield, Middlesex: Guinness Superlatives, 1982.

Bloch, Oscar, and Walther von Wartburg. *Dictionnaire Étymologique de la Langue Française*. Paris: Presses Universitaires de France, 1994.

Blunt, Anthony, and Roger Fry. *Georges Seurat*. London: Phaidon Press, 1965.

Bradfield, Nancy. *Costume in Detail: Women's Dress 1730–1930*. London: George G. Harrap & Co., 1981.

Braudy, Leo. *Jean Renoir: The World of his Films*. New York: Columbia University Press, 1972.

Brooke, Iris. *A History of English Costume*. London: Eyre Methuen, 1972.

Busby, Roy. *British Music Hall*. London and New Hampshire: Paul Elek, 1976.

Castil-Blaze (François Henri Joseph Blaze). *L'Academie Impériale de Musique: Histoire littéraire, musicale, choreographique de 1645 à 1855*. Paris, 1855.

Castle, Charles. *The Folies Bergère*. London: Methuen, 1982.

Charbonnel, Raoul. *La Danse*. Paris: Garniers Frères, n.d.

Cheshire, D. F. *Music Hall in Britain*. London: David and Charles, 1974.

Chilvers, Ian, ed. *The Concise Oxford Dictionary of Art and Artists*. Oxford: Oxford University Press, 1990.

Chujoy, A. *The Dance Encyclopedia*. New York: A. S. Barnes & Co., 1949.

Clarke, Mary, and Clement Crisp. *The History of Dance*. London: Orbis Publishing, 1981.

Courthion, Pierre. *Georges Rouault*. London: Thames and Hudson, 1978.

Crawford-Flitch, J. E. *Modern Dancing and Dancers*. London: Grant Richards, 1913.

Cunnington, Phyllis, and C. Willett. *The History of Underclothes*. London: Faber and Faber, 1981.

Daix, Pierre and Georges Boudaille. Translated by Phoebe Pool. *Picasso: The Blue and Rose Periods*. London: Evelyn, Adams and Mackay, 1967.

Danilova, Alexandra. *Choura: the Memoirs of Alexandra Danilova*. London: Dance Books, 1987.

Dannett, S. G. L. and F. R. Rachel. *Down Memory Lane*. New York: Greenberg, 1954.

Davidson, Gladys. *Stories of the Ballets*. London: T. Werner Laurie, 1949.

Denvir, Bernard. *Toulouse-Lautrec*. London: Thames and Hudson, 1991.

Derval, Paul. *The Folies Bergère* London: Methuen and Co., 1955.

Dorsey, H. *The Belle Epoque in the Paris Herald*. London: Thames and Hudson, 1986.

Durgnat, Raymond. *Jean Renoir*. London: Studio Vista, 1975.

Earnshaw, P. *Lace in Fashion: From the Sixteenth to the Twentieth Centuries*. London: B. T. Batsford, 1985.

Eells, George. *Cole Porter: The Life that Once He Led*. London: W. H. Allen, 1967.

Ewing, Elizabeth. *Dress and Undress*. London: B. T. Batsford, 1978.

Faris, Alexander. *Jacques Offenbach*. London: Faber and Faber, 1980.

Franks, A. H. *Ballet for Film and Television*. London: Sir Isaac Pitman & Sons, 1950.

———. *Social Dance: A Short History*. London: Routledge and Kegan Paul, 1963.

Gammond, Peter. *Offenbach: His Life and Times*. Tunbridge Wells: Midas Books, 1980.

Gänzl, Kurt. *The Encyclopaedia of the Musical Theatre*. Oxford: Basil Blackwell, 1994.

——— and A. Lamb. *Gänzl's Book of the Musical Theatre*. London: The Bodley Head, 1988.

Geffroy, Gustave. *Constantin Guys: historien du Second Empire*. Paris: G. Crès et Cie Paris, 1920.

Glyn, Elinor. *Visits of Elizabeth*. London: Duckworth and Co., 1900.

De Goncourt, Edmond and Jules. *Germinie Lacerteux*. London: Vizetelly & Co., 1887.

Gorham, Deborah. *The Victorian Girl and the Feminine Ideal*. London: Croom Helm, 1982.

Grun, Bernard. *Gold and Silver: The Life and Times of Franz Lehár*. London: W. H. Allen, 1970.

Guest, Ivor. *The Empire Ballet*. London: London Society for Dance Research, 1962.

———. *The Romantic Ballet in Paris*. London: Dance Books, 1980.

———. *Jules Perrot*. London: Dance Books, 1984.

———. *Ballet in Leicester Square* London: Dance Books, 1992.

Guide des Plaisirs à Paris. Paris: 1907.

Haddon, Archibald. *The Story of Music Hall*. London: Fleetway Press, 1935.

Hammen, Scott. *John Huston*. Boston: Twayne Publishers, 1985.

Harding, James. *Folies de Paris: The Rise and Fall of French Operetta*. London: Chappell and Company, 1979.

———. *Jacques Offenbach: A Biography*. London: James Calder, 1980.

Hardwick, Mollie. *The World of Upstairs Downstairs*. London: David and Charles, 1976.

Harrison, Michael. *A Fanfare of Strumpets*. London: W. H. Allen, 1971.

Hollingshead, John. *The Story of Leicester Square*. London: Simpkin, Marshall, Hamilton, Kent & Co., 1892.

———. *My Lifetime*. London: Sampson Low, Marston & Co., 1895.

Huston, John. *An Open Book*. New York: Alfred A. Knopf, 1980.

Hyman, Alan. *The Gaiety Years*. London: Cassell, 1975.

Jacques-Charles. *Cent Ans de Music-Hall*. Paris and Geneva: Editions Jeheber, 1956.

Johnston, John. *The Lord Chamberlain's Blue Pencil*. London: Hodder and Stoughton, 1990.

Jullian, Philippe. *Montmartre*. Brussels: Phaidon, 1977.

Kaminsky, Stuart. *John Huston: Maker of Magic*. London: Angus and Robertson, 1978.

Kislan, Richard. *The Musical: A Look at the American Musical Theatre*. Englewood Cliffs, N.J.: Prentice-Hall, 1980.

Koegler, Horst. *The Concise Oxford Dictionary of Ballet*. Oxford: Oxford University Press, 1977.

Kracauer, Siegfried. *Offenbach and the Paris of his Time*. London: Constable, 1937.

Laufe, Abe. *Broadway's Greatest Musicals*. Newton Abbot and London: David & Charles, 1978.

Laver, James. *Taste and Fashion*. London: George Harrap & Co., 1937.

Lees, Gene. *The Musical Worlds of Lerner and Loewe*. London: Robson Books, 1990.

Leslie, Peter. *A Hard Act to Follow: A Music Hall Review*. New York and London: Paddington Press, 1978.

Littlewood, I. *Paris: A Literary Companion*. London: John Murray, 1987.

MacQueen-Pope, W. *The Melodies Linger On*. London: W. H. Allen, 1950.

Madsen, Axel. *John Huston: A Biography*. London: Robson Books, 1979.

De Margerie, Anne, Marianne Théry and Dominique Brisson, eds. *Le temps Toulouse-Lautrec*. Paris: Editions de la Réunion des Musées Nationaux/Textuel, 1991.

Mariel, Pierre. *Paris Revue*. London: Neville Spearman, 1961.

———— and Jean Trocher. *Paris Cancan*. London: Charles Skilton, 1961.

Marks, Edward B. *They All Had Glamour: From the Swedish Nightingale to the Naked Lady*. New York: Julian Messner, 1944.

De Ménil, F. *Histoire de la Danse*. Paris: Alcide, Picard & Kaan éditeurs, n.d.

Montorgueil, Georges. *Paris Dansant*. Paris: Théophile Belin, 1898.

Morley, Sheridan. *Spread a Little Happiness*. London: Thames and Hudson, 1987.

Moser, Françoise. *Vie et Aventures de Céleste Mogador*. Paris: Editions Albin Michel, 1935.

Nolan, William F. *John Huston: King Rebel*. Los Angeles: Sherbourne Press, 1965.

Paris by Night. London: Rozez and Co., 1871.

Parker, Derek and Julia. *The Natural History of the Chorus Girl*. Newton Abbot and London: David and Charles, 1975.

Pearsall, Ronald. *The Worm in the Bud*. London: Pelican Books, 1971.

————. *Victorian Popular Music* London: David and Charles, 1973.

Plessis, Jacques, and Jacques Crépineau. *The Moulin Rouge*. Stroud, Gloucestershire: Alan Sutton Publishing, 1990.

Pool, Phoebe. *Picasso: The Formative Years*. London: Studio Books, 1962.

Pratley, Gerald. *The Cinema of John Huston*. Cranbury, New Jersey: A. S. Barnes & Co., 1977.

Rabenalt, Arthur Maria. *Voluptas Ludens*. München-Regensburg: Verlag Die Schaubühne, 1962.

Renoir, Jean. Translated by Norman Denny. *My Life and My Films*. London: William Collins, Sons & Co., 1974.

Rewald, John. *Seurat*. London: Thames & Hudson, 1990.

Ribeiro, Aileen. *Dress and Morality*. London: B. T. Batsford, 1986.

Richardson, Joanna. *The Courtesans*. London: Weidenfeld and Nicholson, 1967.

————. *Gustave Doré*. London: Cassell, 1980.

Rearick, Charles. *Pleasures of the Belle Epoque*. New Haven: Yale University Press, 1985.

Rigolboche (Marguerite Badel). *Memoires*. Paris: 1860.

Rose, Millicent. *Gustave Doré*. London: Pleiades Books, 1946

Rust, F. *Dance in Society*. London: Routledge and Kegan Paul, 1969.

Ryan, Marianne, ed. *Toulouse-Lautrec*. London: South Bank Centre, 1991.

Sachs, Curt. *World History of the Dance*. New York: Norton & Co., 1937.

Scott, Harold. *The Early Doors*. London: Nicholson and Watson, 1946.

Searle, Townley. *Sir William Schwenck Gilbert: A Topsy-Turvy Adventure*. London: Alexander-Ouseley, 1931.

Sesonske, Alexander. *Jean Renoir: The French Films, 1924–1939*. Cambridge: Harvard University Press, 1980.

Shaw, George Bernard. *Music in London: 1890–1894*. Vol. 2. New York: William H. Wise, 1931.

Shercliff, José. *Jane Avril of the Moulin Rouge*. London: Jarrolds, 1952.

Short, Ernest. *Fifty Years of Vaudeville*. London: Eyre and Spottiswoode, 1946.

Sorell, Walter. *The Dance through the Ages*. London: Thames and Hudson, 1967.

Souvais, Michel. *Les Cancans de la Goulue*. Paris: Michel Souvais, 1991.

Thomson, David. *Europe since Napoleon*. London: Pelican Books, 1966.

Thomson, Richard. *Seurat*. London: Phaidon Press, 1985.

Toll, Robert C. *On with the Show: The First Century of Show-Business in America*. New York: Oxford University Press, 1976.

Traubner, Richard. *Operetta: A Theatrical History*. Oxford: Oxford University Press, 1989.

Twysden, A. E. *Alexandra Danilova*. London: C. W. Beaumont, 1945.

Van Damm, Vivian. *Tonight and Every Night*. London: Stanley Paul and Co., 1952.

Vandamm, A. D. *An Englishman in Paris*. London: Chapman and Hall, 1892.

Visani, Maria Cionini. *Toulouse-Lautrec*. London: Thames and Hudson, 1968.

Vuillier, Gaston. *A History of Dancing*. London: Heinemann, 1898.

Walker, John, ed. *Halliwell's Film Guide*. 11th Edition. London: Harper Collins, 1995.
Warnod, André. *Les Bals de Paris*. Paris: Les Éditions G. Crè & Cie, 1922.
Weber, Eugen. *France Fin de Siècle*. Cambridge: Harvard University Press, 1986.
Wilmut, Roger. *Kindly Leave the Stage: The Story of Variety 1919–1960*. London: Methuen, 1985.
Zeldin, Theodore. *France 1848–1945: Anxiety and Hypocrisy*. Oxford: Oxford University Press, 1981.
Zola, Emile. Translated by L. Tancock. *L'Assommoir*. London: Penguin Classics, 1970.
———. Translated by George Holden. *Nana*. London: Penguin Classics, 1972.

ARTICLES

Amaya, Mario. 'The Dance in Art 1850–1925'. *Dance and Dancers* (London), December 1960.
———. 'The Little Genius of Montmartre'. *Dance and Dancers* (London), April 1961.
'The Antiquity of the Can-can'. *The Mask* (London), March 1868.
Barker, K. M. D. 'Dance and the Emerging Music Hall in the Provinces'. *Dance Research: The Journal of the Society for Dance Research* (London), 5, no.2 (1987).
Bock, Hans-Michael. 'George Wilhelm Pabst: Documenting a Life and a Career'. Eric Rentschler, ed. *The Films of G. W. Pabst*. New Brunswick, N. J.: Rutgers University Press, 1990.
Gribble, Francis. 'The Origin of the Can-Can'. *The Dancing Times* (London), April 1933.
Guest, Ivor. 'Bal Mabille'. *Ballet* (London), February 1947.
———. 'Cora Pearl plays Cupid'. *Ballet* (London), May 1948.
———. 'The Opéra Balls'. *Ballet* (London), March 1950.
———. 'The Heyday of the Cancan'. In W. H. Holden, ed., *Second Empire Medley*. London: British Technical and General Press, 1952.
———. 'Queens of the Cancan: They Made Paris Gay'. *Dance and Dancers* (London), December 1952.
———. 'The Alhambra Ballet'. *Dance Perspectives* (New York), Autumn 1959.
Hall, Clifford. 'Introduction' to Lillian Browse, ed. *Constantin Guys*. London: Faber and Faber, 1946.
Koritz, Amy. 'Moving Violations: Dance in the London Music Hall, 1890–1910'. *Theatre Journal* (London), December 1990.
Macmillan, James. 'An Age Stripped Bare'. *The Sunday Times Magazine* (London), 6 October 1991.
Majdalany, Fred. 'The Truth about the Cancan'. *The Dancing Times* (London), June 1935.
Russell, John. 'Feast of Life'. *The Royal Academy Magazine* (London), no. 38 (1993).
Shone, Richard 'A Giant Fills the Frame at Last'. *The Times* (London), 5 October 1991.
Sierek, Karl. 'The Primal Scene of the Cinema: Four Fragments from the *Mistress of Atlantis* (1932)'. Eric Rentschler, ed. *The Films of G. W. Pabst*. New Brunswick, N. J.: Rutgers University Press, 1990.
Soldene, Emily. 'How the Alhambra was Shut'. *The Sketch* (London), 30 January 1895.
Williamson, Michael E. 'La Boutique Fantasque'. David Drew, ed. *The Decca Book of the Ballet*. London: Frederick Muller, 1958.
Wise, Sarah. 'Secrets of the Showgirls'. *Marie Claire* (London), February 1994.
———. 'Women with Alter Egos'. *Marie Claire* (London), March 1995.

PERIODICALS AND NEWSPAPERS

Ballet (London), 1947, 1948, 1950.
Black and White (London), 1894.

La Cinématographie Française (Paris), 1953.
The Daily Graphic (London), 1894.
Dance and Dancers (London), 1952.
Dance Magazine (New York), 1959.
The Dancing Times (London), 1927, 1933, 1935.
The Days' Doings (London), 1870.
The Era (London), 1842, 1845.
Everybody's (London), 1953.
Le Figaro (Paris), 1857.
The Independent (London), 1990, 1991, 1997.
L'Intermédiaire (Paris) 1891.
Journal pour rire (later *amusant*) (Paris), 1848, 1850, 1852.
Monthly Film Bulletin (London), 1953, 1959, 1960.
Motion Picture Herald (New York), 1942, 1960.
The Observer (London), 1870.
St. Paul's (London), 1896.
The Sketch (London), 1894, 1895.
The Sunday Times (London), 1991.
The Times (London), 1897, 1991.
Variety (New York), 1952, 1955, 1958, 1960.
Whitehorse Star (Whitehorse, Canada), 1992.
Yukon News (Whitehorse, Canada), 1994.

INDEX